Dialogicality and Social Representations

The Dynamics of Mind

Ivana Marková

CAMBRIDGE
UNIVERSITY PRESS

CAMBRIDGE UNIVERSITY PRESS
Cambridge, New York, Melbourne, Madrid, Cape Town, Singapore, São Paulo

Cambridge University Press
The Edinburgh Building, Cambridge CB2 2RU, UK

Published in the United States of America by Cambridge University Press, New York

www.cambridge.org
Information on this title: www.cambridge.org/9780521824859

First published 2003
Reprinted 2005
This digitally printed first paperback version 2005

A catalogue record for this publication is available from the British Library

ISBN-13 978-0-521-82485-9 hardback
ISBN-10 0-521-82485-0 hardback

ISBN-13 978-0-521-02276-7 paperback
ISBN-10 0-521-02276-2 paperback

Dialogicali
The Dynami

BI 3994406 9

The theory of social knowledge developed in this book is based on dialogicality and the theory of social representations. It is argued that dialogicality, the capacity of the human mind to conceive, create and communicate about social realities in terms of, or in opposition to otherness, is the *sine qua non* of the human mind. Social representations are sharply distinguished from mental and collective representations. Being embedded in history and culture, social representations manifest themselves in public discourses and social thinking about phenomena, which touch in some fundamental ways upon social realities, e.g. political, ecological or health related. The theory of social representations places communication and the concept of change in the centre of social psychology. Ivana Marková's new book is unique in bringing together the concept of dialogue and social knowledge and will make an important contribution to social psychology, social and human science and communication studies.

IVANA MARKOVÁ was born in Czechoslavakia but has lived in the UK since 1967. She is Professor of Psychology at the University of Stirling and has been a visiting professor at the universities of Oslo, Berne, Paris, Linköping, Mexico and Bologna. She directs three international research groups in the European Laboratory of Social Psychology at the Maison des Sciences de l'Homme in Paris. She is a Fellow of the British Academy, a Fellow of the Royal Society of Edinburgh and of the British Psychological Society. Previous books include *Paradigms, Thought and Language* (1982), *Human Awareness* (1987) and *Mutualities of Dialogue* (co-ed.) (1995).

For my mother

Contents

Figures and table

Figures

Table

Preface

If you ask a student or a professor of psychology 'What is social psychology?' you are likely to receive as many different descriptions of social psychology as there are individuals you ask. Contemporary social psychology may cover anything that, in one way or other, could be referred to as 'social'. At one end of the spectrum social psychology has been associated, for a long time, with pathological and clinical phenomena as indicated by the names of the past *American Journal of Abnormal and Social Psychology* and the *British Journal of Social and Clinical Psychology*. At the other end of the spectrum, it has been affiliated with 'applied' fields including diverse subjects like the study of marital discord, racism, health beliefs, occupational and environmental issues, to mention but a few. Still other social psychologists, in their effort to upgrade our field to a scientific discipline, emphasise information processing and social cognition models that can be properly developed only in experimental and laboratory paradigms.

As social psychology covers such a range of diverse and often unspecified phenomena, not surprisingly, it has turned into a highly heterogeneous field including many disconnected areas. A science writer Morton Hunt (1993) maintains that social psychology is so fragmented that it has become a 'no man's land'. Thus he claims that while most other sciences more or less accumulate and deepen knowledge about the phenomena under study, this cannot be said about social psychology. It deals with many different issues that have little in common and that are often fads and 'hot topics'. These issues come and go, and so do their accompanying 'theories'. Therefore, he argues, social psychology does not explore the phenomena under study in any depth. As a result, explorations of these phenomena do not add up to new knowledge. True, Hunt points out that social psychology has provided humankind with some important insights but nevertheless, his final verdict is as follows: social psychology has 'no proper boundaries, no agreed-upon definition and no unifying theory' (Hunt, 1993, p. 434).

Social phenomena, however, are by their nature multifaceted and heterogeneous and it would be equally damaging for social psychology if we attempted to homogenise social diversities into the unifying theory to which Hunt alludes. Nevertheless, Hunt has a point. If everything 'social' can refer to social psychology, the term 'social psychology' becomes nonsensical because it has no boundaries. Meanings of terms are related to specific frames of reference and if there are no such frames of reference, one can hardly talk about meanings.

There is one claim that we can make with some certainty. Traditionally, social psychology has always had something to do with the nature of the relations between the individual and her social world. However, once we attempt to go beyond this elementary claim, we arrive at the first problem: what exactly does it mean to examine the nature of the relations between the individual and her social world?

Since the end of the nineteenth century numerous social psychologists have constantly criticised our discipline for 'individualising the social'. For example, James Mark Baldwin (1910, 1911) was preoccupied with emphasising the interdependence between the 'individual' and the 'social' and he argued that psychological theories of his time ignored this interdependence, in particular with respect to the social origin of knowledge. Therefore, they were inadequate for any purpose and should be discarded in the intellectual attic among old furniture. Following Baldwin, 'crises' and criticisms have inundated the history of social psychology and it appears that today we are no better off than in Baldwin's time. In his scholarly historical analysis Rob Farr (1996) has shown that the 'individualisation of the social' has taken different theoretical paths and that it has significantly shaped our discipline throughout the whole of the twentieth century. Due to inadequate theoretical and/or empirical ideas expounded by, e.g. behaviourism, positivism and cognitivism, the social nature of the individual has been misunderstood, ignored or even rejected. Individuals have been treated as atoms and have been artificially detached from their social contexts resulting in the 'individualisation' of the social. Consequently, psychology deals with two elements: the individual and the social and then it poses questions about their relations.

Even many psychological terms that we currently use imply the detachment of the individual and the social. 'Interaction', 'socialisation', 'intersubjectivity', 'assimilation', 'adaptation', 'exchange' and indeed, 'individualisation' are not neutral social scientific expressions but they express presuppositions that individuals or groups come into interaction, or that individuals become socialised, or that they adapt to or assimilate perspectives of others and so on. These terms are already theory-laden and are part of the specific theoretical frameworks presupposing that relations between the individual and the social are about to emerge or that they have already come into existence. Hence the emphasis of social psychology is on the exploration of these relations.

While much criticism concerning the 'individualisation of the social' comes from within our discipline, interestingly, even outsiders observe that social psychology is concerned, above all, with the individual. Thus Allen Newell (1990), the proponent of artificial intelligence did not have much difficulty in extending his unified theory of cognition to social psychology on the following grounds. He observed that it is *individual psychology* that in fact contributes a model of the *social* person. Therefore, he observed, that social psychology presents itself as being a component of individual psychology! He justified his claim by drawing attention to social psychological theories like attribution, social perception, affiliation and attachment. According to him, these theories are concerned above all with the individual within a social group rather than, as he called it, with 'the social band proper'. Amongst these models, he continued, 'indeed *social cognition* [Newell's emphasis] is exactly the area within social psychology that has attempted to take the stance of modern cognitive psychology and move it into the study of the social band' (Newell, p. 491). Newell concluded by saying that the underlying models of these attempts in social cognition remain shadows of what they should be; they remain static, focusing on the manipulation of independent and dependent variables rather than on the dynamics of social action.

The dynamics of social action, however, cannot be developed from the presupposition of static phenomena that are somehow put into motion. Instead, we need a theory of social knowledge that presupposes dynamics as the point of departure.

The aim of this book is to propose such a theory of social knowledge.

Twenty years ago I published *Paradigms, Thought and Language*, a book addressing some specific issues of the theory of knowledge in psychology. I questioned, at the time, the epistemology, which was based on the presupposition that the origin of thought and language must be sought solely in the cognitive faculties of the individual. Contrary to this presupposition I assumed that thought and language are social in their origin and that, therefore they are – or should be – the main concern of social psychology. My problem was to find the theoretical means that would conceptually link dialogicality and thinking.

It took me a long time to see that Moscovici's theory of social representations could provide the conceptual force in linking dialogicality and social thinking. The theory of social representations conceives thinking and language as captured in common sense and in daily discourse. In contrast to scientific thinking, which attempts to arrive at *scientific knowledge*, common sense thinking arrives at *social representations* of natural and social phenomena. Science searches for truth through the power of *individual rationality*. Social representations search for truth through trust based on beliefs, common knowledge and through the power of *dialogical rationality*. Social representations do not originate from pure reasoning or information processing. They are rooted in the past, culture, tradition and language.

In contrast to many other social psychological approaches, the theory of social representations does not pose questions about how to think about and how to study the emergence and existence of relations between the individual and the social. True, the theory of social representations does not dispute that the contemporary social psychology is concerned above all with the individual. However, the theory of social representations is not preoccupied with the problem of the individualisation of the social. Neither is it critical of questions that are commonly studied in contemporary social psychology like 'how does the individual perform, act, think or communicate in society, or in a social group or in a community?' The critique of the contemporary social psychology by the theory of social representations comes to light through proposing an alternative ontology and epistemology in the study of social phenomena.

Questions about the relations between the individual and the social, that are commonly posed in contemporary social psychology are based on ontology,[1] i.e. the theory of human existence that views the individual and the social as two units. Reflecting on 'the individual-group problem' Harold Kelley (1999, p. 36f) maintains that four themes concerning this 'problem' dominated not only twentieth-century social psychology but also his own work. He summarises his comments on this problem under four 'counterposings of the individual and the group' (the italics in the four questions below are Kelley's):

- The individual *or* the group?
- The individual *versus* the group?
- The individual *from* the group?
- The individual *against* the group?

If the theory of human existence presupposes that the individual and the social are in their origin two units, then, understandably, questions about the relations between the individual and the social are meaningful. Examples of such questions would be the following: How do the two elements enter into interaction and how do they affect one another?

In contrast, the theory of social representations is based on a fundamentally different ontology. The ontology of the theory of social representations presupposes the symbolic and communicative interdependence of the *Ego-Alter* as its point of departure. It is from this position that the theory generates knowledge about social phenomena. Above all, in the human world, *to be* means to *symbolically communicate*.

In the first approach the conceptual difference between the individual/ social and the *Ego-Alter* may not be apparent – after all, words express the meanings that we give them. However, the differences between the individual/social and the *Ego-Alter* indeed become apparent once we consider their meanings in the frames of reference in which they have historically developed and in which they exist in contemporary social science. The difference that I have in mind is in relation to symbolic communication. The processes of the 'individualisation of the social', 'socialisation' and even 'interaction' have often been studied without reference to symbolic communication. Indeed, social psychology has successfully existed for decades without paying much attention to language and communication. In contrast, in social science, the *Ego-Alter* has been defined, since the eighteenth century, as a dialogical relation. There would be no *Self* without *Others* and no self-consciousness without other-consciousness: one determines the other. It would be meaningless to refer to the *Ego-Alter* outside the realm of communication; the *Ego* and the *Alter* are generated in and through symbolic communication. Within this ontology, questions concerning the relations between the *Ego* and the *Alter* cannot be posed in the same way as the questions about the relation between the individual and the social. The individual and the social have been historically and contemporarily conceptualised within monological ontologies, which have presupposed that they are two elements interacting. In contrast, the *Ego-Alter* belongs to a dialogical ontology within which the *Ego* and the *Alter* are interdependent, one constituting the other. Therefore, the meanings of these two pairs of antinomies, i.e. the individual/social and the *Ego-Alter* belong to different frames of reference. Consequently, questions that would be meaningful in one frame of reference, e.g. in the individual/social frame, might be meaningless in the *Ego-Alter* frame of reference and *vice versa*.

This book proposes a theory of social knowledge based on *dialogicality and the theory of social representations*. Dialogicality, it is hypothesised, is the *sine qua non* of the human mind. Dialogicality is the capacity of the human mind to conceive, create and communicate about social realities in terms of the '*Alter*'. This hypothesis provides an alternative to the hypothesis of the mind/brain according to which the brain is a computer and mental states are its software.

The hypothesis of dialogicality can be further expounded as follows. Dialogicality developed throughout anthropogenesis and in history and culture. This means that what has been implanted in the human mind during phylogenesis and socio-cultural history is not only a biological and universal cognitive system (whatever this may be) of the individual, but also dialogicality. We can hypothesise that human thought and language are generated from dialogicality.

In the first instance we need to pose the following question. What evidence is there to postulate the hypothesis of dialogicality as the *sine qua non* of the human mind? In order to provide an answer to this question in this book, we must go beyond the boundaries of social psychology and visit other fields, for example, philosophy, anthropology, history, linguistics and cultural studies. It is social and human scientists who have created, often unwittingly and artificially, boundaries between scholarly fields. Human traditions, often guided by political and territorial interests, constrain our ideas into the strait-jackets of narrowly conceived disciplines, thus depriving us of seeing social phenomena in different perspectives and in the multifaceted realities to which they belong. This is why we must take a broader view in our intellectual effort to postulate a theory of social knowledge.

As a theory of social knowledge, the dialogically based theory of social representations presupposes that social thinking and language are phenomena in *change* and that different kinds of social knowledge co-exist together in *communication*. Change can be experienced as a sweeping storm but it may also remain unnoticed by those who live through it. Whether rapid or slow, *change* rather than *stability* is the presupposition on which this theory of social knowledge will be built. Communication by definition involves movements of thoughts, transformation of meanings and contents of knowledge. Older kinds of knowledge are not eliminated by new kinds of knowledge even if these appear to contradict one another. Just like Kuhn (1962) argued that Einsteinian knowledge of relativity did not eliminate Newton's mechanistic physics – and that each kind of physics remains important for the solution of specific problems, so different kinds of social knowledge can serve different purposes.

This book is structured in such a way that each chapter builds on the ideas of the previous chapter and thus lays grounds for the next chapter.

Chapter 1, *Change: an epistemological problem for social psychology*, shows that there is considerable asymmetry between the concepts of stability and change in terms of their theoretical status. Casual inspection of psychological theories of social knowledge indicates that in general, they foreground stability but not change, as a theoretical concept. The concept of knowledge in European philosophy and in science since ancient Greece has been determined by the historically and culturally established search for stability and certainty. Knowledge, certainty and truth all go together;

knowledge must have a degree of certainty, otherwise it would not be knowledge. However, if thinking and language are dynamic phenomena, what does this imply for the theory of social knowledge? It implies that the concepts of stability and change pose an epistemological problem for social psychology.

Chapter 2, *Thinking and antinomies*, starts with the idea of antinomic or oppositional thinking in ancient Greece and China. This chapter shows that the idea of antinomies in thinking has existed in various guises, although it has often been ignored in philosophy and in science. It has had its peaks and troughs throughout the history of science, mysticism and religion of the Middle Ages until it practically disappeared in the mechanistic science of the seventeenth century.

Only in the nineteenth century, when the concepts of evolution, relativity and interdependence of various phenomena in natural, human and social sciences required a new theoretical underpinning, did thinking in antinomies once again come to the fore. In Hegel's theory of social knowledge there was, for the first time in history, a systematically developed concept of interdependent antinomies in tension as a basis of dialectic movement. The concept of interdependent antinomies in tension presupposes that the two components are created together, like *figure-and-ground*. In post-Hegelian social science the idea of antinomies in thinking has been established by a number of scholars in sociology, in developmental and social psychology and in psychopathology.

Unlike antinomies of thinking, *Linguistic and dialogical antinomies* (Chapter 3) have not been clearly expressed in the study of language until the end of the seventeenth century. Several kinds of antinomies in language can be identified. Focusing on the work of philosophers like René Descartes and John Locke on the one hand, and of Giambattista Vico, on the other, we can detect the first antinomy in the study of language in *a-historical versus historical* approaches. Later on, from the eighteenth century onwards, we can identify, as part of the Romantic Movement of the eighteenth century another antinomy, that of *the social versus the individual* nature of language. Although we can find it in the work of various scholars, like Bernardi, it was most clearly expressed in the work of Wilhelm Humboldt. For him, language was an organism consisting of two interdependent components. Specifically, he conceptualised language as a collective system of signs, on the one hand, and as speech of individuals, on the other. The third kind of antinomies, *linguistic*, can be found at all levels of analysis of language, ranging from phonological, to grammatical and semantic. These have been studied mainly in the twentieth century through the work of the pre-Saussurean linguists, more explicitly by Ferdinand de Saussure (1857–1913), and later on by his followers. Finally, there are *antinomies in dialogue*. Among these, the most fundamental one, which actually defines dialogue, is the antinomy between the '*Ego*' and the '*Alter*'.

Chapter 4, *Thinking through the mouth*, presents the hypothesis that dialogicality is the ontological characteristic of the human mind to conceive, create and communicate about social realities through mutual engagement of the *Ego* and the *Alter* in thinking and in communication. While the *Ego* and the *Alter* are interdependent, they also preserve their autonomy. Antinomies in communication between interdependence and independence and between setting one's own perspective and adopting the perspective of the other create tension and conflict. Through tension and conflict both partners negotiate their position, deepen their understanding and misunderstanding and mutually change each other's perspectives. The specific characteristic of dialogicality is the emphasis on the multifaceted nature of communication. Hidden and open polemics, parody and irony are all ridden with tension, and hence have the potential for different interpretations.

But how exactly do we move from dialogical antinomies to a dialogically based theory of social knowledge?

Chapter 5, *Social representations: old and new*, introduces Durkheimian and Moscovici's theories of collective and social representations, respectively. Durkheim's sociology of knowledge is characterised by a number of specific features. These include the duality of human nature, stability of collective representations, institutional and constraining nature of collective representations, collective monologism of representations and a continuous genesis of collective representations from religion to science. In contrast, Moscovici's theory of social representations uses as its basic theoretical resources dialogicality, change in thinking and communication, polyphasia in thinking, common sense thinking and knowledge.

Chapter 6, *Dialogical triads and three-component processes*, addresses the fundamental question: how can static epistemologies be transformed into dynamic ones? The attempt to answer this question was already suggested by Karl Bühler. He argued that social knowledge is co-constructed by the *Ego*, the *Alter* and Representation. However, it was Moscovici who proposed the *dynamic semiotic triangle Ego-Alter-Object* (or symbol/ representation) as a basic unit of the theory of social knowledge. There are several characteristics that make these triangular relations dynamic and therefore, different from other triadic models. First, the relation between the *Ego* and the *Alter* is a relation in tension. Second, the relations between the *Ego-Alter-Object* take place both simultaneously and sequentially. Finally, the quality of the relation between the *Ego-Alter-Object* points either to belief- or knowledge-based social representations. Three-component processes are illustrated in different spheres of social knowledge, for example in dialogues between those with speech and communication impairment and their partners, in social influence processes and in the creation and change of aesthetic norms in the arts.

Chapter 7, *Understanding themata and generating social representations*, discusses the main concept of the theory of social representations: themata. The structured contents of social representations are generated from culturally shared antinomies that have become problematised. It is when social conditions obtain that these interdependent antinomies become thematised and start generating social representations. Examples of themata, based on such interdependent antinomies entering public discourse are edible/inedible, freedom/oppression and justice/injustice. Among such themata, those derived from the *Ego-Alter*, e.g. morality/immorality and freedom/oppression, generate social representations essential for survival and extension of humanity.

Just as we are born into social representations, we are born into speech and communicative genres, i.e. conventionalised and institutionalised forms of communication. Children adopt speech and communication genres naturally in their social environment as they acquire language and learn to speak in different genres without even realising that they do. Social representations are thematised through communication genres.

Many ideas presented in this book and their development result from my discussions with Serge Moscovici. Over the last few years he has very generously shared his thoughts with me and we have explored ideas from different perspectives; he read drafts of some chapters and commented on them critically and constructively. His broad and deep scholarship has been inspirational for developing my ideas. Since we have extensively discussed these issues, I am unable to distinguish whether in this book I am expressing my own ideas, his ideas or my ideas shaped by his insights and criticism. Therefore, it is impossible to make a proper acknowledgement and I can only apologise to Serge Moscovici for that. This does not mean that Serge Moscovici is in an agreement with everything that I have written. Indeed, he is not and I am taking full responsibility for mistakes in the text.

There are other people who helped me enormously during the thinking about and the writing of this book. Above all, my friends and colleagues from the group *Dynamics of Dialogue* during the years 1987–93 (Jorg Bergman, Rob Farr, Klaus Foppa, Carl Graumann, Per Linell, Tom Luckmann and Ragnar Rommetveit) provided intellectual stimulation for understanding dialogicality and dialogue. Equally important, these relations have led to long-lasting friendships.

Workshops and discussion groups that I have given and attended at the René Descartes University in Paris in the context of our collaboration with the Laboratoire d'Etudes sur l'Acquisition et la Pathologie du Langage chez l'Enfant, have helped me to develop my ideas. I have never failed to apologise there secretly to the spirit of René Descartes for being critical of that great mind. Seminars that I gave at various universities, such as in the Department of Communication Studies in Linköping, the London School of Economics, the Sorbonne University in Paris, universities at Strasbourg, Mexico City, Natal and João Pessoa in Brazil, have also helped enormously to clarify my thoughts. I am very grateful to Professor Per Linell and Professor Jim Wertsch for reading the whole manuscript and for providing critical and constructive comments. Specific thanks are to Sir Geoffrey Lloyd for commenting on Chapter 2. I am also grateful to Professors Augusto Palmonari and Gustav Jahoda, to Drs Anne Salazar and Christian Hudelot for sharing with me their views on various perspectives expressed in this book and for their insightful comments.

The University of Stirling has given me freedom to accomplish my project and I appreciate particularly the help given to me by the Heads of the Psychology Department, Professors Lindsay Wilson and Roger Watt. Bob Lavery was very kind in photographing and scanning the figures that appear in the book and I thank him very much for that. I also acknowledge the generous support of the Carnegie Trust in Scotland for my research abroad.

Most of the work was done in Paris. I am grateful to the Administrateur of the Maison des Sciences de l'Homme, Professor Maurice Aymard; the Director of Maison Suger Monsieur Jean-Luc Lory; Madame Anne Laurent, the Secretary of the European Laboratory of Social Psychology in the Maison des Sciences de l'Homme; and La Mission de la Recherche et de la Technologie du Ministère de la Culture et de la Communication. All these individuals and institutions have provided invaluable support during the years I have worked on this and other projects in Paris.

I am very grateful to Sarah Caro, Gillian Dadd and Paul Watt of Cambridge University Press for their support in the publishing process and to Sara Barnes for editorial help.

My family, Maria, Ivana and Pavel have given me, as always, their warmest support during my work.

NOTE

1. The term 'ontology' as used in this book does not refer to the essence of being in a metaphysical sense. 'Ontology' refers to the nature of human existence. More specifically, it refers to human existence as social existence. It is from such socially conceived ontology that we shall derive the theory of social knowledge.

1 Change: an epistemological problem for social psychology

1 The circle of perfection

Throughout my career as a social scientist I have always been preoccupied with questions as to how, and in what ways, the researcher's work is influenced by implicit presuppositions, which are shared by the cultures, societies and traditions in which she lives. These questions were particularly reinforced by my personal experience, having emigrated from Central Europe to the United Kingdom, from certain kinds of tradition to other ones and from one kind of psychology to another.

We can find many examples in the history and philosophy of science of the effect of implicit presuppositions on thinking and scientific theories, ranging from ethics and aesthetics on the one hand to hard natural sciences on the other. One of them is Nicolson's (1950) fascinating exposition of *the circle of perfection* in the history of metaphysics, science, ethics and aesthetics. The image of God as a circle of perfection had already appeared in Egyptian hieroglyphics and from there it was later adopted by ancient Greeks and by Christians. This image of the circle of perfection dominated science, aesthetics and poetry until the seventeenth century. Nicolson presents evidence not only of how, by the weight of scientific discoveries, this image finally and irretrievably broke down, but also how old habits of the mind are hard to change, due to culture, religion and mythology. For a long time the image of the circle of perfection resisted any attempts to be destroyed. Nicolson points out that 'many great scientists of the past were "poets" and some of them mystics' (Nicolson, 1950, p. 108) and, until the sixteenth or seventeenth centuries, the languages of poetry and of science were complementary and often interchangeable. For example, Newton was influenced by the mystic philosopher Jacob Böhme who developed 'theosophy' as a discipline in which he tried to capture the manifestation of reason through the divine work (cf. Chapter 2).

Like Newton's, so Kepler's mysticism is well known from his writings. In accordance with the dominant religious images of the time, Kepler assumed that planets must necessarily move in the circle of perfection. This presupposition apparently delayed his study of planetary motion. When he could no longer resist his own discovery that orbital movement proceeds in ellipses, he was shattered. Nicolson paraphrases his feelings, saying that he continued to believe that circular motion remains the perfect motion because the circle is a symbol of God. His own finding, showing that planets move in ellipses, indicates *their* limitation and not the limitation of God. The planets simply cannot reach the perfection of their Creator, Kepler thought, and instead, they only imitate the circle by elliptic movement. Their natures permit 'the beauty and the nobleness of the curved' (Nicolson, 1950, p. 134) but not the nobleness of the circle.

Another example of the difficulty of 'breaking the circle' is Darwin's creation, throughout his career, of his theory of evolution (Darwin, 1859). In his analysis of Darwin's creative process, Gruber (1974, p. 174) showed how Darwin's ideas developed gradually, having been originally implicitly embedded in the framework of generally accepted theories of his time. As Darwin, in deepening his knowledge and amassing increasing evidence for his theory of evolution departed from the generally accepted framework, his ideas, from being originally mere hunches, became more explicit. Recognising his own differences from the accepted framework, he was slowly able to reflect upon them and to develop his theory against the scientific majority's point of view. Darwin's original hypothesis, before 1832, included the Creator in the theory of evolution. Darwin thought that the Creator actually made the organic world. Later, the Creator played a smaller and smaller role and finally, he totally disappeared from Darwin's scientific schema. In the final version of Darwin's theory of evolution, the Creator remained, with a question mark, outside the system. Darwin implied that if the Creator existed, he might have initiated the evolution of the natural system. However, he no longer interfered with it.

Thus Darwin, like Kepler before him, deprived God of the responsibility for the worldly phenomena, which he had supposedly created. Having liberated himself, Darwin could then proceed with the formulation of his evolutionary theory. However, it is interesting to note the slow rate in which Darwin only gradually freed himself from the force of implicit presuppositions of the commonly accepted conceptual frameworks and of the various inhibiting factors. Gruber's analysis points to a number of such factors. These included the fear of persecution, hesitation of repudiating his religious beliefs, the fear of loneliness as he isolated himself more and more from the accepted scientific theories and as he entered a field of inquiry into which not many could follow him. Thus both personal and societal pressures were obstacles to his making an essential conceptual transformation into the new system of knowledge.

These examples show how much and how deeply the collectively shared and the implicitly adopted presuppositions of scientific theories are engraved in the researcher's thinking, in particular at the beginning of his scientific journey. Researchers can reject or transform their presuppositions into new ideas only with a considerable effort and only if the weight of argument and/or of evidence becomes irrepressible.

Social psychology, like other sciences, has its deep-rooted presuppositions that are difficult to alter. Among them, the presuppositions of the concepts of stability and change pose particular problems for the theory of social knowledge in social psychology.

2   Stability as the circle of perfection

2.1   Stability and change

In various spheres of life, tendencies towards change and stability are often experienced as a conflict. Let us think of political revolutions. Revolutions, by definition, require renunciation of the past and yet the masters of revolutions latch on to many old values that help them to secure their newly attained power. For example, social interactions and habits of the mind are deeply embedded in culture and they are highly resistant to change. They are part of inter-connected systems of communication, songs, myths, collective memories and traditions.

To illustrate, like other great political revolutions, the Soviet Revolution of 1917 claimed to have broken with the past and to have introduced a new order. Writing about the icon and axe and about the irony that these symbols produced in Russian history, Billington (1966) illustrated how Russia, after the Revolution of 1917, continued to be ruled by Byzantine rituals, but without Byzantine beauty and piety. The revolution disposed of the czar, but rituals based on worshipping and bowing to the tyrant remained unchanged. In a similar manner, Lotman (1990, p. 138) recalls the feudal practices of Ivan the Terrible, who used to execute not only disfavoured boyars but also their families, servants and peasants from his villages. As it is well known, the idea that family is collectively responsible for the actions of its members was maintained by the Soviet regime and even expanded, after the Second World War, to all countries under the Soviet rule.

More recently, in the post-communist countries of Europe, the political and economic revolutions did not necessarily bring about a social psychological revolution. For example, Klicperová et al. (1997), describe a 'totalitarian syndrome' in the minds and activities of the general public produced during the previous regime. It is characterised by patterns of attitudes and behaviours developed in order to adapt to life under totalitarian conditions. These include learned helplessness, specific manifestations of immorality and incivility and lack of civic culture. Such patterns of attitude and behaviour endanger the new state not from outside but from inside and put at risk the democratic awareness of citizens.

We can suppose that 'change' and 'stability' in everyday language are empty terms or without any reference to realities unless we fill them with specific human affairs and with concrete phenomena, which provide them with contents, meanings and passions. We may desire and hope for change just as we may struggle to preserve tradition. We may fear change just as we may hate our existing situation from which we cannot escape. Generally speaking, however, we experience and communicate everything in life *as* change, whether it is saturated with tempestuous and passionate events or gradual, almost imperceptible, transformations.

Language has an immense number of words to express change, movement and passage from one state of affairs to another. Change-words distinguish between fast and slow transformations, intentional or purposeless activities, revolutions and evolutions, and qualities and quantities of adjustments. There are words for ebb and flow, wax and wane and flux and reflux. Yet in order to understand these distinctions, which are built into meanings of change-words, equally, we need to experience and understand non-change. As with pairs of words like life and death, war and peace, fear and hope, limited and unlimited, beginning and end, so with change and stability, we understand the meaning of one word in reference to the other within the pair of opposites.

Not only revolutions, but also our daily routines are experienced as a tension between stability and change when we alter our habits, form and dissolve relationships, choose constancy and disguise old loyalties. Our ability to understand and evaluate events in terms of change and stability is an essential aspect of *commonly shared social knowledge*. Without analysing this term, 'social knowledge' can refer to all kinds of knowing in our everyday life, like common sense, formation and transformation of concepts and social representations, 'know-how' skills, managing interpersonal interaction and relations, among others. Social knowledge is *knowledge in communication* and *knowledge in action*. There can be no social knowledge unless formed, maintained, diffused and transformed within society, either between individuals or between individuals and groups, subgroups and cultures. Social knowledge is about the dynamics of stability and change.

If social knowledge is concerned with creating, understanding and evaluating change and stability, one can expect that the concepts of change and stability will be fundamentally important in the theory of social knowledge. Yet we are badly mistaken if we hold such a supposition. When examining *theories of knowledge* in general and *theories of social knowledge* in particular, the first thing we cannot help noticing is the considerable asymmetry between these two concepts in terms of their theoretical status.

2.2   Stability as a reference point in theories of social knowledge

Casual inspection of psychological theories of social knowledge indicates that in general, they foreground *stability* as a theoretical concept. However, *change* is not treated in the same manner. It is worth considering some examples in social psychology. Theories of social perception are based on the idea that humans, in their desire to control and predict the world in which they live, tend to explain social and natural phenomena in terms of relatively stable attributes (e.g. Heider, 1958; Schutz, 1972). Moscovici (1976b) shows that the studies of social influence have been largely based on congruence and movement towards conformity. Thus these studies have emphasised the tendency for non-change in both thinking and action. Similarly, theories of attitudes and attitude change (e.g. Abelson *et al.*, 1968) highlight people's need for consistency. Conversation analysis, too, searches above all for regularities, rules and principles that remain stable across historical changes in language and across communication genres (e.g. Atkinson and Heritage, 1984).

It is not that change as a social and psychological phenomenon has been ignored. One can find an enormous number of books containing the words 'social change' in their titles. There has been a multitude of research findings concerning the causes of societal change, the analyses of factors leading to social change, the consequences of social change and so on. If this is so, what is the problem, if there is one?

The fundamental issue here is that the criterion for the study of change is the state of stability. It is stability that is presupposed and the questions posed in research concern the causes or reasons for disturbances of stability. For example, social research is often concerned with the question as to why people *change* their attitudes rather than why they *retain* their attitudes. Or, why people *change* their behaviour rather than why they remain *stable* in their habits and activities. Although we have numerous theories about stable universals, their nature, content and form, *we do not have theories of social knowledge based on the concept of change.*

One would think that there must be good grounds on which to evade the concept of change in theories of social knowledge. But what are they? Let us look for an answer in the history of philosophy.

The concept of knowledge in European philosophy and science has been determined by the historically and culturally established search for stability and certainty. The history of European science in general, and social science in particular shows that in order to study change, *the reference point is stability*. Referring to ancient Greek ontology, Lloyd (1994, p. 96) has pointed out that, when Greek philosophers studied change, they analysed phenomena in such a way that they always described the stable characteristics of substances, which they considered as underlying everything that changed. They believed that proper understanding and knowledge could only be obtained from entities, which are permanent.

This line of thinking has also impregnated modern European philosophy. In the seventeenth century Descartes (1628/1911), in his rules for the direction of the mind, pointed out that science must be based only on certain and evident knowledge. According to this traditional Platonic/Cartesian epistemology, which is now often called 'foundational' (Taylor, 1995b), the objective of the theory of knowledge is the search for truth, certainty, unchangeable universals and indubitable principles, which are to be discovered by the mind of the individual. Descartes' epistemological concern was to find out a reliable method, which would verify valid knowledge based on evidence.

In view of the asymmetry between the concepts of stability and change in social psychological theories of knowledge, we need to ask the following question. What kinds of epistemology underlie the theories of knowledge, which foreground stability? We may assume that these theories are based on epistemologies which, again, foreground the concept of stability. If the phenomena that one purports to cognise are conceived as stable, timeless or universal, it must be that their history and their change are irrelevant to one's understanding. It means that we do not need to be concerned with change. In that case, foundational epistemology and an explanation by *a-historical causes and effects* or by *purposes* must be fully adequate.

2.3   Two questions about the nature of knowing

In order to develop my arguments about dialogicality and social representations, I consider it essential, in this chapter, to reflect on the basic presuppositions of foundational epistemologies, which have shaped theories in cognitive sciences. These presuppositions have been mistakenly transferred into social sciences, and more specifically, into social psychology. Only reflection upon them will enable us to conceive of the alternative, *a dialogical epistemology*, for social psychology.

Questions concerning the nature of knowing have undergone surprisingly little variation over the centuries. Although a slight exaggeration, we could claim that, essentially, over the aeons of time, such questions and answers have remained unchanged. Among them, two questions and the answers appear to be particularly significant. First, what aspects of reality can provide humans with knowledge? Second, how do humans represent the world? These basic philosophical questions and the answers to them perhaps would not be of much interest to psychology, if they were concerns only of philosophers. However, they are also theoretical questions asked by psychologists and they have become imprinted in the theories of social knowledge. Consequently, these questions have also been conceived in psychology as empirical ones and they have been implanted into research methods and the analyses of data.

Let us consider the first question, what can count as knowledge. Scholars from Plato to Descartes and Chomsky have provided similar answers. Only knowledge of *eternal universals* can count as true knowledge. Plato postulated the theory of eternal or absolute ideas or Forms, which exist independently of anything that we can perceive through the senses or judge with reason. Particular organisms, like people or animals, or objects like artefacts, or specific attributes like ugly or beautiful, are all perishable. In contrast, the world of Ideas, like the Absolute Man, the Absolute Beauty, the Absolute Justice, Triangularity, Redness or the Absolute Good exist as immanent principles and constitute the objective world, which partake in worldly phenomena to various degrees. The human soul is immortal and already has knowledge of Forms well before the birth of the person in whom it will reside. During life, through a process of learning and acquiring experience, the soul just recollects what it already knows.

For Descartes, the human soul is born with the *innate seeds of knowledge*, and these, as Descartes claims, are clear and distinct ideas. Clear and distinct ideas are universals. They are dispositions, which are like the fire that lies hidden in a flint. They are revealed through reasoning and imagination. For example, the ideas of God, Triangle, Body and so on represent true and immutable essences, which are 'implanted by nature in human mind' (Descartes, 1628/1911, p. 12). This Cartesian point of view enabled Fodor (2000) to emphasise that Chomsky's position of *epistemological nativism* is practically indistinguishable from the one defended by rationalists for centuries – and that his ideas of innateness would be intelligible to Plato.[1] Throughout his extensive work Chomsky has always explicitly acknowledged his debt to Descartes.

Modern psychology has been involved, for decades, in disputes concerning the existence of universals and their natures. The most prominent representatives of cognitive psychology argue that all the most plausible theories of cognition are based on the assumption of innateness of concepts (e.g. Fodor, 1981). The notion of universal, however, has been used very liberally and conveys different meanings to different researchers.

There are weak and strong universals; process and outcome universals; innate and environmental universals; and even universals undergoing change (Marková, 1991).

Considering the second question, the one about representations, we find that the seed of the notion of *representation* already germinates in the ancient Greek idea of *mimesis*, which became particularly important in Plato's philosophy. While, for Plato, the real and objective world was the world of Forms, which were unchanging, universal and incorporeal, perceptible objects of the phenomenal world only resembled or imitated the world of Forms. Plato used the notion of 'mimesis' or 'participation' to refer to particular objects that imitated Forms and were, therefore, inferior to them. For Aristotle, knowing could not be dispensed without images or representations, but in contrast to Plato, Aristotle did not consider mimesis inferior. In the modern studies of cognition, from Descartes through to Chomsky and on until today, a *mental representation* has become an essential concept of all cognitive theories of the mind.

One of the fundamental confusions in contemporary social psychology concerns confounding mental representations and Moscovici's social representations. Mental representations are totally irrelevant to the theme of this book. However, in order to dispel the confusion between mental representations of foundational epistemologies and social representations of dialogical epistemology, I must consider, in this chapter, the main characteristics of mental representations. Then, later the paradigmatic differences between these two, quite incompatible concepts will become much clearer.

2.4   Mental representation

The central interest of foundational epistemologies is to develop a general theory of mental representation. The main epistemological assumption behind this goal is that in order to know something, you need to represent what is outside the mind, to understand the manner in which the mind can construct representations and to express them in language. Thus, 'mental representation' is a term that, in whatever way it is used in the study of the mind, under any circumstances, it cannot be by-passed.

2.4.1   *To make correct mental representations, you must use correct words*
It was René Descartes and John Locke in the seventeenth century who laid down many of the contemporary ideas about mental representations. Specifically, Locke suggested that there is a tight association between language and the theory of knowledge. In his *Essay Concerning Human Understanding* (1690/1975) he raised questions about the nature of

reality and its relation to names, words, signs and language in general. Words can both hinder and facilitate knowledge. They can be abused in many different ways thus preventing the perfection of knowledge. In fact, the wrong use of words, is, according to Locke one of the greatest reasons for the imperfection of knowledge. Among the most significant abuses of words is 'taking them for Things' (1690/1975, book III, Chapter X, paragraph 14) *rather than treating them as representations of things*. This particular abuse is due, according to Locke, to the narrowness of thinking, which restricts one's thoughts to a particular doctrine. In addition, imperfection of knowledge could be due to inconstancy in the use of words, to wrong interpretation, application of old words to new and unusual phenomena, rhetorical use of words, willful faults and neglects and the use of words without having clear and distinct ideas, among many other faults. In order to remedy such defects of speech, words should not be used without precise meanings.

Locke's idea about mental representations as signs of reality restricted itself to the question of truth and falsity of representations. This means that there are correct or incorrect ways in which we represent reality and any imperfection of representations would be due to the use of words without having clear and distinct ideas. In other words, to make correct representations means to use ideas and words correctly. Thus, in Locke's theory of representation we can already find germs of the main characteristics of mental representations as currently studied in cognitive science. There are true and false representations; representations are mirrors or signs of nature; they are formalisations or symbolic structures; they are processes and rules in the brain.

2.4.2   Mental representations are properties of mechanisms   Today, cognitive scientists like Chomsky and Fodor presuppose that the mind is a mechanism or a computer. Chomsky (1980, p. 5) explicitly points out that for him, terms such as 'mind', 'mental representation' or 'mental computation' refer to abstract characteristics 'of the properties of certain physical mechanisms' although these mechanisms remain as yet quite unknown.

However, mechanisms are objects without life history or they are objects in which we can ignore historical changes for the purpose of their study. Mechanisms are decomposable and re-combinable into segments or independent modules and the operations of these segments can be explained in terms of causes and effects or of purposes. Their operations are rule- or algorithm-governed. Mechanisms are self-contained communicational solipsists. Their interaction with the environment is limited to the effect of external forces that they may impose on one another.

Throughout the whole of his career Chomsky likens organs of the body, e.g. vision and its operation in specific cells in the visual cortex, to the operations of organs in the mind/brain. Concerning the confusion in psychology and cognitive science, between the terms 'brain' and 'mind', I could hardly find a more appropriate example of the difference between the two than the one quoted by Rommetveit (1998) that comes from the Hacker (1990) essay entitled 'Chomsky's problems'. There Hacker states: 'What may grow in the brain, e.g. a tumour, cannot grow in the mind, and what may grow in the mind, e.g. suspicion, cannot grow in the brain' (Hacker, 1990, p. 135).

Other cognitive theorists define the mind very abstractly, as a combinatorial space of possible states instantiated in the brain (Jackendoff, 1992). In this conception, mental states, physical and chemical states and computational states are all identical. The brain is a computer and mental states are the software of this computer.

Epistemologically speaking, the mechanistic conception of the mind/ brain is displayed at least in two different ways. The first concerns pleading for the causal explanations of mental phenomena requiring an a-historical and synchronic approach. Traditional epistemologies in European philosophy like those of Plato, Descartes and Chomsky are all based on concepts of universals, certainty, permanent knowledge, immutability and a mental representation. These foundational epistemologies in order to understand and explain natural and social phenomena use *a-historical explanations* (Fodor, 2000, p. 82). Fodor (2000, p. 82) argues that sciences are correct in using a-historical explanations by viewing mechanisms in terms of their synchronic, i.e. existing operations, rather than in terms of their diachronic, i.e. historically contemplated operations. To that extent, 'why couldn't a likewise ahistoric theory of mind/brain supervenience count as explaining how mentality belongs to the causal order?' Indeed, if psychology is concerned with evolution of the phenomena it studies, then it will be '*very* [Fodor's emphasis] unlike lots of other sciences; because in lots of other sciences, it's perfectly OK-in fact, it's the usual case- . . . to be largely or solely ahistorical'. Just like physical sciences provide an aerodynamic explanation of a bird's flight without referring to evolution, so functions of any mind/brain organ should be similarly explained a-historically.

Such arguments should not astonish us because, as already implied, they have been part of European philosophy and psychology for centuries. However, when old ideas in 'new' guises are claimed to be revolutionary turns and when Copernican revolutions entice the psychologist's imagination with promises of the change of paradigm, it may be difficult to reflect on the possibility that the latest fads might be profoundly rooted in history. We may be deceiving ourselves by ignoring this possibility.

The second mechanistic aspect of the mind/brain conception concerns the assumption that the mind/brain consists of a set of independent compartments, which each contain different parts of a machine. While Chomsky emphasises 'mental organs' of the mind, Fodor extends this idea by proposing his conception of 'innate modules'. In both cases, the mind/brain is viewed as containing specialised computational devices; each is designed to treat a particular form of information or to translate information from one specific form into another. Subdividing the mind/brain into specific organs or modules is widely accepted in cognitive and computational sciences.

However, the mind/brain conception has also been extended to social psychology. Jackendoff (1992, p. 17) believes that no matter what takes place in the study of mental representations, the generally adopted view of the mind/brain is fairly robust. He ventures to apply the individualistic computational model into the area of social concepts, by developing an argument for a module or a group of modules called *social cognition* (1992, pp. 67–81). He argues on this basis that 'social organisation' and 'culture' involve the interactions of individuals with each other and that *'each individual's participation in the culture must be supported by cognitive organisation in the individual's mind'* (p. 76, Jackendoff's emphasis). This serves as an argument for the universality of social cognition in the human species and consequently, the essential equality of individuals and social groups in this domain. Jackendoff believes that the causal access to external social relations is obtained through the same channels as in ordinary perception, 'the good old sense organs' (1992, p. 166). However, Jackendoff's ambition goes much further in his attempt to extend the models of individual cognition to social cognition. Specifically, he turns his attention to the possibility of formalisation of social cognition. As he points out, a number of questions still await further research, like the following: how would social concepts look if considered to be formal entities? In what combinatorial space could they be embedded? How could this space be related to the perception of concrete actions?

2.4.3   What do mental representations represent?   Today, the study of mental representations is so vast and diverse with so many contradictory assumptions built into different theories that one can hardly orientate oneself in this complex pattern. Cummins (1996) has summarised the different kinds of questions studied in psychology, cognitive science and philosophy, categorising them under four headings. First, there are questions about *contents* represented in the mind and about the kind of information that is represented in the mind when it is cognising. Contents, however, do not refer to concrete events and to events experienced by the individual but to formalised propositions, concepts, categories or classifications.

Such formalised contents of the mind/brain are assumed to be more or less stable in the mind/brain. Second, there are questions and theories about *forms*, which a mental representation takes. For example, mental representations can take the form of images, symbolic structures and activation vectors. Different forms of representation may be appropriate for different kinds of task. Third, there are questions about the *implementation* of representational schemes in the mind/brain. For example, do they have neural, computational or other implementation? And finally, there are problems of definitions. These require clarification as to what it means to say *that something represents something else*. This issue itself presumably incorporates yet another question. Since mental representations are generally classified as true or false, how do we know when we make errors in representing? As Cummins points out, these four main psychological and philosophical questions impose constraints on one another.

Necessarily, by virtue of such diversities, today there are a number of representational theories of cognition, each claiming to provide a resolution to the above problems.

Since mental representations are conceived as symbols, images, pictures and formalisations, sooner or later, theories of representation become confronted with another challenge: with the relationship between mental representations and reality. This question, again, is a very old one and has been studied since the beginning of the European philosophy. It has produced a variety of answers, ranging from realism to scepticism. However, its current versions in the most important quarters of cognitive science seem to be losing any grip on reality by offering more and more extreme solipsistic positions. In these versions, by being excluded from the study, reality is deprived of any theoretical significance and, to that extent, of any human significance. For instance, Fodor's argument of methodological solipsism is based on the idea that mental states and processes are computations and computational processes to acquire environmental information. However, one cannot really say anything about the nature of reality. If mental processes have a formal character, which Fodor believes to be the case, those processes have access to the formal properties of such representations of the environment only to the extent sensory faculties can provide them. This in turn means that these formal processes have no access to semantic properties of such representations, which include properties such as being true, false, having referents or indeed having the property of being representations of the environment (Fodor, 1980). In other words, all that psychology can do is to account for the mind's mental representations purely in terms of a syntactic machine and be concerned with the internal workings of its cognitive mechanisms. The mind/brain has a built-in innate formalised language, which can operate both as a medium of representation and a medium of computation. Mental representations do not tell us anything about reality.

In the end, it appears that the notion of a mental representation may totally lose its ground. Jackendoff (1992) expresses his own position concerning mental representation with some hesitation:

A representation is not necessarily *about* anything; if you like, it does not strictly speaking *represents* anything . . . The point of this notion of representation is that it can in principle be instantiated in a purely combinatorial device like the brain as I understand it, without resort to any miraculous biological powers of intentionality such as Searle (1980) wishes to ascribe to the brain (Jackendoff, 1992, p. 162).

Having disposed of reality as an object of knowledge, theories of the mind/brain have reinforced their solipsistic presuppositions concerning the specificity of independent modules, of formal computations, of synchronic cause-effect structures or of teleological characteristics of mental representations. At the same time, doubts seem to be creeping in about what the cognitive science has achieved. While praising the computational theory of the mind as far the best and a strikingly elegant theory of cognition, Fodor (2000) acknowledges that this theory accounts for no more than a little part of truth. There are things that are right and wrong about the idea that the mind is a computer and that the structure of the mind is largely modular. And he concludes:

In fact, what our cognitive science has done so far is mostly to throw some light on how much dark there is. So far, what our cognitive science has found out about the mind is mostly that we don't know how it works (Fodor, 2000, p. 100).

3   Breaking the perfect circle of stability

3.1   What can replace foundational epistemologies?

Opponents of foundational epistemologies, cognitivism and the computational modelling of mind/brain, hold just as diverse views as do those whom they criticise. However, there is one common point in their criticism: both the term 'epistemology' and 'representation' have lost scholarly credibility.

It has been suggested by many that the term 'epistemology' should be replaced by other terms evoking different kinds of association than those of mechanism and mental representation. According to Rorty (1980, p. 325) hermeneutics is 'what we get when we are no longer epistemological'. For Taylor, epistemology entails above all an attempt to explain the knowing activity in mechanistic terms and by means of 'the whole representational construal of knowledge' (Taylor, 1995b, p. 8). In 'Overcoming epistemology', Taylor (1995a, vii) talks about the Hydra epistemology which, in its attempt to get at the bottom of knowledge without drawing on our life-experience, has become a 'terrible and fateful illusion'. Borrowing Bakhtinian terminology, he replaces this monological Platonic/Cartesian perspective with a dialogical point of view, according to which an integrated agent is engaged in a dialogue with her social environment. Like Bakhtin (cf. Chapter 3 and 4) Taylor (1995d, pp. 173–4), rather than using the term 'knowledge', refers to 'social understanding' as being fundamentally reflexive. 'Reflexivity' here does not mean mirroring of nature but a profoundly social and interactional capacity of humans to engage in a dialogically based construction of knowledge. Having conceived representations only in their foundational sense (rather than in a dialogical sense, see later in this book), Taylor finds Bourdieu's 'habitus' to be one of the key terms that reflects this dialogical perspective. In contrast, mental representations of the foundational epistemology, whether 'outside' or 'within', are monological and disembodied.

Putnam's (1988) argument against mental representations, again, is based on epistemological grounds. He shows that if mental representations are in the mind, then certain logical conditions must be fulfilled to satisfy the relations between words and mental representations. While he does not deny in principle the existence of phenomena like mental representations, he argues that none of the logical conditions, on which the notion of mental representation is based, are fulfilled. First, each word is not necessarily associated in the mind of the speaker with a certain mental representation. Second, he disproves the claim that two words are synonymous only if they are associated with the same mental representation by different speakers using these words. Finally, the mental representation does not determine what the word refers to. Instead, Putnam (1988) argues that language is a co-operative activity of a 'linguistic division of labour'. A reference is socially fixed and it is not determined by conditions in individual mind/brains.

In social psychology Rommetveit (1974, 1990, 1991) vehemently argues against mechanistic and representational models in various areas of human cognition and communication. He shows that even the study of most fundamental concepts in social psychology, like that of interaction, is still dominated by a mechanistic epistemology. Most conceptions of interaction are based on the presupposition that two or more independent entities, e.g. individuals, groups, etc. or variables, for various reasons become mutually dependent and start affecting one another. Each takes a turn in order to exchange ideas. But meanings, implied by terms like 'exchange' or 'turn-taking', are highly misleading. They evoke an image of *external*, rather than *internal*, relations between the interacting participants. If entities, e.g. objects or participants in conversation, are conceived to be in *external relations*, this unavoidably means that each of them is an independent entity and that their relations can be modelled on mathematical or formal logical functions. For example, if a conversational partner describes someone as 'friendly' and the other participant describes the same person as 'intelligent', unless either of these claims is opposed by either of the participants, the truth value of these two claims, in terms of formal logic, becomes 'he is friendly and intelligent'. In other words, elementary conversational contributions can be mechanistically composed and decomposed into their parts by connectives like 'and', 'not', 'but', and so on. Such connectives bind elementary propositions externally as parts of a mechanism. Similarly, Rommetveit argues, 'turn-taking' implies that two (or more) individuals can both make a contribution to the dialogue, with each contribution being the sole responsibility of a single participant. Likewise, 'exchange' evokes an image of two or more independent give-and-take sequences, with each participant being responsible for either 'give' or 'take'.

In contrast to the position of 'exchange', Rommetveit (1974) argues that both participants jointly generate all dialogical and interactional contributions. Human cognition and communication is dual, always orientated both towards the speaker and the listener, who adopt simultaneously the roles of active participants. Self and others always dyadically share social realities because the human mind is dialogically constituted. In communication the participants reciprocally adjust their perspectives by drawing the focus of attention to what is being talked about from the position of temporal 'atunement to the atunement of the other' (Rommetveit, 1992, p. 23).

The main attack on the foundational epistemology comes from various brands of 'construction', 'social construction', 'constructivism' and 'social constructionism'. 'Construction', as an approach, is not new and can be found throughout the whole hundred years of the history of psychology, from Baldwin, Vygotsky, Piaget, Karl Bühler and Peirce, to more recent scholarly approaches, like the social construction of knowledge by Berger and Luckmann (1966).

Among constructivists, Arbib and Hesse (1986) challenge the positivist or verificationist foundational epistemology by drawing attention to a tradition, according to which reality is constructed rather than given. In their attempt to develop a constructivist information-processing theory of the mind, referring to Marx, Durkheim and Weber these authors describe their constructivist model as a social one. In their model, the unit of representation is a 'schema' and it consists of both a synchronic and a diachronic aspect of knowledge. While the former aspect refers to the socially cumulated and schematic knowledge, which is mutually and culturally shared, the latter refers to a newly acquired knowledge of the individual. Avoiding the term 'epistemology', Arbib and Hesse consider cognitive science to be a potential basis for their new theory of 'the construction of knowledge' and the schema-theory a new framework for this cognitively and schema-based holistic system.

However, it is the most recent 'revolutionary turn' that distinguishes itself from earlier constructivisms of Baldwin, Vygotsky, Luckman and Berger. It is *critique* that is the major goal of the latest wave of constructivism (for a review of this approach see Danziger, 1997). There is no unified ontology and epistemology underlying these 'postmodernist', as they call themselves, versions of social construction. On the contrary, it could be claimed that as new interpretations of social construction emerge and further diversify, social psychology becomes more and more disintegrated. 'Postmodernism' presents itself as an essential critique not only of the foundationalist psychology, but also of all psychology that is not 'postmodern'. It emphasises deconstruction, dispersion and fragmentation of concepts, of theories and social phenomena themselves.

Paradoxically, in its most extreme versions, the 'postmodern' social constructionism is ontologically and epistemologically close to the most extreme versions of mental representation theories in the cognitive and computational science. Both individual solipsism and social solipsism reject the possibility of knowing reality. Just like Fodor and Jackendoff, who reject reality as something, about which nothing can be said, so Gergen (1994) is mute to ontology and adopts a profound relativism in epistemology, destabilising all kinds of knowledge. All knowledge is relativist. There is nowhere to go either from the individual solipsism of cognitivists or from the social solipsism of postmodernists. In both approaches reality loses 'reality' and becomes unreal.

Despite the range and profundity of their thinking, the majority of these scholarly critiques did not propose a viable alternative to foundational epistemologies. They put their fingers on the main characteristics of foundational epistemologies, such as their mechanistic conception of knowledge, static and formalistic nature of mental representations and the static theory of the mind. They argue that human agency is a historical agency, that the mind is dialogical and that the individual and social must both feature in the theory of knowledge. Yet, we are still lacking a theory of social knowledge that would bring the dynamics and dialogicality of the mind to a theoretical fruition.

The concept of change remains an epistemological problem.

3.2   Change: an epistemological problem

Social and human scientists have been for a long time well aware that change, temporality and historicity play essential roles in human and social affairs. For example, Gergen (1973), in his influential paper on social psychology as a history maintains that phenomena studied by social psychologists are historical phenomena. He is critical of contemporary social psychology because it examines social phenomena as if they were static and not historically embedded. Social psychology should not model itself on natural sciences like physics and chemistry, which try to explain objects of their study in terms of causes and effects. Humans are agents who act with intentions and therefore they are different in nature from physical phenomena. They do not act in identical, repeatable and predictable ways, as do physical phenomena.

However, if human agency is a historical agency, what should be the characteristics of a historical explanation? Surely, such characteristics would involve more than a description of successive events in which the human agent is involved. However, Gergen does not pose this question. His analysis does not concern the fundamental problem as to what kind of theory of knowledge is required in order to provide historical explanations of social phenomena. Therefore, we need to go one step further than Gergen. Not only should we claim that the human agency is a historical agency. In addition, we must propose a theory of social knowledge that will provide *a historical explanation* of human agency.

First, since the concept of stability has dominated theories of knowledge for centuries, we need to break the perfect circle of stability. Yet, our intellectual heritage, based on the concept of stability as the sole starting point of inquiry, is deeply rooted in European thinking. In her attempt to break the circle of perfection of stability a researcher might think that she has accomplished 'the revolutionary turn' through a fundamental criticism and through denuding all the presuppositions on which the Platonic/Cartesian paradigm rests. Yet she may totally deceive herself in thinking that she is presenting a genuine alternative. Without even being aware of it, there is a danger. Our concepts, theories and scientific methods may become, in no time, stealthily filled once again with presuppositions of foundational epistemologies. Let us reflect on some examples of the difficulty that the concept of change has presented for other researchers.

3.2.1   Saussure's problem   Since the eighteenth century the idea of stability and change in knowledge has been associated with the concept of relatively stable socially and culturally shared traditions of thinking and

language on the one hand and with that of more variable individual agency in thinking and language on the other. The problem that has been the crux of the matter was how to conceptualise the interdependence between the relatively stable and variable characteristics of thought and language. The attempts to conceptualise this double-sided, relatively stable and at the same time variable, nature of the human mind ran into problems.

The founder of semiotics, Ferdinand Saussure (1857–1913), conceived of language as a relatively stable social phenomenon, which changes through the speech of individuals. His monumental work in linguistics exemplifies, more than any other work, the theoretical problem of studying *change* in social phenomena. He viewed language as a social fact. Speech, in contrast, according to Saussure, was an individual act. How can *change* be scientifically studied in linguistics, which is concerned with such a complex phenomenon that is both social and individual, both relatively static and dynamic, both passively adopted and reflectively created?

For Saussure it was a general semiotic fact that continuity over time is bound up with changes in time. He emphasised that 'This question of the necessity of change deserves further consideration, for not enough light has been thrown on it' (Saussure, 1910–11/1993, p. 100). He pursued the question of the static and the dynamic linguistics assiduously, pointing out that the rudiments of any change in a language are brought in only through speech and that every kind of change is started by a certain number of individuals (Saussure, 1910–1911/1993, p. 118). In order to consider the gravity of the problem for Saussure of change in language, let us consider the quotation from his work:

I now come to the duality of the object which features in the title of this chapter. Linguistics comes to its second crossroads. (The first crossroads: should we study the language or speech?) Should we study synchronic linguistic facts or diachronic facts [?] (In fact, these are two disciplines.) You cannot mix the two approaches. This is the place to add, since at the first crossroads there was a choice between the language and speech, that everything diachronic <in a language> is born in speech. The rudiments of any change in a language are brought in only through speech . . . They will only become linguistic facts when they have come to be accepted by the collectivity. As long as they remain in speech, they do not count (speech being individual). When the change becomes linguistic, we study it.

But changes always begin with facts of speech (Saussure, 1910–11/1993, p. 118). After giving many examples of changes in language, he makes a decision:

On reaching the bifurcation <static linguistics and dynamic linguistics>, I choose to pursue *static linguistics* (1910–11/1993, p. 125).

Saussure's critics, however, rarely recognise his theoretical problem of conceptualising change. While he admitted that he did not know how to study facts in language (synchrony) and changes in speech (diachrony) simultaneously, he has been criticised, often light-heartedly, for having studied language only *synchronically*, i.e. as a stable system, rather than *diachronically*, i.e. in its change. For Saussure, these two issues belonged to two different scholarly disciplines, which could not be mixed. And since he thought that they could not be mixed he chose to pursue static linguistics.

And thus, according to Saussure, one can only capture changes in language by studying the sequences of stable, i.e. synchronic states – something like a succession of stable pictures which, if projected sufficiently quickly, would give an impression of a moving film (for more details, cf. also Chapter 3).

While Saussure was well aware of the problem of change that he could not solve, many contemporary psychologists are struggling with the same problem but, apparently, without Saussure's insight into their conceptual difficulty. Valsiner and his colleagues (e.g. Valsiner, 1989, 1998; Dodds, Lawrence and Valsiner, 1997; Valsiner and Lawrence, 1996) have brought this general problem to the open. They have discussed the difficulty, in psychological theories, of conceptualising interdependencies with respect to the personal and social phenomena. These authors argue that, although the human individual has both personal and socio/cultural attributes which should be conceived together, it is common in psychological theories that one or the other is ontologically denied.

Concerning the socio/cultural accounts of personal development, the main problem that arises is that they tend to split the individual from the social. As Dodds, Lawrence and Valsiner (1997, p. 484) maintain, 'their attempted resolutions focus on the constitution of the personal within the social through dialogue, discourse, fusion, joint or mutual activity, narrative or voice'. Such accounts, however, the authors argue, have difficulty in explaining the interdependence between the personal and the social, because they conceive them as primarily, i.e. ontologically, separate. This means that the individual is primarily conceived as one unit and society as another unit. Consequently, these theories have difficulty in explaining how the individual and society can interact and how they maintain their interdependence.

3.2.2   *Is 'equilibration' the answer to the problem of change?*   While Ferdinand Saussure was concerned with change in language, Jean Piaget was concerned with developmental changes in thinking. Saussure did assume that the change in language has something to do with the interdependence between the relatively stable, social aspect of language and the dynamic, individual aspect of speech, but he did not know how to address this problem. In contrast, Piaget's theory of equilibration takes into consideration both stability and change in the development of a child's thinking. Despite that, however, Piaget's theory does not solve the problem of change.

Piaget posed the question of the development of thinking in a different way to Saussure with respect to the development of language. While for Saussure language was above all a social phenomenon, for Piaget, thinking started in the mind of the individual.

Like all great scholars, Piaget developed and reformulated his theory throughout his whole life. Therefore, one might be mistaken in focusing rigidly on a specific aspect of his theory that was postulated at a certain period of his life and ignoring the fact that he changed or developed his views on the subject as time went on. Nevertheless, we are fairly safe in drawing attention to the following issues. According to Piaget, the individual is engaged in the dialectical relationship with his environment. Moreover, Piaget acknowledged the historical and cultural effects of society on the individual's process of thinking. However, as Chapman (1992) points out, Piaget did not present any account as to how thinking could be affected by social factors because he was not concerned with these questions. Instead, his primary aims were to explain 'the *generativity of intelligence* and the *progressive increase of rigor observed in intellectual development*' (Chapman, 1992, p. 46). In other words, in contrast to Saussure, Piaget did not pose for himself the epistemological question of the interdependence between the social and the individual nature of thinking.

Piaget's theory of a child's thinking is based on the postulated developmental stages that become progressively more complex with the child's age. The less complex stages form the necessary ground for the next ones in the hierarchy. Within each stage Piaget explains stability and change as an equilibration of cognitive structures. Equilibration is a process of reorganisation of the existing cognitive structures, which occurs when new contents and the newly formed knowledge are integrated. He views cognition as an open system interacting with the environment through assimilation and accommodation, which provides the necessary conditions for equilibrium (Piaget, 1985, p. 170). Piaget insists that his cognitive equilibria are totally different in nature from equilibria in mechanistic physics. Equally, they are also very different from thermodynamic equilibria in physical sciences because cognitive equilibria, in contrast to physical equilibria, are open systems: they assimilate environment into their structures.

When cognitive structures within a given developmental stage can no longer cope with the environmental pressures coming from new knowledge and new contents, the whole structure transforms to the next level. However, as many critics have pointed out, equilibration, a central concept of the dynamics in Piaget's theory, refers only to activities within each stage. Piaget does not explain how any given stage changes into the next one in the hierarchy. Beilin (1992) comments that Piaget agreed with this criticism on several occasions.

Interestingly, Piaget himself viewed similarity between his theory of stages and Saussure's synchronic analysis of language and he referred several times to some sort of dynamic equilibrium when he spoke about Saussure's system. Piaget's concept of equilibrium refers to a state of relative stability during which the system can accommodate new structures and contents without any conflict that would disturb the existing level of development. His theory of equilibration is a sophisticated device which involves actions of the individual's cognition that operate within the boundaries of the existing stage of the development, just like the synchronic system of language allows for novelty within its limits.

3.2.3   'History' with a goal   If foundational epistemologies argue for an a-historical explanation, let us turn to historically based explanations. For example, teleological and functional explanations consider phenomena in their development and see them as purposeful. Teleological and functional explanations are based on the idea that organisms, throughout their histories and development, strive towards a pre-determined goal. Piaget's theory of cognitive development can serve as an illustration of this point.

The concept of the development of child's logic in Piaget's theory is based on hierarchically postulated stages, which are *universalistic*. All children are expected to go through the same stages, as the child's cognition unfolds, progressing from illogical to more logical thinking. As Piaget (1970, p. 35) says, if we study children all over the world, 'in Geneva, Paris, New York or Moscow, in the mountains of Iran or the heart of Africa, or on an island in the Pacific' we find similar ways in which children conduct social exchanges. We observe them between children as well as between children and adults and they take place 'regardless of the context of information handed down through education'. By the age of approximately 12 the child's thinking reaches the stage of formal operations and therefore, of logical thinking, where development arrives at its peak.

Later in his life Piaget placed more emphasis on the constructivist possibilities of the mind and he focused more on the mind as an open system with further possibilities of cognitive development. However, while he emphasised the dialectic of forces between the individual and

environment, his theory of stages, which is based on the intellectual development of the individual and which has a universalistic orientation,
did not allow him to develop this dialectic any further. Universalistic theories never pay sufficient attention to the world in which organisms live
and Piaget's theory of stages is not an exception. Despite the fact that
Piagetian scholars emphasise Piaget's constructivism, his theory has a
predetermined goal: to achieve the operational stage.

Such teleological or functional 'histories' with a predetermined goal are
based on the notion of continuity in which each stage is a firm preparation
for the next one. However, living organisms have their personal histories.
Life and its history, moreover, imply a degree of unpredictability and this
contradicts the point of view according to which change is predetermined
by some final cause, e.g. by achieving the final stage in a predetermined
hierarchy.

The ideas of final causes, goal-directed behaviour, means-ends models
and teleological explanations in evolution and development are common not only in psychology but also in functionalist approaches in other
sciences, like biology and linguistics.

In biological sciences, for example, a teleological explanation became
fashionable in the 1940s in the study of voluntary movements of organisms (Rosenblueth et al., 1943). Later, with the development of cybernetics, teleological explanations became widespread during the 1950s
and 1960s. The question 'for what purpose?' dominated the anticipatory
models in biological evolution. Biologists of that period, e.g. the reputed
Soviet scientist Bernstein (1967) argued that the purposeful aspect of
organisms and their movement dominates every response of an organism with respect to any motor problem. Motor actions of an individual,
whether of an animal or a human being, are attempts to find solutions to
specific kinds of problems.

The idea that intelligible human behaviour must be viewed as the pursuit of goals was not only generally accepted but also there were many
theories put forward to show how sciences aimed to define these goals.

These theories tried to understand the use of information and the ways
information is organised in the organism. It was believed that sciences like
embryology, ontogeny and phylogeny, all show purposefulness in their
activities. It became commonplace to argue that the developing organisms
strive for the maximum of negative entropy and for vital stability. For
example, a fish develops fins in order to swim; and birds develop wings
in order to fly (for criticism of these functionalist theories see Lewontin,
1990). The teleological explanation was behind any changes in the human
brain. Drawing on investigations of fossils, Eccles (1989, pp. 56 and 95)
argues that the change in the habitat of hominids from living on trees to

living on the ground required a redesign of their nervous system and was 'a challenge to develop a language of sounds for communication'. Thus, teleological assumptions were also implicit in the explanation of the development of language, the self, and in the emergence of consciousness and self-consciousness.

In linguistics, a teleological explanation was developed and defended by Roman Jakobson in his genetic approach to language. Jakobson's means-end model of language seems to have been inspired by several factors. First, Jakobson objected to the synchronic approach to language by Saussure and to Saussure's idea that changes in language are arbitrary (see Chapter 3). Second, Jakobson was a Hegelian scholar and no doubt was influenced by Hegel's finalistic conception in philosophy. Moreover, he accepted and commended the idea of purposefulness in the work of his linguistic predecessors like Baudouin and Kruszewski as well as in the social philosophy of the Czech social scientist and humanist T.G. Masaryk (Jakobson, 1958/1985, II, p. 416). Third, later in his career, Jakobson was strongly influenced by cybernetics and information theory and by the notions of teleology in these disciplines, which he applied in linguistics.

We can only conclude that histories with a goal are *a-historical histories*: their focus is on the predicted final outcome. Any unpredictable development can take place only within the limits of that predicted outcome. Whether these explanations are suitable for the biological development of an organism, I am not qualified to comment. However, their suitability for the study of the interdependence between the socially shared knowledge and human agency is more than questionable.

In the end we are left with a series of unanswered questions. What is in and through the mind, if not mechanisms and mental representations? If knowledge is both socially and individually generated, how can we conceptualise this interdependence? On what presuppositions can we postulate a theory of social knowledge?

4   The mind in dialogue

In order to attempt to answer these questions, let us take a different tack.

Let us characterise the mind as the capacity of human beings to communicate, to make sense of signs, symbols and meanings in their experience as well as to create new signs, symbols and meanings. Let us further presuppose that this capacity is rooted in history and culture. It is specifically activated in social events that matter to humans and that humans experience as fundamentally important for life and its extension.

Such phenomena that touch and disrupt in some fundamental ways the lives of individuals, groups or societies, are phenomena in communication and in tension. They make social change not only possible, but also unavoidable.

These propositions explain why the theory of social representations is fundamental to developing my arguments. In the last four decades, the theory of social representations has shown its theoretical power in the study of phenomena, which have had fundamental effects on social thinking and communication all over the world.

Thus in order to explain dialogicality of the mind, we need to view the mind as if it was not a mechanism without history but a historically and culturally constituted phenomenon in communication, tension and change. For something to be alive, it must withstand tension and conflict within itself and must have the force to endure the conflict and tension, because antinomies in the mind are the source of all movement and vitality (Hegel, 1830/1873). The analyses of many scholars and humanists concerned with the nature of the human mind as well as the insights of magnificent writers guide us in the same direction. For example, thinking in oppositions or antinomies saturates all of Bakhtin's (see Chapters 3 and 4) writings. Oppositions, through polemics, collisions and quarrelling, all of which are ridden with tension, always leave a loophole, exposing human dialogue to an openness of different interpretations and therefore to novelty. Where there is dialogue, there is human activity. Words want to be heard and similarly, ideas are live events and they want to be understood and answered by others from their positions.

One of the masterpieces of the twentieth century, *The Magic Mountain* of Thomas Mann, swells with oppositions in characters, situations, internal dialogues and also with interpenetration of contraries at different levels of thinking and dialoguing. Antinomies in thinking and dialogue are, for Mann's heroes, the criteria of life and realities:

We dispute. We quarrel until blood nearly every day, but I confess that oppositions and hostilities of his thoughts become attraction the more I am acquainted with him. I need friction. My fundamental convictions live only to the extent that they have opportunity for fight and I am then confirmed in them.

In the next chapter we turn our attention to oppositions and antinomies of the mind.

NOTE

1. I do not claim that there is no difference with respect to these questions and answers between Plato, Descartes and Chomsky. These scholars lived in different epochs, which prioritised different issues. Theories of knowledge do

not exist in a vacuum but in societies. For example, religion was a different issue for Plato than it was for Descartes and Chomsky. Thus, Plato included God among universals. Descartes did so too, although one is not sure whether Descartes would have done so if there had not been pressure by the Church. Chomsky and Fodor leave God out of universals. One could give other examples of issues affecting the theories of knowledge like a well-developed mechanistic theory of the world, which was part of Descartes', Chomsky's and Fodor's theories but not that of Plato. Darwin's evolutionary theory influenced Chomsky and Fodor but not Plato and Descartes; and so on. Nevertheless, with these concessions, we observe that the reference to the nature of universals, as timeless monuments of knowledge, has undergone little change.

2   Thinking and antinomies

1   Making distinctions

Before we can develop a theory of social knowledge in social psychology, we need to ask the question about the precise assumptions on which this theory will be based and which will distinguish it from foundational epistemologies. In order to do this, let us start pondering about one essential capacity of all living species: *making distinctions*. No living organisms could survive without this essential capacity. Animals, just like humans distinguish between danger and safety, 'us' and 'them' or food and poison. Making distinctions is fundamental for living; in humans it is also essential for thinking and communication.

It has long been established that processes such as perceiving, thinking, knowing, feeling and expressing meaning start from making distinctions. For example, in fixing eyes on an object, i.e. *in perceiving*, the perceiver depicts it from the field of his perception. He brings the object into the foreground and perceives it against the background of other things. From that moment on, the object becomes the focus of attention and, as a consequence, it stands out from its background. In other words, perceiving is making distinctions. In the nineteenth century, the psychologist Alexander Bain (1868) characterised making distinctions as an essential feature of intelligence. For him, the beginning of thinking, knowing or having ideas started with the discrimination between opposites or antinomies such as, e.g. 'heat and coldness' or 'red and blue things'. Making distinctions and expressing them in thinking, for Bain, was as old as is human thinking. He considered that discrimination between different things is a basic and a self-evident property of intelligence that required no further elucidation. Therefore, no specific chapter in his book on psychology was dedicated to it (Bain, 1868, p. 82f.).

Making distinctions is such a fundamental capacity of intelligence that it makes one wonder, whether, and if so, how, it is related to the omnipresent human potency of thinking in polarities, oppositions and antinomies. The latter have been evident throughout the history of humankind in

26

Table 2.1 *Symbolic dualisms (adapted from Faron, 1962 and from Middleton, 1968)*

Attached to right and left hand in Mapucheland		Attached to order and disorder in Lugbaraland in Uganda	
Right	Left	Order	Disorder
Good	Evil	Man in society	Man outside society
Life	Death	Normality	Inversion
Health	Sickness	Moral	Amoral
Ancestral spirits	Evil spirits	Lugbaraland	Alien lands
Fullness	Hunger	Kinship, marriage	Incest, cannibalism

various kinds of epistemology, cosmological systems, religions, myths and philosophies. Scholars of very different pursuits like philosophers, anthropologists and sociologists have observed that thinking in antinomies is widely spread in diverse cultures, tribes and societies all over the world and they have also noted the tremendous varieties of thinking in antinomies. Heterogeneous kinds of polarities and antinomies appear to be underlined by very diverse beliefs about the nature of the world and by different theories of knowledge.

Classifying phenomena in the world into, for example, *good* and *evil* or *light* and *dark*, can be found both in ancient Persian philosophy and also in modern societies with the highest technological development. The Dutch historian Fontaine (1986, 1987, 1988), in his three volumes on *The Light and the Dark: A cultural history of dualism,* paints a fascinating picture of oppositional thinking in science, religion, literature and myth in the early classical periods of Greek history. He reminds us that it would be fatal to think that dualisms can be found *only* in history and in old mythical and religious doctrines like those of Zarathustra, of Ormuzd and Ahriman, light and darkness or good and evil. Rather, the tendency of thinking in distinctions, opposites, antinomies and counterparts in nature and culture, is common across race, age and culture (Needham, 1973; Lévi-Strauss, 1962) (Figures 2.1 and 2.2 and Table 2.1).

Making distinctions, thinking in antinomies, oppositions, polarities and dualities and their expressions in language have been the subjects of scholarly interest in many societies and cultures. For example, we can find specific forms of making distinctions and polarities in thinking and language since early Greek Homeric literature and rhetoric (Lloyd, 1966, pp. 90–4). Nevertheless, there is no evidence that these two kinds of capacity, i.e. making distinctions and thinking and expressing polarities in language have the same root in human intelligence. Therefore, while we can assume that the two phenomena are related in one way or other, we

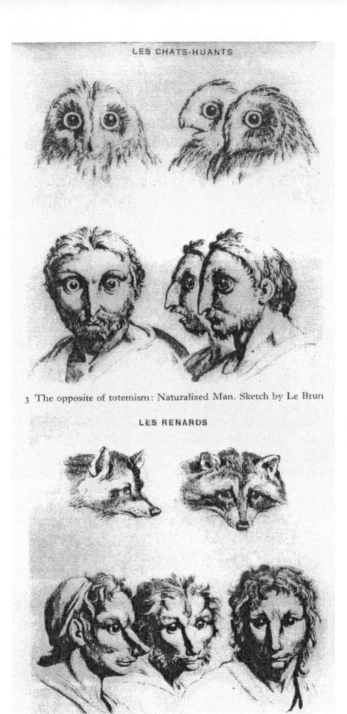

Figure 2.1 The opposite of totemism: Naturalised Man. Sketch by Le Brun. From Lévi-Strauss (1962). Cliché Bibliothèque nationale de France, Paris. Reprinted with permission.

Figure 2.2 Mexican opposition of sun/moon

must cautiously treat them as parallel capacities.[1] We can hypothesise, though, that making distinction and the tremendous variations of thinking in antinomies and polarities may both indicate something about the dialectic and dialogical nature of the human mind.

2   Polarities and antinomies in different cultures

In his outstanding book on *Polarity and Analogy*, Lloyd (1966) reviews the extensive evidence about thinking in polarities, and the widespread classifications of realities into opposites in ancient and modern societies. Although his main focus is to document thinking in polarities in ancient

Greece, Lloyd provides anthropological, historical and sociological evidence that he has found in various societies and cultures from all over the world. He shows that classification of realities, natural phenomena, societies and cosmological systems into dichotomies is extremely common. Moreover, Lloyd draws attention to the multiple kinds of such dualistic classifications, in human cultures. They extend to classifications of plants, animals, colours and artificial objects. Lloyd points out that it is very difficult to come to any systematic understanding of their natures. Some societies might classify the world in terms of left-right, female-male, coast/seaside versus land/mountainside, west-east etc. (cf. Lloyd, 1966, p. 33), while other societies might employ different polarities. Due to use of different classification criteria, specific societies produce totally different tables of opposites.

Lloyd (1966) shows, moreover, that polarities and antinomies have been conceived in a variety of ways. For instance, some kinds of polarities, such as 'black and non-black', are mutually exclusive, while others, such as 'black and white', are not. Some polarities, like Chinese Yin and Yang are mutually interdependent, while others, such as those found in Aristotle's law of non-contradiction (i.e. a thing cannot both be something and not be that thing at the same time), are strictly separate. Certain polarities belong to the same kind of reality, like 'hot and cold'; whereas others, like Plato's Forms and Particulars, are parts of different kinds of reality. For Plato, the world of Forms belongs to the divine, uniform and immortal reality, while the world of Particulars is part of human, diversified and mortal reality. In some pairs of opposites, e.g. 'odd' and 'even', the components have an equal status, at least in some cultures. In other pairs of opposites one component is superior to the other, like Yang (superior) and Yin (inferior) in Chinese thought. Some opposites are mutually exclusive, like male/female, others are relational, like hot/cold. Indeed, the criteria used for classifications of opposites, contraries, contradictories, dualities and polarities, represent an enormous variety and are based on very different qualities of the phenomena in question. We can find different kinds of dualism in magical traditions, religions and mysticism and in philosophical teaching (Fontaine, 1986, 1987, 1988).

Just as there are many different ways of thinking in antinomies, which do not fit into any unified and homogeneous pattern, there are also many different terms, which refer to thinking and communicating based on making distinctions. Understandably, such terms, like 'antinomy', 'opposition', 'polarity', 'contradiction', 'contrary', 'binary', 'dyad', 'pair', 'duality' and 'dualism' have different and heterogeneous meanings. What interests us at the moment is the very idea of thinking in antinomies; a tentative answer as to why thinking in antinomies is so widespread will be suggested later in the book.

In order to bring to attention the pervasive and heterogeneous nature of thinking in antinomies and oppositions, I shall use, in this chapter, the original terms that were used by their authors when they referred, in their own work, to antinomies and oppositions in thinking. For example, Hegel used the term 'contradiction'; Ogden or Tarde spoke about 'opposition'; Jung was preoccupied with 'opposites' and so on. Sure, these terms are often underlined by different characteristics of thinking in antinomies, but this is not important at the moment.

We could expect that if making distinctions and if thinking in anti-nomies and polarities are such fundamental characteristics of the human mind, then, surely, they will constitute basic features of the theories of knowledge as well as the theories of scientific thinking. However, there is lack of evidence to support such a hypothesis. Lloyd (1966, p. 27) expresses surprise that, given that there are masses of theories and expla-nations in Greek philosophy and medicine, which are based on opposi-tions, this recurrent feature of Greek thought has attracted little atten-tion by scholars and historians of ancient philosophy.

In a similar vein, in his book on *Opposition* Ogden (1932/1967) dis-cussed different kinds of oppositions and their importance in sciences. He produced a diagram of different kinds of oppositions (Figure 2.3) and was dismayed by the neglect of oppositional thought in various nat-ural and social sciences throughout European history. He argued that we could pinpoint, in European history, a number of discontinuous periods of rise and fall, of climax followed by the downfall of the emphasis on thinking in antinomies and oppositions.

It appeared that in the 1960s, after the long downfall of oppositional thought, interest in oppositional thinking was suddenly growing. In the Introduction to Ogden's (1932/1967) re-edition of his book on *Opposition*, Richards (1967, p. 7) maintains that were Ogden still alive, he would be gratified to note how fully his ideas about the role of opposition have been justified. Richards thought that sciences such as crystallography, physics, biology, cultural studies and psychology have all finally recognised the im-portant role of oppositional thought in their methodologies and concepts. Yet, Richards' optimism was short lived. Today, neither the theories of knowledge nor scientific theories integrate thinking in polarities and anti-nomies into their basic conceptual presuppositions.

3   Antinomies, oppositions and polarities in ancient Greece and China

In many of his scholarly writings Lloyd (e.g. 1966, 1990, 1994) com-pares and contrasts the ancient Greek and the Chinese civilisations. He draws attention to their broad parallelisms in technological, political and

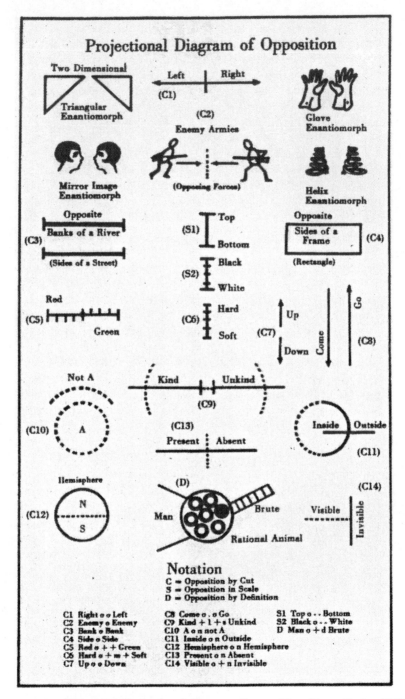

Figure 2.3 Projectional diagram of opposition. From Ogden (1932)

intellectual spheres. For example, there is a resemblance between these
two civilisations with respect to philosophical diversities, pluralistic political situations and technological innovations which took place in approximately the same time periods. Lloyd refers not only to the contrasts
between Greece and China in various historical periods with reference to
ethical, political and philosophical speculations, but also to their scientific, logical and epistemological presuppositions.

In comparing and contrasting scientific thought in the ancient Greek
and Chinese sciences, Lloyd implies and at times explicitly states that
both scientific systems were characterised by thinking in antinomies or
polarities. This means that when Greek and Chinese scholars considered
the contents of concepts and the meanings of words or phrases, for example of 'darkness', they also thought about the opposite of 'darkness',
e.g. 'lightness' or simply 'not-dark things'. In other words they always
understood meanings with reference to something else.

Most importantly, Lloyd maintains that, while we can compare various similarities and differences between the ancient Greeks and Chinese,
the ways in which the two civilisations conceptualised antinomies, oppositions and polarities, have no parallels in the history of mankind. These
unique ways of thinking about oppositions have led to very diverse speculations about *the change* and *the coming-to-be*.

As a first approach in the analysis of this issue, we can say that in the
majority of their theories, the Greeks viewed *the components in a pair of
opposites as excluding one another*. For example, if something was considered to be true, then that thing could not, at the same time, be considered
as false. Similarly, if something was dark, then, for the Greeks, it could
not be light at the same time. The Greek theories of being, i.e. ontology,
and the theory of knowledge, i.e. epistemology, were both based on the
search for truth and certainty. The Greeks sought to discover the invariant states in nature, science and the human mind. Thinking in opposites
was a good example of this logic based on invariant states, in which the
opposite sides of things could not be mixed together.

Nevertheless, we must not ignore the fact that the Greeks also used
relational antinomies. For some Greek philosophers, the relational oppositions formed the bases of their philosophical systems. They built some of
their ontologies on the relational antinomies, as in the case of Heraclitus
who was preoccupied with the dynamic nature of the world. However,
generally speaking, relational oppositions did not form the basis of Greek
'scientific' arguments.

In contrast, in ancient Chinese theories *the two components in the pair of
opposites were mutually interdependent*, being in a perpetual cycle of wave
motion. The Chinese ontology and epistemology was based on the assumption of *continuous change* and cyclical phases in all world phenomena.

For example, darkness already anticipated light just as light included the seed of its opposite, darkness. One could never have *either* one *or* the other, because both co-existed in a context of movement and perpetual change.

These were the fundamental divergences with respect to the nature of opposites or antinomies in Greek and Chinese thought and they led, in both cases, to the development of original scientific thought. Lloyd (1990, p. 143) maintains that throughout their long histories, both systems have remained faithful to their basic ideas based on opposites. As a result, these divergences are still embedded, today, in scientific presuppositions and in common knowledge of these different systems of thought.

3.1   Opposites in Plato and Aristotle

Concerning the ancient Greek culture, Lloyd (1966) documents and analyses thinking in polarities, i.e. in pairs of opposites, in philosophy, religion and mythology, in cosmological doctrines and medicine, as well as in theories and explanations of natural phenomena, e.g. physiology and pathology. He comments that one can hardly ignore the tremendous variety and frequency of theories based on various kinds of opposites. Both in pre-Socratic texts and in Plato's *Dialogues* one can find recurrent appeals to different kinds of opposites. In Plato's *Dialogues*, the most important opposites were 'being and becoming', 'Forms and Particulars' and 'what is' and 'what is not' (Lloyd, 1966, p. 113).

Plato attempted to clarify differences between various kinds of argument in speech and in dialogue. In particular, he was critical of the Sophists who, instead of seeking objective truth through deduction, which Plato considered as the correct way of thinking and speaking, adopted an empirical-inductive method in arguing, teaching and philosophy in general. Plato considered the Sophists' method to be wrong. For example, if the Sophists found empirically that an argument was persuasive, then they would use it, because they thought that it was useful. Rhetoric provided them with the practical means of persuasion and teaching. Plato devoted several of his *Dialogues* to the criticism of the eristic art of rhetoricians, i.e. to disputes aimed at victory rather than the truth.[2] Rhetoric produces *belief* rather than *knowledge*. Its strategy is flattery and pretence, it is like wearing a mask (Plato, *Gorgias*, 457a). In contrast, Plato showed that dialectic is *the science of eternal and unchanging being*, it is the true knowledge (Plato, *Philebus*, 57e-58b). This is so because only dialectic thinking is underlined by the ability to discern similarities and differences between things by means of critical and rigorous thought.

Aristotle, who was also very much preoccupied with oppositions, pointed out that all philosophers before him had conceived oppositions as *the* principles of thinking. This also included those philosophers who were primarily concerned with atoms and elements rather than with dualities and opposites.[3] The most common oppositions included the following: limited and unlimited, odd and even, one and plurality, right and left, male and female, resting and moving, straight and curved, light and darkness, good and bad, square and oblong.

In addition to the already existing lists of oppositions, which were constructed by his predecessors, Aristotle contributed another important pair of oppositions: potentiality and actuality (e.g. Aristotle, *Metaphysica*, Book Omega, 8, 1050a).

By adding this pair of opposites, potentiality and actuality, Aristotle could then conceptualise *change and development* (see below). He also systematised, and above all, formalised, different types of opposites. These were applied not only to terms, e.g. 'limited/unlimited', but also to propositions, on the condition that these did not involve contradictions. These formalisations were the basis of Aristotelian syllogistic logic and his laws of thought.

3.2   *The strict separation of antinomies in ancient Greece*

We must not forget that Greek cosmologies and philosophical systems used an enormous amount of variety and criteria for classifying antinomies and polarities, e.g. into relations, asymmetries and categories. Despite this, it is important to draw attention to the fact that in the majority of these cosmologies and systems, the components of a pair of opposites or polarities in Greek thought were strictly separated one from another. The emphasis was on the impossibility of their co-existence: if there is one, there cannot be the other; if one is true, the other one must be false; and so on. This impossibility of co-existence of polarities was built into the most important of Aristotle's laws of thought, *the law of non-contradiction*. It not only underlined the concept of rationality, logic, science and philosophy in ancient Greece, but it also gave direction to all systems of knowledge, which were influenced by that law. It followed from this conception of opposites, which rigorously excluded one another, that Greek science was strictly exact, axiomatic, deductive and definitional. Thus, logic and science were based on the same principles. It was essential that deduction and its outcomes were not only logically correct but that they also corresponded to the basic facts of science (Aristotle, *Analytica Posteriora*, 76a, 26–30).

Deduction and geometrical thinking were also the main principles of mathematics. The Greeks attempted to deduce the whole of mathematics from a few axioms and definitions. This way of thinking extended to other disciplines, such as biology, medicine, politics and music. In biology, for example, dilatation and contraction of arteries was seen as corresponding to the upward and downward beats which were analysed by the Greeks in the theory of music. This idea was also applied to medicine in an attempt to express pulse mathematically, as an analogy in the science of harmonics (Lloyd, 1990, p. 94).

The principle of opposites was extended even further. In medicine, the famous physician Galen thought that opposites were to be cured by opposites although, as Lloyd (1966) pointed out, it was often very unclear what he meant by opposites. Lloyd (2000) maintains that the Greek geometrical style of thinking became more than an ambition of intellectual rigour. It became an obsession, a tool in disputes with opponents. It was sometimes upheld artificially and counter-intuitively and often led to absurdities.

3.3   The concept of change in ancient Greece

In ancient Greece, it was a pre-Aristotelian scholar Heraclitus who was the philosopher of change. First, he postulated the theory of flux, claiming that everything in the world is in a continuous – even if imperceptible – change. For him, the world was dominated by change and change always involved strife or war. He also emphasised the interdependence and the unity of opposites. He proposed the conception of unity in diversity, which was based on the notion of tension and conflict. Tension and conflict of opposites and their unity was for Heraclitus fundamental to all reality. Amongst the existing fragments of his work we can find a number of claims that many centuries later would appear in mediaeval magic and much later in Michail Bakhtin's writing on dialogicality (Chapter 3). Amongst these fragments are those which postulate that the same thing is both living and dead, and that a person is both young and old. We can interpret these fragments as the attempts to express the logic of change and the dialectic of movement. To Heraclitus, flux and opposition is in the nature of everything that is alive. If strife between opposites were ever to cease, the world as such would stop existing (Kirk and Raven, 1957, pp. 182ff).[4]

In contrast to Heraclitus' concept of continuous change, Aristotle's (*Metaphysica*, 1049b) concept of change, as we have already remarked, is derived from the pair of opposites *potentiality* and *actuality*. In introducing this pair of opposites Aristotle linked together *matter* and *form*: 'matter exists in a potential state, just because it may come to its form; and when it exists *actually*, then it is in its form' (*Metaphysica*, 1050a). Actuality, for him, was something in the making, for example, the act of building, of weaving, of seeing or of theorising. Any movement produced by an agent was something actual. Aristotle maintained that the word 'actuality' is derived from that of 'action' and thus, it refers to reality in its completeness. One can say that the reality in its completeness is a form and a movement: in other words, it is an action. In accordance, Aristotle thought that nature was alive and that it should be conceived as a unity. Moreover, he believed that all natural and alive things have an innate tendency towards *becoming actuality*.[5] However, as with other opposites, Aristotle conceptualised potentiality and actuality as mutually exclusive. The thing either is in potentiality or in actuality. It cannot be both at the same time.

Aristotle's concept of change, based on separation of potentiality and actuality dominated European thinking until the re-emergence of dialectical thinking in the eighteenth and nineteenth centuries. However, dialectical thinking did not totally disappear from the European scene; some forms of dialectical thinking penetrated and survived in mediaeval theology and in magic.

3.4   Antinomies and oppositions in ancient Chinese thought

In Chinese, like in Greek philosophy, the world was conceived in terms of oppositional forces. In Chinese thought, the concepts of oppositions, both in theories of being (ontology) and theories of knowledge (epistemology) were very different from those in Greek thought. From approximately the fourth century BC Chinese philosophy was based on the opposite forces Yin and Yang. Examples of these two forces were represented in many different ways, like light and dark, male and female, up and down, convex and concave and sun and moon. These opposite forces controlled all natural phenomena with their oppositional regular and predictable courses, alternately waxing and waning, the one being inversely proportional to the other. In ancient Chinese philosophical thought the opposite forces were considered as dynamically interdependent: one could not exist without the other.

Although in asymmetric relation, with one superior to the other, they were always reciprocal. It was their balance that was essential for wisdom and for science.[6] Yin and Yang were parts of a unity. In no way could they be thought of as two separate forces. Instead, Chinese philosophers conceived them together as a wave. If one was flourishing, the other was declining.

3.5   The Chinese concept of change

The Chinese philosophy conceived of the whole universe as undergoing slow pulsations of fundamentally opposed – but mutually

Figure 2.4 Yin and Yang

necessary – basic forces. The well-known 'diagram of the supreme ultimate' illustrates the dynamics of Yin and Yang. Various individuals and institutions have adopted this diagram symbolically as a representation of their own philosophy (e.g. the Danish physicist Bohr; the Department of Communication Studies at the University of Linköping in Sweden). The diagram shows the two complementary shapes: 'The Yang returns cyclically to its beginning; the Yin attains its maximum and gives place to the Yang' (Needham, 1962, p. 6). There are also two small circles in each shape, indicating that when the force reaches its maximum, it already contains the beginning of its opposite (Figure 2.4). In this sense, nothing could be only *either* Yin *or* Yang.

In Chinese thinking in general, there was a fundamental preference for what can be called a wave conception, with one force coming up and the other going down. Whenever the operations of Yin and Yang are described, it is always as a process of a maximum and a minimum. This conception of waves explains the cyclical change of mutual production or mutual conquest in the dominating Chinese natural philosophy.[7]

Chinese science and scholarship did not have any interest in axioms, as the starting point of mathematics. Despite this, the Chinese achieved, without axiomatic thought, remarkable results in mathematical sciences (Lloyd, 1994, p. 94). Their emphasis was always on change and dynamics rather than on the static structures of axioms. Although they did not reject stability, change was the starting point of their thinking. While change represented the process, stability was its continuation: the latter did not exist without the former and vice versa. Chinese reasoning, while employing critical procedures in evaluating the process of thought, was concerned with pragmatic usefulness rather than with the abstract principles of thinking and a theory for its own sake.

The conception of the pulse in Chinese and Greek medicine serves well as a demonstration of the contrasting ways of thinking in antinomies in those two civilisations. It also shows their different cultural values. Lloyd (1990, p. 94) maintains that the concept of pulse was very important in the study of health and disease both for the Chinese and the Greeks. Lloyd observes that, for the Greeks, problems of pulse were related to internal disorders of humours, e.g. blood and bile. The Greeks were preoccupied with the elaboration of theoretical classifications of the types of pulse and with different possibilities of expressing in mathematical terms the dilatation and contraction of vessels. In other words, their ambition was to turn any subject matter into an exact science. In contrast, the Chinese were always concerned with the feel of the pulse; they studied the modalities of breath, the flow in the vessels and passages and links in the body. Their focus was on the dynamics of the body, on process and change, rather than on static structures and classifications.

We need to reflect on the differences between antinomic thinking in the Greeks and the Chinese in a more general way and view them as part of a broader spectrum. These differences cannot be captured by focusing on isolated strategies of thinking, based, in the former case, on static structures, separate opposites and axioms and in the latter case on processes, interdependent opposites and the concept of change. Above all, these differences should be viewed globally as expressions of cultural distinctions, values and particular mythologies of those societies, in which these different systems of thought are embedded. Such cultural distinctions are also apparent in other spheres of life, for example, in different education practices, in different responses to socio-political pressures and in specific moralities dominating those cultures.

For example, in a totally different context, Lele and Singh (1987) describe educational practices of teaching classical Hindu grammars and Gracco-Roman grammars in these two ancient societies. The culture of ancient Greece based on deductive thinking seems to be reflected in pedagogical principles described by Lele and Singh. The authors point out that Graeco-Roman grammars start from pedagogical principles, aiming to teach barbarians good language. They are written as manuals showing how to write correct language; they teach grammar and rules and they are well organised in order to correct the speech of the uneducated. In contrast Panini, representing the classical Hindu grammar, is written in a manner that totally ignores pedagogical assumptions as they were conceived in the West. Written by a native speaker for a native learner, Panini does not intend to teach grammar but it discovers a grammatical order together with the readers, making sense of language together with them. Disregarding definitions, its main interest is *not* 'to freeze what is dynamic in the community of native speakers of his language' but to arrive at meanings through dynamic intersubjectivity (Lele and Singh, 1987, p. 51). We can suggest that the focus on deduction and the static rules, on which ancient Greek thinking was based, have their parallels in pedagogical principles. In contrast, inductive thinking and the presumed dynamic in language seem to be reflected in Hindu pedagogical principles.

4   From the Greek polarities to science and mysticism

Although opposites played a crucial role in Greek philosophical thought, the way they were conceptualised clearly implied that one component of a pair of opposites was correct and the other was wrong or at least that one was preferable to the other one. For example, in the polarity stable/unstable or dialectic/rhetoric, the former component in each pair was considered superior to the latter and therefore more suitable for a scientific endeavour. In the Plato concept of polarities, only Forms, i.e., immutable and God-like ideas, e.g. Soul, Beauty, Goodness, constituted the basis of philosophy. In contrast, things we see, touch and hear, although they bear the same name as Forms, like a soul, a beauty or goodness, are changeable, unstable and perishable, and therefore, in Plato's philosophy they were degraded.

We can also speculate that, because the components in a pair of opposites were considered as separate from one another and because only one component in the pair, e.g. 'stable' in stable/unstable or 'dialectic' in dialectic/rhetoric, was believed to be 'right', thinking in opposites finally lost its significance. Polarity was not needed and could be reduced to the 'right' component because only the 'right' component mattered in philosophical and scientific thought. The 'right' component constituted the element of thought. This speculation would be consistent with the already established presuppositions, which characterised much of ancient Greek philosophy and science: Forms, static structures, the emphasis on geometrical method, on deduction and the search for certainty.

European philosophy and science emerged from ancient Greek thought and adopted its presuppositions about the nature of the world. It has equally adopted Greek epistemological principles, which were geared towards the development of exact sciences based on secure knowledge, truth and certainty. We can find these principles in mediaeval science and in its aftermath, in Galilean/Newtonian science.

Despite the domination of non-antinomic thinking, a line of antinomic thinking, nevertheless, can be traced from Plato to Descartes, through St Augustine (AD 354–430). Antinomies were prolific in St Augustine's philosophical and religious system. Like Plato, St Augustine considered one component in the pair of opposites as having a higher standing, i.e. as a correct and more preferable one to the other, and lower component, which was inferior. However, Taylor (1989, pp. 127ff) observes that despite using various kinds of oppositions in his philosophical system, Plato did not include the opposition inside/outside. It was only St Augustine who developed a theory, according to which the actions of the soul, i.e. actions coming from the inside, have moral superiority over the bodily and worldly actions.

St Augustine elaborated the opposition inside/outside, i.e. spiritual versus bodily. In contrast to Plato's philosophical system, this opposition became the centre of St Augustine's philosophy of self-knowledge. Consequently, inner/outer became the most important antinomy in religious scholastic philosophy. As Taylor puts it: 'this same antinomy of spirit/matter, higher/lower, eternal/temporal, immutable/changing *is* [Taylor's emphasis] described by St Augustine, not just occasionally and peripherally, but centrally and essentially in terms of inner/outer' (Taylor, 1989, pp. 128–9).

It appears that interest in the opposition inner/outer in the writing of St Augustine stems from his belief that human consciousness, i.e. the inner, incorporeal activity, is highly superior to the outer, corporeal activity. He excellently describes the inner aspects of the human soul in his psychological passages on memory and on the contents of memory (St Augustine, *Confessions*). For him, the mind is memory itself and its wonders, like reflection, awareness and images, enable the soul to reach God. For Plato, the highest principles are in the world of Forms, that is, in the outer world. In contrast, St Augustine shifts the centre of attention from the world of objects to the inner world, to the activity of knowing and self-knowing and to reflexivity. This is where God is to be found (Taylor, 1989, p. 130).

Although St Augustine's descriptions of the faculties of the mind are remarkably similar to those of modern psychologists, in contrast to the latter St Augustine saw the mind is a unity which could not be decomposed into individual faculties, like memory, sensation, understanding, will, feeling and so on. He perceives them as a whole, as the united mind. The most inward of all kinds of knowledge for him is 'I know that I am alive' (St Augustine, *The Trinity*, XV, 12.21–12.22). This point of view about the agent and the perspective of the agent, who is the greatest source of knowledge that is certain, comes from his mind, that is from inside.

Although more than a thousand years separated St Augustine from Descartes, as many scholars have acknowledged, there is a clear connection between them. The first-person pronoun dominates the theory of knowledge of both philosophers. The stance of radical reflexivity, the self as a thinker and a knower, determines what is considered to be true. While for Augustine the outer world is inferior, in Descartes, the outer world is thrown into doubt and scepticism.

Following St Augustine's thinking in antinomies, Christian theology was preoccupied with the conception of God as the 'ultimate principle' and with the question of how to harmonise the multiplicity of finite worldly things with the 'ultimate principle'. The 'ultimate principle' was usually described symbolically as a unity of two opposites, such as infinite versus finite. The implication of the idea of this unity was the question of how to conceptualise pantheism in the face of monotheism. For example, how can one account for good and evil, for negative things in the world in which God is ever present (pantheism) with the view that God is the supreme good which created the world (monotheism)? These and similar questions about oppositions and dualities preoccupied mediaeval theology, theological logic and the varieties of religious symbolic forms. This continued to be the case during the Renaissance.[8]

4.1   Antinomies in the Renaissance

Today, the notion 'Renaissance' brings to the mind the idea of an outburst of artistic spirit, new developments in science and liberation of the human mind from dogmatic theology. Yet, Renaissance was by no means a homogeneous period, but a complex mixture of different tendencies, ranging from mysticism and magic on the one hand, to scientific discoveries and new philosophical priorities on the other. Oppositional thinking flourished in all those tendencies.

During the later period of Renaissance, towards the end of the sixteenth century, two main intellectual tendencies could be discerned, influencing cultural life at the time. One tendency manifested itself in mechanistic science in the effort to better understand the rationality and logical faculties of the human mind. Science was now quickly developing and new discoveries in various disciplines, such as medicine, physics, chemistry, together with technological innovations, were rapidly changing everyday life, at least of some parts of the population. These advancements, one could say, were sound proof of the newly discovered powers of the individual. The human spirit as a microcosm with its dignity, morality, self-determination and responsibility, about which Pico della Mirandola wrote so enthusiastically, made itself visible by changing its social world.

The second tendency went in an opposite direction. While the emphasis on powers of the individual with both its positive and negative features galvanised European life, this tendency rejected the applications of mechanistic science and instead, reached for non-science and heterodoxy. It delved into mediaeval and Renaissance magic and mysticism. These tendencies had origins in ancient Egyptian magic and were later adopted by the Greeks and the Arabs. Magic and mysticism had a tremendous influence on mediaeval culture in Europe. It became apparent in various disciplines ranging from cosmology, astrology and alchemy to medicine and wizardry. In all these disciplines magical proponents aimed to transcend the reality and to transform matter into something else in various spheres of natural phenomena. Alchemy, which, it seems, had its most significant period at that time, attempted to produce the philosophers' stone and elixir.[9]

In contrast to mechanistic science, which was based on the notion of automata and static structures, heterodoxy and mysticism of the late Renaissance was based on antinomic thinking. Alchemy principles were derived from the interaction of the pairs of elements through transmutations. The laws of hermetic relativity assumed a universal bipolarity of all existence, of its antinomies and analogies. Antinomies were assumed to be bonded by their synthesis; it was thought that there was really nothing that could not be viewed in terms of antinomies (de Lasenic, 1997). It is as if the struggle for the increase of rationality and enlightenment led to the loss of magic, which Weber called 'the disenchantment of the world'. As if stripping the world of its charm through mechanistic science and rationality led to the desire to re-enchant it again (Moscovici, 1988/1993, 1998a, 2002b) through hermetic disciplines, astrology, alchemy and similar tendencies involving organic powers.

Many of these trends of thinking were based on some elements of dialectic. One of the most important documents of dialectic hermetic thinking was inscribed in the Emerald Tablet from the mediaeval Byzantine. Amongst its dialectically formulated pronouncements one can find those, like 'what is above is also below', expressing hermetic efforts to understand tension and struggle between parts and the whole of universe. This way of thinking, based on interacting antinomies, was characterised by a preoccupation with the holistic point of view and with the relations between meaning and senses (Kratochvíl, 1997).

Analogies, too, were conceived in terms of antinomies, connecting various kinds of worldly and celestial phenomena. The main emphasis of this philosophy of analogies in antinomies was based on the assumption of the unity of the universe. Of those analogies, perhaps the most important one was that of microcosm and macrocosm, uniting the human being and God. The idea of microcosm reflecting macrocosm penetrated the work of the Renaissance philosophers from Ficino to Pico della Mirandola, and of scientists like Kepler and Newton. It pointed to the intimate relationship between science, poetry, mysticism and symbolism, creative energies and the power of imagination.[10]

4.2   Antinomic thinking of Jacob Böhme

Amongst those who apparently had a significant influence on the development of modern antinomic thought was Jacob Böhme (born in 1575 at Altseidenberg, a small village in Lusatia on the borders of Bohemia). Böhme was a mystic with a great deal of imagination, for whom the real world was a place in which to achieve self-realisation. He had no education and because he did not know Latin he wrote his works in German. Hegel often acknowledged his debt to Böhme, who, according to him, was the first real German philosopher. Although much of what he wrote was unpolished and obscure and his accounts of spirits and angels made Hegel's head swim, as Hegel himself pointed out, he also appreciated Böhme's dialectic thinking (Haldane, 1897)[11] and his rational mysticism. Haldane (1897, p. 151) reminds us that according to Hegel 'all that is real is actually rational, and that the rational is real'.

Böhme had done intuitively what Hegel accomplished later with full awareness: he presented a dialectical conception of development based on interdependent antinomies, passing through contradictory stages bound by internal, rather than external relations. The notion of contradiction is essential to Böhme's conception of development, just as it is fundamental for Hegel. In his most important work, entitled *Mysterium Magnum* (1623/1958) (Ch. xxix (11)), Böhme makes it quite clear that all things can be a source of dialectic movement: nothing was created evil, even evil itself must be the cause of something good. Therefore, rather than concluding that the truth does not exist and that nothing is permanent, speculative mysticism responds that the truth is revealed through reason. Rejecting the view that truth is the absence of contradiction, speculative mysticism searches for new conceptions in philosophy and religion.

It thus seems that speculative mysticism of the Renaissance scientists, like that of Jacob Böhme, freed up the human mind of scholastic restrictions and helped to bring antinomic thinking back on the road. And, of course, the *Zeitgeist* of evolutionary thinking was already looming up.

5   The problem of antinomies for Kant

Yet, it was Kant, whose treatment of antinomies signified the breakdown of the Platonic/Cartesian paradigm. He was preoccupied with antinomies throughout all his life without resolving the problem of their mutual relations. Kant was first concerned with the nature of the antinomy in his pre-critical period. Specifically, he treated this matter in his essay entitled *Versuch den Begriff der negativen Grossen in die Weltweisheit einzufuhren* (1763) (An attempt to introduce the concept of negative quantities into philosophy). Kantian scholars rarely discuss this essay, and when they do, it is in the context of his ideas on morality. This essay, however, is very interesting for its treatment of antinomies and it is here that Kant distinguished between logical and real antinomies. Logical antinomies, just as we saw them in Aristotle, are mutually exclusive and cannot both be valid at the same time. Real antinomies, i.e. those referring to real life issues, are not contradictory in the same sense as logical antinomies. Instead, although real antinomies they are two activities working in opposite directions, one posits the other one.

It seems to me that at this point Kant was very close to the notion of antinomies reciprocally making and conditioning one another as mutually interdependent forces. For example, Kant insisted that people never desire an object without positively detesting its opposite. Therefore, the intention to achieve pleasure is not just to contradict displeasure but also to actively avoid it. Explaining this thesis in the context of moral feeling of internalised law, he claimed that one could conceptualise the negative attribute only in the context of the positive virtue of consciousness.

Kant also referred to new discoveries in physics, such as magnetism and electricity. He gave examples of the interdependence of antinomies that Hegel himself used later on. However, in contrast to Kant, Hegel, in his *Logic*, underlined these examples by new theoretical speculations of his time. Amongst these examples are those of magnetic and electric forces. One cannot separate opposite magnetic and electric forces because they mutually condition one another: one cannot have the positive pole without the negative one and vice versa.

Kant viewed his own considerations about antinomies as tiny theoretical beginnings, which were to open up new prospects, and which could have an important impact on philosophy. Having studied antinomies in early periods of his life, Kant returned to the problem of antinomies much later in the *Critique of Pure Reason* (1781/1929). At that point he clearly recognised the difficulty, which he could not resolve. In dealing with the concepts of understanding, imagination and intuition, he also tried to explain the fundamental antinomic relations such as inner/outer, unity/multiplicity and activity/passivity. However, despite his recognition of the problem, he never broke the barrier of static philosophy, which locked him together with Descartes. It was Hegel who finally accomplished the leap into dialectic (Marková, 1982).

6   Hegel's dialectic

The Cartesian theory of knowledge, based on 'certain ideas' such as elements of knowing, was in harmony with mechanistic science. It lasted without being seriously challenged until the eighteenth century. However, new discoveries in natural sciences during the eighteenth century, i.e. in physics, chemistry, biology and geology, the discovery of electric and magnetic fields and the looming ideas of evolution, demanded something more than just a mechanistic explanation. We have already noted Kant's problem concerning the indivisibility of the opposite magnetic poles. Science could no longer progress within its 'normal' trajectory as a mechanistic science. Instead, it had to take into consideration development, dynamics, processes and changes in the phenomena under study.

Discoveries in natural sciences were accompanied by fundamental, though gradual, changes in the socio-economic life. An increased knowledge of other cultures, their languages and civilisations, provision in public education and improvement in literacy and experiences gained through travel, were some of the factors that shook the static and universalistic paradigm based on elements. The notions of development, evolution and change penetrated life and sciences; yet, the concepts underlying these notions were still not theoretically mastered. Therefore, different questions were then asked about science and human phenomena. These required different theories of knowledge than those based on static and mechanistic ideas.

In the theory of the mind, it was Hegel who made the conceptual breakthrough. In contrast to Kant, who tried to solve the specific problem of antinomies, Hegel's starting point was not such a specific problem. From the very beginning, Hegel's philosophical presuppositions started elsewhere. His ancestors were Heraclitus, Aristotle and Böhme, rather than Plato and Descartes. It was a holistic, pantheistic and dynamically orientated approach, which was already present at the start of his philosophical journey.

Nevertheless, before discussing Hegel's dialectic antinomies, a word of caution is required. It is not an exaggeration to say that few philosophers in the history of ideas are more controversial than is Hegel. For example, the American philosopher and semiotician Charles Sanders Peirce (1931) fluctuated throughout his life between adopting and rejecting Hegel's philosophy. Thus he kept switching from considering Hegel as 'in some respects the greatest philosopher who ever lived' (1.524), to wanting to resuscitate Hegel 'though in a strange costume' (1.42), to rejecting his philosophy totally (1.368). Peirce's triangular conception of knowledge in his semiotic system is reminiscent of Hegel's dialectic.

Critical evaluations of Hegel's contributions range from those who, like Peirce, have adopted some aspects of his philosophy to those, who have totally rejected him for obscurity. Equally, interpretations of his system amongst philosophers differ enormously and a discussion of these interpretations would not advance my argument. As with any theoretical system, one does not accept it as a dogma but selects those aspects and those interpretations that make meaning in one's own theory. Rather than describing Hegel's system, logic and dialectic, I shall keep, as much as I can, to concrete examples he used to illustrate his points about interdependent antinomies and dialectic, avoiding his complex terminology. While a philosopher will, no doubt, consider such a strategy rather simplistic, it will be meaningful with respect to the core question I am asking in this book: how can we develop a theory of social knowledge which is based on the concept of change?

I regard Hegel primarily as a philosopher who tried to deal with the question as to how one can develop the logic of change. Such logic, he assumed, would provide an explanation of the evolution of social realities and nature. Above all, it would account for the mind's journey towards social knowledge.

In developing his own dialectic epistemology of change, Hegel always acknowledged his debt to Aristotle. He appreciated Aristotle's vitalistic and holistic conception of nature, but also built on his concept of potentiality and actuality. It is crucial to point out that, in contrast to Aristotle, in Hegel's conception of change, potentiality and actuality were no longer separate oppositions but they were interdependent forces. For Hegel, nothing could be *either* in rest *or* in movement: the two opposite components are simultaneously co-present like parts of one whole, like a figure-and-ground. He frequently expressed this idea in his writings, claiming that one has to comprehend nature as a purpose which is 'immediate and *at rest*, the unmoved which is also *self-moving*' (Hegel, 1807/1977, p. 12). Thus, in contrast to Aristotle, no unmoved Mover is required. Activity is the principal characteristic of natural and social phenomena.

6.1   From an unhappy beginning to a happy end

Like Aristotle, Hegel makes a distinction between potentiality and actuality and he regards activity and striving for goals as the essence of nature and culture. In his *Phenomenology of the Spirit* he refers constantly to dialectic in the development of nature and history. In history, it is important that each stage constitutes a basis for its next stage and to that extent predetermines the historical or developmental course. In nature, for example, an acorn gives way to a tree; a bud disappears when it bursts into a blossom, only to be succeeded by a fruit. These forms, Hegel says, are moments of an organic unity, one being a necessary step for the other and in the end, constituting the life of the whole. Similar logic can be found in history, as one culture succeeds another. The development of the mind, the phenomenology, is the journey of the mind towards science.

The concept of the journey of the mind towards science illustrates the difference between Cartesian doubt and Hegel's doubt. Descartes' doubt led him to scepticism as he rejected the truth of sciences and as he found the only certainty in his own mental activity of doubting based on clear and distinct ideas. For Hegel, in contrast with Descartes, and in agreement with Jacob Böhme, the method of doubting is based on the assumption that 'truth' and 'falsity' are interdependent phenomena rather than independent antinomies. For him, truth is not a minted coin, which is available in its ready-made form (Hegel, 1807/1977, p. 22). Truth must be reasoned about, searched for and discovered in a step-by-step process during the journey of consciousness. Hegel calls this voyage an unhappy 'journey of despair'. As he poetically puts it, this process, this journey of despair, represents 'the struggles of Mind to know itself, to make itself objective to itself, to find itself, be for itself, and finally unite itself to itself' (1837/1956).

It is through scepticism towards one's own thinking and representation of realities that one must struggle in order to reach a more adequate understanding. Scepticism towards thinking and rejection of the previous truth, though, is never purely negative. It also has a positive aspect (cf. Böhme's claim that one can find goodness in evil). The rejected forms of consciousness give rise to more adequate forms: as consciousness transforms into another form (or level), so does the reality to which that form refers. The final product is a new unity, the new consciousness of the new reality. In other words, consciousness does not passively accept reality, but it creates and re-creates a new reality. In this process, *unhappy* consciousness reaches its *happy* end in self-realisation.

At this point we need to emphasise that Hegel adopts a *teleological* position with respect to history, the present and the future. This means that for him, history has a goal and the purpose of history is to accomplish this goal. We have already referred to such a goal-orientated explanation as *a-historical*. A process can hardly be a *historical* one when the outcome of that process is already known! Moreover, goal-directedness in history and development also implies a universalistic explanation – as we have already observed it in Piaget's theory of developmental stages (Chapter 1).

Despite our criticism of a-historical explanations in the study of human social phenomena, we do not reject such explanations in principle. A-historical mechanistic explanations may well serve as explanations of mechanisms, which do not have a history. Teleological explanations might perhaps serve as explanations of some characteristics of biological organisms and as explanations of some universalistic phenomena. However, under no circumstances are a-historical explanations suitable as explanations of human phenomena because these involve interdependencies between societies, groups and individuals and therefore between creative agencies. The movements and changes of human social phenomena have neither predetermined goals, nor do they necessarily lead to a progress.

6.2   The father-and-son relationship as a unit

The concept of interdependent antinomies 'truth' and 'falsity' and the voyage of consciousness towards more adequate forms of truth in Hegel's theory of knowledge expresses his general logical principle of dialectic. Antinomies do not start as two independent elements, which for one reason or the other come together. Instead, antinomies condition one another. They come to existence together, like *figure-and-ground* (Marková, 1982, 1990). Hegel's (1830/1873) example of father-and-son demonstrates this point. A man can be in different kinds of relationships with different people. He can be a boss, a friend, a husband, an uncle and so on. However, it is precisely at the moment when his son is born that the father-and-son unit comes into being. The man's relationships that pre-existed this specific father-and-son unit were relationships between him and other people or between him and other things. The father-and-son relationship comes into existence together both as a *whole*, i.e. father/son, and as the *split* between the two complements, 'father' and 'son'.

Another example Hegel used to illustrate this point was that of a magnet, which is already found in Kant. A bar of metal cannot be magnetised only at one end. When you split a bar of magnetised metal, each part, once again, will have two poles. Each part of magnetised metal generates its complementary opposite. However, while Kant used this example *to demonstrate the existence of a problem*, a problem which he could not solve, Hegel used the same example as the most obvious demonstration of the interdependence of complementary opposites, which nobody can even attempt to separate. It is a demonstration of his dialectic of nature. In other words, it is not a demonstration of a problem but the statement of his point of departure for new philosophy and new science.

6.3   Antinomies exist in tension and conflict

For Hegel, as for Heraclitus, all living phenomena involve internal tension of contradictory forces. Hegel postulates contradiction in reality, nature, society and thought as 'the very moving principle of the world and it is ridiculous to say that contradiction is unthinkable' (Hegel, 1830/1973, p. 223). Hegel uses the term 'contradiction' instead of 'antinomy' or 'opposite'.

Hegel's defence of his term 'contradiction' does not mean to deny Aristotle's laws of thought claiming that a static thing cannot both be and not be at one place. However, while Aristotle was concerned with contradiction in static phenomena, Hegel's contradiction pertains to reality and life, which is ever changing. Anything that lives is part of reality and it is in reality that contradiction in unavoidable. In his *Logic* he conceives of contradiction as an intense antinomy (on this see also Inwood, 1992, p. 65). In Hegel's sense, there could be no dialectic in nature if the tension of interdependent contradictions did not keep it going.

We can distinguish, in Hegel's philosophy, at least two kinds of dialectic, both treated in his *Phenomenology of Spirit* (1807/1977) and in *Logic* (1830/1873).

First, Hegel views dialectic as *a moving principle of reality*. This is his response to the Zeitgeist of the evolutionary and developmental thinking of the end of the eighteenth and the beginning of the nineteenth century. For him, dialectic is the basic *ontological principle* and science has the task to discover this dialectic in real phenomena.

The second way in which Hegel treats dialectic in *Logic* and in the *Phenomenology of Spirit* is *dialectic as the nature of thought*. From this point of view, dialectic is *social epistemology* and it is complementary to its former, ontological sense. The mind is the realisation of world development. It is a process of self-education and self-recognition in its own activity. The *Phenomenology of Spirit* contains a complex argument that self-knowledge can be nothing else but social knowledge: ' "I" that is "We" and "We" that is "I" . . . they *recognise* themselves as *mutually recognising* one another' (Hegel, 1807/1977, p. 110).

The thought in its very nature is dialectical. As thought is by its very nature dialectical, it must, because of its dynamics, fall into contradiction. Therefore, it pushes itself forward in order to resolve the contradiction that it has created. One of the main lessons in Hegel's *Logic* is to show this movement through contradictions in thought and the very necessity to resolve them.

Viewing dialectic as a resolution of contradictions, just like viewing an object of thought from opposite perspectives and arguing for and against, was already well developed by ancient Greeks following on from Parmenides. A pre-Socratic philosopher Heraclitus already proposed the idea that the world is a process in the dialectical development of a struggle between contradictions.

Hegel, however, did not present dialectic as an idea but as a well-developed system of rationality. He showed the *fundamental necessity of dialectic involved in the development of rationality, reality, history and thought.* For him, the mind is the realisation of world development, it is the mind's self-recognition of its own activity.

7   Thinking in antinomies in psychology after Hegel

Although no immediate and no dramatic consequences were brought about in social and human sciences as a result of Hegel's epistemological efforts to show the voyage of the mind through dialectic contradictions, the idea of thinking in oppositions was gradually gaining currency. The concept of development that dominated natural, social sciences and human sciences after Hegel, could hardly be based on static epistemologies. Heterogeneous accounts of thinking in oppositions and their multi-faceted natures became appealing in various branches of social sciences and humanities. In order to give credence to these claims, let us make a brief and casual exploration of oppositional thinking after Hegel in psychology and related fields.

7.1   *The universal opposition*

For the French sociologist Tarde, opposition, alongside imitation and adaptation, was one of the essential social processes. In his monumental book *L'Opposition Universelle* (1897) Tarde presented a perspective according to which opposition is a primary concept of absolutely everything, from logic to cosmology. In his very detailed treatise he proceeded in a systematic way, considering oppositions in science, mathematics, psychology, philosophy, the states of being and in actions. He provided a comprehensive classification of oppositions of various kinds, for example, static versus dynamic and qualitative versus quantitative. In fact, the doctrine of the strife, to him, was the key to all change and the condition of progress. The law of opposition, according to him, is a fundamental force in all kinds of struggle for existence, starting from brain cells and finishing with conflicts of groups and societies.

Social life, in any of its forms, e.g. in economics, linguistics, politics and religion, is supposedly based on forces working in opposite directions and it is through their battles that evolution and progress take place. The law of opposition also provides an essential conceptual tool facilitating the understanding of social movements and the development of public opinion.

Unfortunately, however, despite Tarde's fame and significant recognition at the time, his treatise of opposition was not much noticed by his contemporaries and has now been largely forgotten.

7.2 Jung's obsession

Across the psycho-pathological literature, from Charcot, Janet, to Freud and Jung, one can find numerous theories of and comments in relation to antinomic thinking. Amongst these, Jung was perhaps the one who used the idea of oppositional thinking most explicitly.

One could say that, whether for good or bad, the whole Jungian system is based on antinomic thought. Casual inspection of the Index of his *Collected Works* (Jung, 1979, vol. 20) reveals several pages referring to his treatment of opposites. Many titles of his book chapters and their sections contain the word 'opposition' or 'opposites'. For example, he wrote about 'The alchemical view of the union of opposites', 'The Brahmanic conception of the problem of opposites', 'The opposites' or 'The personification of opposites' and so on. Moreover, the Index to his collected works lists approximately 120 pairs of opposites analysed at various stages of his monumental life work, e.g. action/non-action, analysis/synthesis, Christ/Antichrist, classic/romantic, and so on.

In his analysis of the Jungian psychological system and in particular of dialectic, Rychlak (1968) refers to a letter, in which he asked Jung whether and if so, to what extent Hegel influenced his work. Jung was emphatic in his negative answer and did not acknowledge any influence of Hegel, saying that in the intellectual world in which he had grown up, Hegelian thought played no role at all. He never studied Hegel properly and Hegel's dialectic, he could safely say, had no influence at all as far as he knew himself. Jung admitted, however, that there was 'a remarkable coincidence between certain tenets of Hegelian philosophy' and his findings concerning the collective unconscious (Rychlak, 1968, pp. 342–3). Rychlak comments on Jung's letter, pointing out that despite his rejection of Hegel, one can find many similarities between Jung's work and Hegel's thought, for example: his emphasis on the collective history of people; the role of supra-individual forces in human life and above all, the identical interpretation of the dialectic. I would also add that the Jungian notion of opposites, too, belongs to Hegelian heritage.

It is of course plausible to 're-invent' ideas independently of their first creator. However, it is also possible that as the ideas of Hegel, in this particular case, became part of the collectively shared knowledge, they circulated in society without even being attributed to any specific individual. Their 're-invention' makes even the re-inventor unaware of their proper origin.

In his paper on the contrasts between himself and Freud, Jung (1961, vol. 4, 333–40) refers, among other things, to their differences with respect to the treatment of opposites. Thus he says, 'I see in all what happens the play of opposites and derive from this conception my idea of psychic energy' (p. 337). He explains that for him the interplay of opposites is essentially involved in all kinds of human energies, from psychic to mental. Jung maintains that Freud, at least before they became enemies, had been concerned only with opposites in sexuality (however, more on Freud below).

Jung's interest in opposites had a very broad cultural basis. He studied them in the context of Eastern and Western religions, literature, philosophy, alchemy and mysticism. He frequently pointed out in his work that opposites and their symbols are so common in human thought that even to cite evidence for that would be superfluous. They symbolise conflict and attraction. The most intense conflicts are expressed in symbols like fire and water, height and depth and life and death.

Jung's book on opposites in alchemy was completed in his eightieth year of life and he had worked on it for approximately thirteen years. This book finalised his project on oppositional thinking, which preoccupied him during many years of his life. He pointed out in the book that the tremendous role, which opposites and their union played in alchemy, helps us to understand why the alchemists were so much interested in paradoxes.

Jung sometimes compared psychotherapy to alchemy (e.g. Jung, 1966, vol. 16, p. 200). Psychotherapy uses many different procedures, which may last from one day to several decades. The tensions between some psychic pairs of opposites ease off only gradually and therefore, like an alchemical end product, psychotherapy may take a long time. Moreover, just like in alchemy, where the unity in the end product is never achieved, the personality will never lose its innate duality. Thus duality of man is a product both of collective life and his individual identity.

7.3   Freud's unresolved conflicts

The idea of opposition also permeates much of Freud's work. Ernest Jones (1955, p. 320), Freud's biographer, refers to the prominence of opposites and the contrasts in Freud's work, analysing one pair of opposites after another. He maintains that interest in oppositions illustrates a peculiar feature of Freud's thinking throughout his whole life and his constant proclivity to dualistic ideas. He also refers to Heinz Hartmann, (1955, p. 422) who described Freud's dualistic tendency as a 'very characteristic kind of dialectical thinking that tends to base theories on the interaction of two opposite powers'. Similarly, Philip Rieff (1979, p. 16) speaks about the dialectical bias in Freud. One could say that unresolved antithetical ideas, like wanting something and not wanting it at the same time, constituted, in Freudian thought, the basis of hysteria and various unresolved conflicts. Freud's terms, too, like 'repression', 'defence mechanism', 'adjustment mechanism', 'compensation' and 'substitution', all imply the idea of antinomic mechanisms (cf. Jones, 1955; Rychlak, 1968).

Freud was also concerned with antinomic thinking in dreams, slips of the tongue, jokes and irony. He pointed out (Freud, 1900/1953, IV, p. 318) that the ways in which dreams usually treat the category of contraries and contradictories is remarkable because in dreams, these categories are simply disregarded. In dreams, he maintained, it seems that the category 'no' does not exist; there appears to be no censorship on what can be dreamt. Dreams simply seem to combine contraries into unity and represent them as one and the same thing. Turning a thing into its opposite or denying it totally is one of the means of representation most favoured by the dream work and one which is capable of employment in the most diverse directions (Freud, 1900/1953, IV, p. 326). Also, jokes in general are based on reversals of various kinds. Freud's (1905/1960, VIII) analysis of jokes, in particular of Jewish jokes, illustrates this point particularly well. Thus he maintained that more than other ethnic groups, Jews are well aware both of their faults and their good characteristics and of their relationships, and that this is what Jewish jokes express. Moreover, humour and jokes reduce hostility in aggressors and persecutors. Freud also analysed tendentious jokes, i.e. jokes expressing aggression or criticism against those who claim to be in authority. Tendentious jokes liberate us from the pressure of inhibitions and repression, defuse aggression against the oppression and enable us to laugh at our own misery.

Finally, in order to complete the illustration of Freud's preoccupation with antinomic thinking, it is worth referring to the following controversial example. Freud (1910/1957, XI) referred to an unsupported observation (see Benveniste, 1966, on this issue) that the ancient Egyptian languages contained a number of words with double meanings, where one meaning was the exact opposite of the other. For example, one and the same word had two opposite meanings such as 'strong' and 'weak' or 'to command' and 'to obey'. Moreover, there were also words expressing polarities such as 'old/young', 'outside/inside', 'far/near'. Abel rejected the popular explanation of this phenomenon as a feature of the primitive and illogical state of human thought. Instead, he argued that our concepts are based on comparisons. According to him, every concept is meaningful only in terms of its opposite. For instance, the concept of 'strength' can be formed only as contrary to 'weakness'. Therefore, the word denoting something that is 'strong' contains simultaneously a recollection of something which is 'weak', because these two meanings come to existence together:

In reality, this word denoted neither 'strong' nor 'weak', but *the relation and difference between the two, which created both of them equally* [my emphasis] . . . Man was not in fact able to acquire his oldest and simplest concepts except as contraries to their contraries, and only learnt by degrees to separate the two sides of an antithesis and think of one without conscious comparison with the other (quoted by Freud, 1910/1957, XI, pp. 157–8).

These double, contradictory meanings of the first words were apparently also common in Semitic and Indo-European languages. This unsupported idea suggests that only later, when concepts became more established in people's minds, were their antithetical components separated and individual words were created for a concept and its opposite.

This example, just like many of those in ancient Greek thought show, that an absurdity, a myth or an unsupported belief, simply everything is allowed in the pursuit of 'science' and glory leading to immortality.

7.4   Children think in 'le couple' (in a pair)

In developmental psychology, it was the French psychologist Wallon (1945) who persistently pursued the idea of antinomic thinking. In his book on the origin of thinking in the child Wallon argued that at all levels of the development of thinking, the concept of opposition is essential for the development of reasoning and language. For him, any term about which we can think, requires a complementary term, from which it is differentiated. In other words, all terms are determined by their opposites. He argued that this idea is so basic that the progress of a child's thought and language cannot be achieved in any other way. In his experimental work he showed that a child's responses in terms of antinomies exist practically in all psychological situations. His examples ranged from negativism in motor reactions, to emotional responses, to thinking at a pre-conceptual level, before the theoretical intelligence takes place, to abstract thinking at all levels of complexity. He also referred to Koehler's descriptions of discrimination in pairs by animals. From discrimination in animals one can move to simple discriminations in children.

Thinking always takes place in 'le couple' (in a pair), whether in analogical thinking, complementary thinking, circular responses or any other kind of thinking in antinomies. The pair expresses at the same time an identity and a differentiation: identity becomes divided, the division unites itself and finally, what is different is brought again to unity. Through gradual differentiation in the development of thinking antinomies become more complex. While at the beginning they are all combined in undifferentiated conglomerates, later they become differentiated. Wallon insists that his analyses show that it is the resolution of conflicts and tension in antinomies that lead to new and more complex forms of thinking.

Like Piaget, Wallon used a clinical method in interviewing a child. He found that there is constancy in the way a child employs the simple formula of identification, in order to unite two terms which have some relationship of contrast. To some extent Piaget, too, viewed child development in terms of antinomies. However, in contrast to Wallon, rather than viewing development in terms of contradictions and tension, Piaget referred to equilibration through accommodation and assimilation, as the processes through which the child adapts to his environment.

7.5   Polarities, contradictions and antinomies in thinking in current psychology

The idea that we think and evaluate phenomena in terms of polarities or in terms of the opposing poles of some continua, has become widespread in various forms of empirical and theoretical psychology.

From an empirical perspective, the idea of evaluation of various psychological characteristics using bipolar dimensions is colossal. One can include here personality scales such as those measuring extraversion versus introversion, externality versus internality, excitement versus depression, individualism versus collectivism, bipolar attitude scales, Kelly's repertory grid and so on. Osgood's semantic differential also uses the idea of bipolarity in evaluating objects as good/bad, active/passive and powerful/weak. Referring to many of these examples in the construction of psychological scales, Rychlak (1968, 1994) goes even further. He claims that although the idea of thinking in antinomies has been embedded in many empirical investigations in psychology, it has not been recognised as such. He views oppositions as a basic characteristic of human thinking and argues that this fact has not been recognised by the major psychological approaches like behaviourism, cognitivism or computational psychology, which have built their theories on inputs and outputs, matching, stimulus-response or on formal logic. All these mechanistic approaches, Rychlak argues, are modelled on Newtonian physics rather than on the dynamic positions of Mach, Einstein, Heisenberg and Bohr. In contrast with Newtonian physics and in accord with the latter kinds of physics,

Rychlak's logical learning theory is based on the premise that humans take an active position with respect to sense-making and sense-creating of reality. The logical processes of affirming, denying, or qualifying something are activities, which serve specific purposes. The task of psychology is to examine broad patterns of meanings intended by these goal-directed responses, which all involve thinking in antinomies.

Clearly, the notion of polarities, opposites and antinomies in empirical psychology today represents a mixture of different underlying theoretical perspectives. Some of them presuppose a continuity of gradated antinomies, whereas in other cases they are discontinuous contradictions of the type 'either' 'or', or contraries of the type 'either', 'in-between' and 'or'.

From a theoretical point of view, Michael Billig, in *Arguing and Thinking* (1996) made a significant contribution to the study of antinomies and contradictions. Thinking is by nature argumentative and it develops through confrontation of opposite views. Billig traces it to the ancient tradition of Greek dialogue, with its multivoiced and dialectic nature, and compares it to modern experimental social psychology, from which the voices and dialectic are removed. Instead, they are substituted by 'the idea that thought processes are based upon the categorisation of information' (Billig, 1996, p. 35). However, if 'Protagoras's maxim is correct, then each form of thought can be contrasted by an opposing form of thought' (1996, p. 36).

Our emphasis on thinking in oppositions should not lead to an impression that we exclude or deny other forms of thinking. Indeed, this book will insist that thinking comes about in many different forms and takes on different routes. For example, some kinds of thinking are analogical; there is inductive and deductive thinking; there are scientific, artistic and common sense kinds of thinking; there is practical and theoretical thinking. Different problems require different kinds of thinking. Nevertheless, there is a specific reason for bringing into focus thinking in antinomies.

Thinking in antinomies will constitute a fundamental conceptual tool in the development of the theory of social knowledge. However, before developing the maxim of thinking in terms of interdependent antinomies and oppositions, we must address another issue: antinomies and oppositions in language.

NOTES

1. I am grateful to Sir Geoffrey Lloyd for drawing to my attention the danger of confusing polar expressions in language and antinomies in thinking. He himself makes this distinction in *Polarity and Analogy*.

2. In his *Republic* Plato made a clear distinction between rhetoric on the one hand and dialectic thinking on the other. He was critical of the eristic art of rhetoricians who mixed up rhetoric aiming to persuade, with dialectic thinking searching for objective truth. Arguments, for Plato, were to be based on rationality, on *logos*, rather than on the art of persuasion. Thus, true philosophy must be distinguished from the inferior modes of reasoning based on contentious philosophy. One of the claims of rhetoric and sophistic was that one can make weak arguments appear stronger by the skilful use of language. In another of his Dialogues, in *Gorgias*, Plato was critical of rhetoric because of its manufacture of persuasion. The orator has the power to speak about anything and by means of persuasion he can diminish the reputation of others.

3. In *Metaphysica*, in reviewing the work of his predecessors on opposites, Aristotle discussed the possible mutual influence of Alcmaeon of Croton for whom 'most human affairs go in pairs' and that of Pythagoreans. Pythagoreans were more rigorous than Alcmaeon in their claims about pairs of opposites. They had arranged the fundamental principles into two columns of antinomies (Aristotle, *Metaphysica*, Book A 5 986a–b) as a starting point of their philosophy.

4. Lloyd (1990, p. 117) remarks that even Heraclitus' logic followed the general way of the Greek logical thinking in extremes. The Greek thought was extremist both in its conceptualisation of movement and change on the one side of the range, and in the conceptualisation of absolute stability on the other side of the range. Heraclitus insisted on a total change, for him there was no stability in the world. At the other end of the spectrum, Parmenides asserted inertia, for him what existed, was changeless and without movement.

5. Despite this, however, although they are alive, things in nature do not change on their own accord. Although they have a potentiality for movement and change, in order to become actuality, they must be given a purpose to move towards their proper place. This purpose is given to things by the ultimate source of movement, which is a Mover who, on its own, is unmoved.

6. They were manifestations of Dao, the all-embracing reality, which united the order of nature. The fundamental feature of Dao, translated as the Way, was the cyclic nature of everlasting change.

7. This philosophy included five components, namely Wood, Fire, Earth, Metal and Water, which were in constant change (Needham, 1970; Lloyd, 1994). In contrast, atomism was alien to Chinese thought and one can hardly find any traces of it there. Needham maintains that the original idea of the atom, as that which cannot be divided, is either Greek or Indian, whereas the original idea of waxing and waning waves seems to be Chinese (Needham, 1970, p. 77).

8. These ideas of symbolic oppositions were particularly represented in the work of Nicholas de Cusa in the fourteenth century (1954, p. 49ff), for whom God symbolised the reconciliation of contraries. In the work of Nicholas de Cusa, antinomies form an essential theological and epistemological foundation. Using mathematical examples, he showed that in God, the maximum coincides with the minimum, an infinite line coincides with an infinite triangle, and an infinite circle with an infinite sphere (1954, The First Book). In other words, the finite worldly things have multiple natures and qualities and these are all transcended in God. Having entitled his work *Of Learned Ignorance*

(De Docta Ignorantia), he maintained that people learn about God through a considerable struggle; the more a person is aware of his ignorance, the greater his learning (pp. 8–9). In his theory of knowledge Nicholas de Cusa discerned three stages of knowledge. The lowest stage is sense perception, which does no more than to affirm what the individual perceives. In contrast, the reason, which is a higher stage of knowledge, both affirms and denies. The reason is discursive and is governed by the principle of contradiction. The activity of reason brings us to an approximate knowledge of God. The highest knowledge, the knowledge of God, is attained by intellect, which is a superior activity of the mind. In this conception, the activity of intellect and the use of language are interrelated.

9. These activities were thought to be inferior to science but also irrational, perverse and dangerous for the political and religious masters in Europe. They were viewed with suspicion, because these activities represented liberal thinking, humanism and a kind of intellectual antinomy against the newly established political regimes. Many humanists and representatives of these heterodoxies were seeking asylum in various places in Central and Eastern Europe, of which Prague, during the rule of the Czech King and a Holy Roman Emperor Rudolph II, became the most important. During the peak of that period, some 200 alchemists and their helpers, were employed by Rudolph II, who was interested in magic, esoterism, hermetic disciplines, astrology, alchemy and kabbala. As a result, the Renaissance scientists and mystics like Tycho de Brahe, Kepler, Dee and Kelley, were either invited by Rudolph II or came to Prague being attracted by its liberalism.

10. In mediaeval and Renaissance mysticism and magic, we must distinguish between wizardry on the one hand, and speculative mysticism (Haldane, 1897), on the other. The latter aimed 'to go beyond information given', that is, it strove to overstep the frontiers of reality by means of experience, imagination, creativity and symbolism. If we cannot grasp reality on the basis of experience, we may turn, in our search for wisdom and knowledge, to alternative traditions. Magic and mysticism, therefore, covered a wide spread of approaches and practices. At one pole of the spectrum there was the perspective that reality exists beyond what is available to our experience here-and-now. This perspective attempted to grasp this unknown reality by various forms of extended consciousness. At the other end of the spectrum there was wizardry, trying to reach the unknown by witchcraft and sorcery.

Most scientists whom we celebrate, today, as the founders of 'true' science were both scientists and mystics. Nicolson's (1950) dramatic exposition of breaking the circle of perfection (Chapter 1) in the history of metaphysics, science, ethics and aesthetics, makes very obvious the fact that the borders between science and mysticism were very grey. Kepler himself had no problems in using terms such as 'dynamic power' pointing out that the 'Creator has in himself not only the geometrical archetypes of all things that he has made but also the divine plan for all the phenomena still to be created. Hence the earth-soul reflects in itself the image of the zodiac and of the firmament; evidence of the interrelation and the homogeneity of terrestrial and celestial things' (Nicolson, 1950, pp. 130–1). Religion and mysticism, rather than science first attracted the young Kepler to the ideas of Copernicus.

Kepler's astronomy and astrology remained penetrated with mystic analogies and mystic meanings throughout his life. In those he tended to respond to nature like a poet rather than as a scientist. Kepler was not only an astronomer, who formulated three laws of the movement of heavenly bodies, but also an astrologist who devoted himself to the production of horoscopes, both for himself and members of his family, as well as for Rudolph II and Duke Albrecht of Waldstejn in Prague.

However, even in Newton, the founder of modern mechanistic science in the sense of Galileo and Descartes, one can find more than a scientist preoccupied with mechanistic physics:

there was another Newton, more concerned with his interpretations of Daniel than with the mechanical laws of the universe; a Newton who added the last mysterious passages to the *Principia*, and who in both *Principia* and *Opticks*, presupposed "cosmic spirit", pervading all things, exciting sensations and volition in men and animals who were less mechanical than animate (Nicolson, 1950, p. 135).

Newton too was much influenced by natural magic and by the work of Jacob Böhme. He assumed the existence of ether as linking the sublunary realm with the cosmos, which has a strong resemblance to 'spiritus'. At the same time he assumed that the underlying structure of the world is mathematical.

One could conjecture even more about this speculative mysticism, attempting to go beyond the information given. Could it be that the discovery of instruments such as microscopes and microphones was facilitated by efforts to uncover realms not normally perceived by the unaided senses? Don't we see, today, examples of similar intents in the preoccupation with virtual reality and the Internet? Viewing magic of the late Renaissance from this point of view, it is possible that the efforts of Rudolf II to go beyond immediate reality, to capture what is beyond the 'disenchanted world', may be natural rather than extraordinary.

11. If Böhme were to be a mystic in the sense that mysticism means a preoccupation with something not comprehensible by senses, something which would be connected with superstition and would be lacking reasoning, then, such mysticism would be very remote from Hegel's rationalism. Haldane makes the point, that Böhme's mysticism, however, just like the mysticism of many of his contemporaries, was of a different kind. It was a kind of mysticism, which was akin to speculative thought. Böhme lived at a time when scholastic philosophy dominated scholarship and when knowledge was conceived as a doctrine, and therefore, not as something to be questioned. At those times, inhospitable to new ideas, Böhme was questioning, at a much earlier date than Descartes, some eternal truths that nobody dared to address or doubt. Böhme's speculative mysticism attracted Hegel because it was rational, it went beyond understanding phenomena of his time and tried to reach phenomena beyond the senses which are here-and-now.

3   Linguistic and dialogical antinomies

Investigations of language and linguistic phenomena have been the focus of attention in the world's oldest sciences going back some 4000 years. They were mostly concerned with the grammatical norms and rules, with logic and rhetoric. The foundations of modern science of language in Europe were laid down in the seventeenth century and since that time we can identify several kinds of antinomy that have become the foci of interest in the philosophy of language and in linguistic studies.

1   A-historical/historical antinomy in language

1.1   Language without history

Although René Descartes did not write much about language, his philosophy and scientific method and his mechanistic conception of physical objects and biological organisms influenced the movement aiming to develop universal grammars.[1] Universal grammars of the seventeenth century conceived of language as a mechanism consisting of elements that could be composed and decomposed into parts. Descartes thought that, in order to construct a universal language, one should find a suitable way of arranging ideas in clear and simple units, in the same manner as one can arrange numbers in mathematics (Descartes, 1641a/1970). Several attempts were made at the time to establish universal grammar on these principles. Among them, the Port-Royal *Grammaire générale et raisonée*, published in Paris in 1660, is best known. The seventeenth century German philosopher G.W. Leibniz, aimed at a logical analysis, that would systematically synthesise all the elements of cognition and the signs of language, which, again, would bring out their universal character.

The mechanistic conception of language, just like the mechanistic conception of organisms, did not require any theoretical consideration of *change*. Instead, the widespread point of view was that language had a universal character. For Descartes language was a matter of scientific interest only to the extent that it could be subjected to rational thought and analysis using mathematical methods.

This idea continues through the following centuries. An eighteenth-century scholar James Harris (1751/1968), in his treatise on language and universal grammar, adopts a strictly mechanistic approach to all aspects of language. According to him, just as a statue can be divided into several limbs, so speech can be divided into its constituent parts, like articles, nouns, verbs and so on.

Descartes' strict scientific thinking excluded other ways of obtaining knowledge, in particular, through culture. Although he acknowledged the effect that culture had on people (cf. Jahoda, 1992), it was in the context of his general observation about life and not in the context of science. For him, historical studies were not concerned with human rationality and with the search after truth. Language could be studied scientifically only through logic and mathematics.

In contrast to Descartes, who based his theory of knowledge, and by implication, of language, totally on a-historical assumptions of innate ideas and on universals, John Locke's a-historical theory of knowledge heavily relied on experience and learning. Locke's mechanistic ideas, which dominated his conceptions about thinking, also penetrated his ideas about language. For him, fashions, customs and habits of a nation bring out certain combinations of complex ideas that are exclusive to a specific language and do not exist in any other language. Some nations have words for phenomena of customs, which exist only in their own culture: 'where there was no such Custom, there was no notion of any such action; no use of such Combinations of *Ideas*' (Locke, 1690/1975, II, XXII, 6). From these considerations Locke came to the observation that languages constantly change over time, they 'take up new, and lay by old terms' (1690/1975, II, XXII, 7). He thought that these changes are due to variations in customs and to newly formed opinions. Such social changes create new combinations of ideas and transfer them into language. Where there are new things, people need to think and talk about them. Interestingly, though, Locke's acute observations about change in language did not lead him to ask questions about the concept of change as such. Thus change was not an epistemological issue for John Locke and therefore, it did not play any essential part in Locke's theory of language. He considered change to be arbitrary due to variations in customs. His epistemology remained, like that of Descartes, totally a-historical.

1.2   Vico's New Science

Scientific theories and philosophies, which stimulate interest, are bound to provoke anti-theories and anti-philosophies. This was true about the

Cartesian/Lockean epistemology. Giambattista Vico (1668–1744) was amongst the first of modern scholars who explicitly rejected the Cartesian/Lockean a-historical approach to language and the notion of clear and distinct ideas as the ultimate constituents of knowledge.[2] Vico argued that just as a lamp lit at night illuminates an object but hides the surroundings, so the mind, by perceiving the object in question clearly and distinctly in the Cartesian fashion, loses sight of what is in its shadow. And such a narrow-minded approach precludes proper understanding of that object.

Image of the Port-Royal universal grammar based on logical and mathematical rules and axioms, Vico argued, was totally irrelevant to language. Instead, in *New Science* Vico (1744/1968) presented a picture of language as originating from historical, social and cultural processes. In contrast to his contemporary French scholar Condillac, Vico did not view language as a product of individuals who, in order to communicate, had agreed on a common code. He argued instead that people are born into a communicating society. He suggested that in early historical stages primitive people did not communicate by words. Speech was born from mute gestures as a sign language (1744/1968, p. 401) and from gestures which had some relations to the ideas that people wanted to express. Later in history, such 'mute acts' became words. The first language, according to Vico, was poetical and was used by theological poets.

Vico emphasised the role of poetry both in the origins and in the subsequent historical evolution of language, in culture, creativity, folk psychology and emotional expression. He also maintained that the first language was not reflexive, because, among other things, it did not express *irony*. The use of irony, for him, was based on a meta-communicative ability, i.e. the ability to reflect on one's own and on others' communication. When we ironise something, we must be able to reflect on language itself (1744/1968, p. 408). For example, we negate by confirmation but we demonstrate that we are not serious by other means of communication, i.e. tone of voice, accent and non-verbal gesture. Irony relies on a shared understanding of negation. We use irony with others as well as with ourselves and we use different kinds of irony for different purposes and aims. These ideas of meta-communication in Vico's conception of language, though, are nowadays rarely mentioned. We could say that these ideas were very early germs of what in the twentieth century Bakhtin calls '*double-voicedness*' (Chapter 4). Discussing parodistic discourse, Bakhtin (1984b, p. 194) likens it to irony and to other kinds of *double-voicedness*. Double-voicedness refers to the use of someone else's words in order to express one's own intentions and meanings that are hostile to others' words. By that he means that in our own speech we often repeat the words of other people if we want to ironise them or to give them meanings that they originally did not have. Bakhtin clarifies this as follows:

In the ordinary speech of our everyday life such a use of another's words is extremely widespread, especially in dialogue, where one speaker very often literally repeats the statement of the other speaker, investing it with new value and accenting it in his own way – with expressions of doubt, indignation, irony, mockery, ridicule and the like (Bakhtin, 1984b, p. 194).

While Giambattista Vico was a highly original thinker, we must also see him as a child of his epoch. It was an epoch, in which the preoccupation with subjectivity and intersubjectivity was something new and the literature of his time was full of various characteristics of interpersonal relations, like deception, pretence, insincerity and differences between what was real and what only appeared to be real. In the twentieth century it was Erwin Goffman in particular who brought these characteristics to attention.

Preoccupation with subjectivity, intersubjectivity and otherness was an essential aspect in the rise of European individualism from the sixteenth century onwards. The emergence of new literary genres such as biographies, the growth of literacy and a rapidly developing interest in letter writing – all went alongside the cultural changes in the concept of self and personal identity. Trilling (1972) has magnificently captured these changes, reflected in language, in his analysis of the literature of the period. He showed that the growth of awareness about 'sincerity' and 'insincerity' and the preoccupation with these terms in the literature was related to the new meaning given to the concept of personhood. Much of the great literature at the time was preoccupied with role playing, understanding the difference between reality and appearance, the use of different speech genres and the ability to use language in order to hide what one does not want to reveal. All these language games could take place because the individual was developing, at a broad level, the ability to see himself through the eyes and the language of the other. In other words, he has become able to reflect on himself as author and co-author of his dialogical contributions.

Emphasis on subjectivity and otherness reflected itself in the emergence of conversation as a form of dialogue that is carried out primarily for social reasons and that does not have specific aims apart from talking for pleasure, a game or politeness. In his study of conversation, Tarde (1922) pointed out that he could not trace it in history further back than to the fifteenth century in Italy and the sixteenth and seventeenth centuries in France. Slightly later conversation as a genre emerged in England and in the eighteenth century he found it in Germany. Tarde drew attention to conversation as a social encounter giving attention to the other person, to negotiation, battle, tension and mutuality. He also pointed to its ethical and moral nature. Conversation destroys hierarchy between people and forms a preamble to the exchange of services, something that became important in the emergent individualism, in the development of stock markets and in the new kinds of social activities and services calling for negotiation.

The emergence of the modern notion of the self was later accompanied by new insights into grammatical aspects of language. These appeared in the eighteenth century from the linguists like Bernhardi and Vater, who drew attention to the existence of pronouns like I, Thou, You. These pronouns are parts of speech acts and are tied to verbs that call for trusting relations like I promise, I will do, I respect.

Not surprisingly, viewing language as dynamic and contextualised, Vico discarded the distinction between literal meanings of words and metaphors. He argued that people in more primitive historical stages used metaphors naturally as part of their thinking; what we call today 'literal meanings' in the past were metaphors. Vico discussed the use of metaphor in great detail, pointing out that a large part of metaphors in all languages were related to the human body, senses and passions. He viewed metaphors as a highly creative and imaginative feature of early people in their effort to understand their world (Vico, 1744/1968, p. 405). Emphasising the power of imagination and the use of language in context, imagination was for him a creative possibility of the human mind to make choices of its environment. Moreover, choices so made could then be integrated into new and meaningful wholes.

2   Social/individual antinomy

2.1   Speech and reflection are social

Johann Gottfried von Herder (1744–1803), who was Hamann's[3] student, contributed to yet another revolutionary turn in the conception of language. Herder elaborated three important ideas.

First, like his predecessors Vico and Hamann, Herder studied primitive cultures and their expression in folk, e.g. poetry and popular myths. He argued that to properly appreciate other cultures and their traditions, one must attempt to adopt their own perspective and their own point of view. He acknowledged, though, that it is difficult enough to empathise with a single individual and understand his feelings and actions let alone the whole culture. Therefore, it is an enormous task to empathise with other nations. Herder argued that in order to 'feel oneself into everything' (cf. Marková, 1982) that concerns other nations, one must have the ability to picture their ways of life, habits, desires and characteristics of their environment. Such reflexive ability, for Herder, was particularly important with respect to language. According to him, language must be studied as a historical creation of people. It expresses the collective experience of a nation and it represents a nation's actions, history and emotions. His way of thinking about language has gone far beyond designation. He has opened up a wide spectrum of different uses of language serving different purposes and situations. Above all, both speech and reflection are expressions of human nature, which is social.

Herder's second major contribution, which was connected with the first one, was his attention to self-consciousness. Here again, one can trace ideas that resemble those of Vico. By emphasising self-consciousness, he brought into focus the concept of subjectivity in language. In his analysis of Herder's work, Taylor (1995c) implies that Herder is a philosopher at a cross-roads. Taylor's analysis underlines those features of Herder's thought, which pre-empt the concept of heterogeneity in language, thus opening the road towards the dialogicality of language and the mind.[4] There are several issues implicit in Herder's work. Above all, humans use language in multifaceted, polysemic and heterogeneous situations. Therefore, we need to understand the different ways in which situations can be interpreted. In other words, we must be able to choose what is to be interpreted from *all* or, at least, from *many different senses*. For example, we must understand the meanings in interaction and use them properly in the commonly shared communication of genres and sub-genres.

Second, we must know how to show and interpret expressions of emotions, like indignation, admiration or shame, how to show respect and how to acknowledge or ignore the other interlocutor. Irony, laughter, jokes and the use of metaphors – all require understanding of common communication codes. All these activities take place simultaneously in linguistically defined situations.

Moreover, language activities are meta-communicative. They communicate something about themselves and in doing that, they reveal what it is to be human. In order to express and comprehend meta-communicative aspects of language, we must be self-conscious and reflective. For example, in order to ironise, the speakers must be able to reflect on what is supposed to be real and what is supposed to be apparent in communication.

Finally, Vico's echo can be discerned in Herder's holistic conception of language. Herder insisted that we do not learn language by acquiring single words. We are born into language and into culture and well before we acquire the first actual word, we have already appropriated the whole repertoire of language-based cultural practices, even if still in an abstract and not-yet-expressed form. Herder's holistic perspective is also manifested in his conviction that reason and language develop together from the nature of humanity: 'without speech man would have no reason and no reason is possible without speech' (Herder, 1771/1967, V, p. 40).

In conclusion, we could say that Herder was a scholar on the crossroad of epochs in at least two senses. First, through his work the antinomy *a-historical/historical* became sharp: he rejected universalistic and atomic conceptions of language and separated them from cultural awareness, holism and other-orientation. Second, through elaborating on these issues, Herder anticipated the emergence of another antinomy, that of *social/individual*.

2.2   Vitalism of Humboldt

Wilhelm Humboldt (1767–1835) elaborated many of the ideas about language outlined by Herder. Like Vico, Hamann and Herder, Humboldt emphasised historicity in the study of language. In contrast to them, he carried out systematic linguistic observations in studying many different languages, e.g. Kawi, Malayan and Sanscrit, and thus became a founder of comparative linguistics. He argued that language arose instinctively from the social nature of human beings and he claimed that language plays an essential role in the development of the human mind. In contrast to his contemporaries like Condillac, Humboldt's (1836/1971) view was that language did not arise from any sort of social pressure. It was the inner need of people to communicate with one another that had led to the development of language. People are reflective animals and they express their emotions in songs and poetry.

Like Herder's, so Humboldt's fundamental conception of language was holistic. He conceived of language as an organic whole, as a living organism, which is creative and always active, never a finished product but always an ever-changing, dynamic process. The true definition of language may be only genetic. The finest features of a language cannot be understood as diverse and separate elements taken from a connected discourse. Breaking language down into single words and rules is 'a lifeless tour de force based on scientific dismemberment' (Humboldt, 1836/1971, p. 27), which has nothing to do with the reality of language. His holistic conception led him to maintain that language is one universal organism and the differences between languages exist only within that universal language. From his view of oneness of language he proceeded to the notion of oneness of humanity: humanity consists of individuals who all have their similar human powers. Humboldt often conveyed his holistic perspectives in his writings, but perhaps most explicitly he expressed his holistic views in a letter to his friend Schiller in 1795. He claimed there that language must possess at any moment of its life the features that make it a whole. As with any other organic phenomenon, all aspects of language are mutually interdependent (Nerlich and Clarke, 1996, pp. 31–2). From today's perspective, these claims could be considered as extravagant in their exaggerated emphasis on the all-embracing nature of language, but we must see them in the context of Humboldt's time. On the one hand, they challenged the mechanistic positions in the study of language. On the other hand, they were part of the vitalistic point of view in Humboldt's time, emphasising the organic unity of the universe.

Philosophically, Humboldt's terminology is Kantian. However, in his analysis of Humboldt's work Shpet[5] (1927) points out that Humboldt is, in his world outlook, more similar to Hegel than to Kant. Shpet refers in this respect to broad-mindedness, boldness of ideas and the depth of Humboldt's analysis. Above all, Shpet draws attention to the philosophical perspective looming at the time, according to which all human social phenomena must be conceived both as *substances*, i.e. something more or less permanent, and *subjective activities*. These ideas were implicit in Humboldt and later on they were present and further developed in Hegel's *Phenomenology of the Spirit*. Like Hegel, Humboldt postulated two mutually interdependent components of language: first, language as a persistent phenomenon, in the sense that it is the product of humankind. At the same time, it is transient and ever changing through the activity of speaking individuals. Humboldt expressed this idea in his well-known claim that language is not a finished product, *ergon*, but activity, *energeia*. It is a phenomenon in the making. In Humboldt's conception of language, *ergon* and *energeia* are inseparable but ergon, the relatively stable component of language, restricts energeia in its creativity.

Humboldt (1836/1971, p. 23) made it clear that the permanence of language, that is, 'the work of nations' must precede the activities of individuals. Nevertheless, the two aspects of language, permanent and transient, are intertwined and simultaneous. In his linguistic theory Wilhelm Humboldt formulated, for the first time, clearly and openly, the interdependence between language as a social phenomenon, or in his words, the soul of people on the one hand and the intellectual activity of the individual on the other hand. In this way Humboldt explicitly introduced the *antinomy social/individual*, which created a puzzle not only for him, but also for many of his followers. Language is an external manifestation of people's minds but when the individual uses language, she does not mirror language as a collective product. Rather, Humboldt emphasised individual creativity and individuality of speech action. Individuality, however, for him, reflected language as a collective product. Humboldt was aware of the difficulty of showing how exactly individuality and collectivity are interdependent. For him, it was at that time an incomprehensible issue, concealed from perception (1836/1971, p. 24).

Humboldt's vitalistic and organic approach to language stood in sharp difference to the Lockean mechanistic conception according to which objects and words could be decomposed down into their attributes. No longer can we find in Humboldt's approach the criterion of truth and falsity of knowledge defined by the correct and incorrect use of language and leading to correct or wrong representations of an object.[6] Instead, Humboldt presented a socio-cultural and dynamic concept of language, and insisted that 'the individual creativity and the culture are . . . interdependent, as the urgencies of their natures demand' (1836/1971, p. 8). Creativity of the individual, however, is constrained by the environment, in which the individual lives and through which he expresses agency. Humboldt explains in many different ways that each individual builds on what is commonly understood by others. The two components, i.e. language as a social manifestation and the individual's intellectual power, 'do not proceed consecutively and separately with respect to one another, but are absolutely and inseparably the very same activity of the intellectual capacity' (1836/1971, p. 24). Humboldt never conceived of these two factors as separate but they formed, for him, an organic unity from the beginning to end.

Humboldt expressed strong opinion that communication by means of language stimulates intellectual life and provides the human mind with convictions. According to him, the force to think is necessarily fired by language and equally language is fired by thinking. It is appropriate to recap, once again on Locke's ideas about knowledge and communication. While for Locke words in communication distorted knowledge and were obstacles to truth, for Humboldt, communication led to an increase in 'objectivity' of knowledge. According to Humboldt 'objectivity' and 'subjectivity' are dialectically interdependent. This can be seen in the following example. Humboldt appreciated the role of *'alterity'* brought into language. It is the experience of *'otherness'*, which enables us to be reflective or meta-communicative. The word from a stranger opens, for the individual involved, new possibilities for the use of language. The word from a stranger makes us reflect, forces us to try to understand the unfamiliar other and, consequently, enriches our own language. It serves as a test for comprehensibility and thus through such use of language we become aware of those aspects, which otherwise would be taken for granted. At the same time, the word from a stranger, as it is used for others, transforms itself into something that becomes 'objective', i.e. part of the common heritage. These views of Humboldt anticipate Bakhtin's notion of 'strangeness' (*ostranenie*) as well as that of the appropriation of the word of the other (Chapter 4).

2.3   Saussure's choice

There are as many critics of Ferdinand de Saussure (1857–1913) as there are admirers. The critics focus on the fact that he separated the study of language as a static system of signs (*la langue*) from spoken language (*la parole*) and thus introduced 'hard' linguistics and semiotics, relegating the real language of everyday life to a non-science. His admirers, on the other hand, value the very same thing: by separating the essential from arbitrary, Saussure established the real science of linguistics and semiotics.

Saussure used three basic terms in his theory, which make better sense in French than in English, because in English there are no separate words for the phenomena that Saussure analysed. I shall therefore use the French terms in italics when referring to these three phenomena. '*Le langage*' (Language) for Saussure is the faculty of human beings to use a specific '*langue*' (language again in English) (Saussure, 1910–11/1993, p. 6). This ability of *le langage* is given to every individual with the language organs he develops, and with what can be produced with these organs. However, such organs provide no more than a faculty, a capacity or a potentiality for language acquisition. This capacity would not come to much if it were not for *la langue* (i.e. language as a system of signs) and also for *la parole* (speech). *La langue* is the social component of language (ibid. 1910–11/1993, p. 70); it is a social product. It is passive and resident in the collectivity: it is a social fact. In contrast, *la parole* is active and individual.

Until recently, the main source of Saussure's ideas was *Le Cours de Linguistique Générale*, which was compiled by Bally and Sechehaye (1915) on the basis of three sets of lecture notes for lectures given by Saussure at the University of Geneva during 1906–11. *Le Cours* appeared two or three years after Saussure's death and it represents the editors' view of Saussure's conception of language. Moreover, it is *not* organised chronologically, as Saussure's lectures were given year by year, but according to the principles of Husserlian philosophy, which was influential at the time (Saussure, 1910–11/1993, p. xi). These two facts have led to some significant distortions of Saussure's ideas about *the concept of change* in language.

In contrast, the three volumes of *Le Cours*, published in the 1990s are organised chronologically, covering Saussure's lectures from 1907 until 1911. They provide new insights into the problem that Saussure experienced with respect to the antinomy between *la langue* and *la parole*.

The third volume of *Le Cours* contains the most important notes taken by Constantin which were not used in the original version of 1915. In more recent versions of *Le Cours* only fragments of those notes were published (Saussure, 1910–11/1993, p. xiii). In fact, in these notes, and in particular in the *Notebook VIII*, we find the most important evidence of Saussure's problem with the concept of change in language. These notes were taken towards the end of the Cours III, that is, in 1910–11. The notes state that '*la langue* is a social fact' (1980,11/1993,VIII, p. 97) and that this gives it a centre of gravity. It is bound with time and with its past. Time actually curtails freedom of *la langue*. The notes further state that, although theoretically *la langue* can be considered independently of time, *la langue* changes as it is transmitted from generation to generation. There are shifts in the acoustic image, in signification and in the relation between idea and sign. In other words, the changes occur through usage of language:

The language can be controlled as long as it is not in circulation, but as soon as it fulfils its function you see the relations shift (Saussure, 1910–11/1993, p. 100).

What a paradoxical claim in contrast to Humboldt! We can control language *by not using it!* Saussure pondered about this issue further by raising the question about the artificial language of Esperanto. Would Esperanto, which is not the language of any compact community and is not learned as a natural language, start changing like an ordinary language, when it becomes social?

These quotes and references illustrate Saussure's hesitation over the question of change in language. Before the publication of Constantin's notebooks, this issue was a matter of superficial criticism of Saussure for not dealing seriously with *la parole*. The above quotes show, however, that Saussure was well aware of the problem and that his work was at a crossroads (see also Chapter 1 on this issue).

Yet it is also at this point that we can see clearly the difference between Humboldt and Saussure. Saussure posed the same questions, about the interdependence between the social and individual nature of language, as did Humboldt. However, Humboldt adopted the concept of interdependence between the social and individual characteristics of language without resolving the question as to how they are interdependent. Saussure, too, considered *la langue* and *la parole* to be interdependent, but he resolved the problem by the strict analytic separation of the two aspects of language. *La langue* and *la parole* had to be *studied as independent* from one another. In a Durkheimian manner (Chapter 5), he saw *la langue* as a social institution, as a social fact, which is passive and therefore *analytically* totally separated from *la parole*, the activity of the individual.

Thus Saussure concludes that the two aspects of language, *la langue* and *la parole* presuppose one another and that one cannot exist without one another. Nevertheless, they are so little alike in nature that each requires a separate theory. Any chimerical attempt to bring these two parts of language together from the same point of view will only result in a rather muddled discipline: 'You cannot take both roads simultaneously, must follow both separately or choose one of them. And I have said, it is the study of *la langue* that I am pursuing for my part' (1915/1959, p. 92). *La langue* is an objectively analysable system of signs. Each sign is an interdependent union of acoustic image and meaning (Saussure, 1915/1959, p. 32).

By separating *la langue* from *la parole* Saussure separated the social and essential from the individual and accidental (1915/1959, p. 30). Towards the end of Cours III in 1911 he was so assiduously preoccupied with the question of *change*, that one wonders how he might have developed his ideas should he have lived longer. Unfortunately, he died less than two years later.

Saussure's emphasis on *'la langue'* as a social fact and his dramatic proposal that *semiotics should be a science of social psychology* has had no effect. Neither psychology of language, nor linguistics, psycholinguistics or cognitive science have been much concerned with the antinomy *social/individual*. These sciences have treated language as a capacity of the individual. Until the rise of pragmatics, discourse analysis and conversation analysis during the 1960s and 1970s, the main emphasis in the study of language was on individual capacity or faculty – on what Saussure would call *'le langage'*.

3   Linguistic antinomies

To my mind, the most significant linguistic antinomy during the twentieth century is that between synchrony and diachrony. It exemplifies the problem in the study of language as to how to conceptualise *change* in language. This problem has penetrated all levels of linguistic analysis from phonemes to meanings of lexical items and to grammar and pragmatics.

3.1   *The original contribution of Vilém Mathesius*

Vilém Mathesius was the founder of the Prague Linguistic Circle in 1926. In his paper *On the Potentiality of the Phenomena of Language* (1911/1964), presented in 1911 to the Royal Bohemian Learned Society, Mathesius made a distinction between synchronic and diachronic linguistic problems. In this paper he argued for the synchronic approach in the study of linguistics. He introduced the notion of potentiality in language, which refers to a *static oscillation*, as opposed to a *dynamic change*. By static oscillation he meant instability within various aspects of language at a given period of time. He claimed that there are idiosyncratic kinds of oscillation in speech amongst the individuals speaking a particular language; there are also oscillations in semantic characteristics of speech, with words having semantic potentialities rather than strictly rigid meanings. There is some resemblance between this idea of static oscillation in meanings of words by Mathesius and Piaget's idea of equilibration of cognitive structures. Both refer to dynamic changes – or oscillation *within* a certain relatively stable period of time (Mathesius) or a developmental stage (Piaget).

In view of these ideas, Mathesius defined linguistics as 'a science whose task is to analyse, in a static [=synchronistic, J.V.] manner, the language materials used by a language community at a given time, and, in a dynamic [=diachronistic, J.V.] manner, its historical changes' (Mathesius, 1911/1964, p. 22). Mathesius argued that linguistics should examine the speech of an individual speaker in order to reveal 'the full extent of the potentiality of the concerned language'. He also admitted that his own theory was not entirely new and that other thinkers had already presented some of the ideas he had. It is here that Mathesius declared that the distinction between static and dynamics was 'first clearly envisaged by the present writer when he was reading, during his university studies, T.G. Masaryk's remarks on linguistics' (1911/1964, p. 32) in 1885.

As he himself pointed out later on, Mathesius had made this distinction several years before Saussure's (1915/59) *Cours de Linguistique Générale* was published. Unfortunately, Mathesius' important paper, which he read in 1911 to the Royal Bohemian Learned Society, was ignored and not a single question was asked by those present (Wellek, 1976). As Vachek (1964) points out, one of the greatest linguists of the twentieth century, Roman Jakobson, then declared that had Mathesius delivered his lecture 'not in Prague but in Moscow, it would have caused there a veritable revolution in linguistics'.

In contrast to Saussure, who separated synchrony from diachrony, Mathesius held that linguistics must study both synchrony and diachrony. Indeed, it must study the speech of individual speakers, in order to arrive at the full potential of language. However, although Mathesius advocated both the synchronic and diachronic approaches to the study of language, once again, it is not clear in concrete terms, how these two processes might be intertwined. Much of what Mathesius described were intuitions rather than theoretical proposals as to how the concept of change in language could be developed and how language change could be studied.

3.2   *The dialectic of synchrony/diachrony in the Prague Linguistic Circle*

The Prague Linguistic Circle, and more generally, the Prague School of Semiotics, established itself as a leading scientific, artistic and humanistic movement in Czechoslovakia in the early years of the twentienth century.[7] The theoretical aims of the Circle were formulated and developed into a programme in the *Théses* (1929), presented to the First International Congress of Slavonic Languages in Prague in 1929. The *Théses* dealt with a variety of issues concerning theoretical, methodological and pedagogical problems of Slavonic languages. One of the main aims of the programme was the study of the relationship between synchrony, i.e. the study of language as a system at a particular time, and diachrony, i.e. the study of language as a system in change and development. The *Théses* stated at the very beginning that, in contrast to the claims of the Saussure school, one should not make a strict separation between the synchronic and diachronic approaches in the study of language. The *Théses* emphasised, instead, that in order to examine the system of language in terms of its functions, it was necessary to study how it transforms itself. One should not presuppose that linguistic changes are destructive. Rather, the study of linguistic changes facilitates the understanding of the stability of language and its functions. Moreover, the study of the synchronic system would be incomplete without an investigation of its evolution, because the language system, as it exists in its present form, not only contains elements that are about to disappear but it already anticipates its future developments.

Among those who most vehemently argued that synchronic and diachronic approaches in the study of language are interdependent, were Roman Jakobson and Jurij Tynjanov. For Tynjanov and Jakobson (1928/1981), pure synchronism[8] was only an illusion, because every synchronic system has its past and its future. Every system exists only as evolution and, on the other hand, evolution is inescapably of a systematic nature:

> The opposition between synchrony and diachrony was an opposition between the concept of the system and the concept of evolution; thus it loses its importance in principle as soon as we recognize that every system necessarily exists as evolution, whereas, on the other hand, evolution is inescapably of a systemic nature (Tynjanov and Jakobson, 1928/1981, p. 79).

The phrase that 'evolution is inescapably of a systematic nature' expresses Jakobson's teleological view of the 'historical' development of language. Jakobson's teleological perspective is understandable. He thought that to introduce teleology in the development of language means introducing dynamics and diachrony. He thought that we are obliged to seek a purpose of change. Like Hegel, Jakobson believed that history has a goal. Each change in the phonological system is purposeful (Jakobson, 1932/1971, I, p. 232; Jakobson, 1971/1985, II); changes in sound can be understood only from a teleological perspective. He expressed this very same point of view in a number of papers on sound and phonology and often argued against the superstitious fear of teleology. This point of view, while it emphasises evolution and history, adopts a finalistic perspective that I have characterised in Chapter 1 as a-historical.

This a-historical and teleological point of view sharply separates Hegel, Jakobson and Piaget on the one hand and the historical point of view emphasised by Bakhtin, Benjamin and Moscovici on the other. This also separates Hegelian dialectics from Bakhtin's dialogicality (Chapter 4).

3.3   Why is it not interesting that a tree is not a horse?

For Roman Jakobson, the idea of opposition in language was seminal (Jakobson and Waugh, 1979/1988, p. 22) and he studied oppositions at all levels of language: in phonetics, phonology, morphology and semantics. He viewed, at all levels of linguistic structures, oppositions as the two integral characteristics that were strictly relational (e.g. Jakobson, 1972/85, p. 85). He argued that every single constituent of any linguistic system is built on the antinomy of two logical contradictories: the presence of an attribute ('markedness') in contraposition to its absence ('unmarkedness'). In fact, oppositions interpenetrated all Jakobson's work; an opposition became almost an obsession for him and it would be difficult to do justice to his work on oppositions. Jakobson showed that antinomies underlie the whole phonemic structure of language (e.g. Jakobson, 1982/1988). Opposites are so 'intimately interconnected that the appearances of one of them inevitably elicits the other' (Jakobson, 1972/1985, p. 76).

Jakobson argued against the particular way in which Saussure conceptualised opposition. He (1982/1988) maintained that Saussure confused *opposition* with *difference*. This means that if we simply say that two things are *different*, it can mean that we talk about contingent or isolated things. For example, I am different from you, the letter *m* is different from the letter *p* and a tree is different from a horse. In contrast, Jakobson argues, *oppositions* are of such nature that one component in a pair of opposites inevitably elicits the other: we cannot speak of *long* without simultaneously evoking *short* (or whatever we may consider to be the opposite of *long*) or *expensive* without evoking its opposite, e.g. cheap. They are co-present like the figure-ground configuration. This configuration constitutes a relational whole, one cannot exist without the other. They co-exist and are integral complementarities and are both *sequential* and *simultaneous*. Jakobson argued that Saussure's oppositions deal only with sequentiality and with difference. For example, *sequentiality* in phonological phenomena may pose the question of how the speaker pronounces a particular phoneme depending on what precedes and what follows. While this aspect is important, oppositions are also in simultaneous relation to each other. This concerns the question of the meaning that the phoneme evokes, i.e. its opposition to another phoneme, as in the figure-ground configuration. For Jakobson opposition implies both a *simultaneous and sequential* relation.[9]

Sergej Karcevskij (1884–1955), one of the founding members of the Prague Linguistic Circle and another emigrant from Moscow, made an extraordinary contribution to the study of opposition. Like Jakobson, he argued that it is wrong to confound opposition and difference. In his study of the Russian verb, as early as in 1927, he observed that it became fashionable to affirm that linguistic values existed only in terms of their oppositions. But to talk about opposition as if it were a difference, Karcevskij says, is an absurdity:

A tree is a tree because it is neither a house nor a horse nor a river . . . Opposition pure and simple necessarily leads to chaos and cannot serve as the basis of a *system* [Karcevskij's emphasis]. True differentiation presupposes a simultaneous resemblance and difference (Karcevskij, 1927, pp. 13–14).

Karcevskij's basic presupposition was that language has life and that therefore, it is in constant flux. It is both *general* (which I read as *social*) and *individual*. It must be a means of communication, which is orientated towards others and at the same time, it is a means of self-expression of each individual in the community. In speech, there is a constant antinomy and tension between these two dimensions of language. Most importantly, *the self-expressive* usage of *the individual* can never be reduced to *the social* usage just as *the social* usage cannot be reduced to *the individual* usage. These two kinds of usage, Karcevskij argues, make linguistic signs both static and dynamic at the same time (Karcevskij, 1929/1982, p. 50).

3.4   Karcevskij's concept of change in his theory of meaning

Karcevskij's views on linguistic opposition are perhaps best expressed in his paper on *The asymmetric dualism of the linguistic sign* (Karcevskij, 1929/1982) which, I would argue, goes in some respects far beyond Wittgenstein's conception of the meaning. Karcevskij takes, for the purpose of his analysis, one antinomy, that of homonymy/synonymy. This antinomy, for him, is concerned in an essential way with *linguistic change*.[10]

Let us start with an example to explain homonymy and synonymy. Let us imagine that we are in a conversation and we use a word we have never used before and have never heard of being used in a similar situation. We say about someone that he is 'studený' because we wish to express that he has an *unsociable, distant personality*. When we use such a new expression, we do two things. First, we create a self-expressive *homonym*. We generate a particular association between a certain psychological or individual characteristic (e.g. unsociable) and the word expression (in this case 'studený'). Second, as we have created a self-expressive *homonym*, we have also added this new word to a series of generally used *synonyms*. This means that we have added a new expression, i.e. 'studený' to those, which in ordinary public usage refer to the phenomenon in question by different words, e.g., phlegmatic, impassive, 'a fish' or unsociable. However, if the use of the new word 'studený' simply created a kind of *static oscillation* in meaning, as Mathesius would call it, we could not speak about language change. We could only speak about a kind of oscillation or equilibration. Karcevskij, however, goes beyond the notion of oscillation.

His theory goes like this. The meaning of each word can be established only in the concrete situation (or to use Wittgenstein's term, in a specific language-game). We can thus say that the meaning and the situation, in which it is used, are complementary like figure and ground. This means that the speaker always generates, through the use of a word, a new representation of the concrete situation. In other words, any time we use the word, we *transpose* the semantic value of the sign, even if very slightly. For example, any time we use the word 'studený', the contexts, in which we use that word, are by necessity different. Thus, any time we use the 'same' word STUDENÝ, it obtains a slightly different meaning through intonation, the immediate linguistic context, the topic, which is discussed, and so on.

As a result of these considerations, Karcevskij argues that every meaning of a word can be expressed as an intersection between the two coordinates, homonymity and synonymity. But another point is important. If all this meant no more than that there are two orthogonal axes and that the meaning shifts along each axis separately, we would not have sufficient conditions for the change in meaning. All we would have would be fluctuations of a meaning but no real change in it. However, Karcevskij's claims are more fundamental. He emphasises that '*the intersection of the coordinates, and not the coordinates themselves*' (my emphasis) (1929/1982, p. 50) is the key to his theory. In other words, the lack of fit between the meaning of the word or the sign and its representations keeps their *relation in tension* and thus makes it *dynamic and flexible*. Linguistic values, Karcevskij argued, exist only by virtue of their antinomies to one another.

It is essential that it is *a relational*, rather than *an arbitrary antinomy*: there must be a simultaneous resemblance and difference between the two and this relation is in tension.

Due to this tension meanings are transposed and *cannot return to their point on a single axis*. Both axes affect the transposition and therefore there is no possible return. So, while Karcevskij continues to use the notion of *unstable equilibrium*, in fact, his concept is that of *change* and not of an *unstable equilibrium*, as we found in Mathesius or in Piaget.

The crucial point to Karcevskij's dynamic theory of meaning is that each sign has a number of semiotic functions and equally, each situation, in which it is used, can be expressed in a number of different ways. Should a sign have one function only, each sign would denote one situation and there would be no ambiguity between the word and what it signifies and there would be no reason for language to change and develop. It would be like a road-sign, or a learning instruction to do this or that. However, the main feature of language is not to provide information using road signs or to instruct how to learn. As Karcevskij argues, 'the exact semantic value of a word can be adequately established only as a function of a concrete situation' (1929/1982, p. 52). Karcevskij was a student of Saussure and I would like to suggest that this is the exact point at which he departed from his teacher. Although Saussure was aware that language changes through speech, he did not want to take this fact into consideration because, as he said, he would not know what to do about that unpleasant fact. He regarded language change as arbitrary, unsystematic and therefore not a subject for scientific exploration. For Karcevskij, however, language change was the very issue that required scientific examination.

4   Dialogical antinomies

4.1   *The sphere of between I and Thou*

The idea of interdependent relation between self- and other-consciousness that shaped Romantic social sciences in the eighteenth century, was re-born in the early part of the twentieth century in the religiously orientated neo-Kantian movement, flourishing particularly in the German town of Marburg. The neo-Kantians adopted many of Hegel's ideas and particularly those related to the self- and other-consciousness. The perspective that the individual acquires self-consciousness together with other-consciousness, which was the essence of Hegel's master-slave allegory (see Chapter 7), became one of the fundamental ideas in neo-Kantian philosophy.

The neo-Kantians based their philosophy on the 'dialogical principle', which involved the relationship between 'I' and 'Thou', that is, the relation of co-authors in communication. In addition to Hegelian philosophy, their dialogical principle came also from Judaism and from Christianity. It was found in the Old Testament as the cultural and communal spirit. The dialogical principle, the neo-Kantians argued, is established and maintained through speech and communication. Communication expresses the life experience of people, their emotions, concerns and the making of their social realities. At the time, the dialogical approach not only drew attention to the social nature of humankind but, in accordance with Kantian philosophy, it placed considerable weight on the idea that the activity of thought creates human realities (e.g. Cohen, 1919).

The scholars, who came with the provocative and original ideas of the dialogical principle, are now largely forgotten or are studied in the context of religion or Judaism. However, they were all very good social psychologists because their starting point was not individuals but the relations of the *Ego-Alter* in dialogues. Amongst the most significant members of the neo-Kantian movement who studied the dialogical principle were Herman Cohen, Franz Rosenzweig, Martin Buber, Eugen Rosenstock, Ferdinand Ebner and Gabriel Marcel. The dialogical principle of the neo-Kantians seemed to have been one of the most significant bridges connecting philosophy and religion in the early part of the last century. In addition to the 'dialogical principle' they coined other terms like 'existential dialogism' (Rosenstock, 1924), 'I and Thou' (Rosenzweig, 1921) and 'the sphere in between' (Buber, 1923/1962). Their anti-individualist approaches to the study of social thinking and language were broadly based, ranging from religion to philosophy, linguistics and politics.

Among those who specifically reflected on the individualistic presuppositions in human and social sciences and in the studies of language in the early part of the twentieth century was Eugen Rosenstock. He pondered about individualism embedded in the grammars of different languages and specifically in their morphologies. Ancient Greek grammar was constructed on the basis of grammatical cases and their declinations and such constructions have then become constitutive of most European languages. These grammars start with the first case, the nominative, which poses the questions: Who? (e.g. I, you) and What? (e.g. a table, a window). All other grammatical cases are derived from the nominative and they are, again, questions about individual entities. For example, the second grammatical case, the genitive, asks 'Whose? 'Of what?' The Dative, the third case asks 'To whom' and 'To what'?

Reflecting on the grammar of cases, for Rosenstock (1963, I, p. 754) there was one essential question: To whom is directed *the thought in these grammars*? He answered this by suggesting that the thought be directed to the individual. Yet he himself was dissatisfied with such an answer. It does not correspond, Rosenstock suggested, to 'the grammar of the soul'. The grammar of the soul, Rosenstock argued, does not start with the *I* or *We* but with the *Ego-Alter*.[11] But if the natural grammar of the soul starts with the *Ego-Alter* relation, why is it that the ancient Greeks developed grammar along the nominative, the *I*?

We can only speculate about possible answers to this question. One answer was already suggested earlier in the discussion of Greek antinomies (Chapter 2). Most conceptions of the antinomies in ancient Greek thinking were strictly conceived as separated one from another. Aristotelian philosophy, despite its interest in oppositions, was above all categorical. Greek science was deductive and axiomatic and Greek grammar followed this suit.

However, there is room to speculate further. If we adopt Rosenstock's suggestion that the grammar of the soul is based on thinking in communication, from where does the grammar of the soul originate? For Rosenstock, the origin of the grammar of the soul was in religion. He maintained that the dialogical relation between *Ego-Alter* is part of religion in ancient Egypt, in Christianity, Hebrew and Islam. We can find it also in Russian Orthodox religion. Religious thought is social thought and we can hypothesise that it originates in *common sense thinking and communication*. In contrast to scientific thought, which has become more individualised, religious thought has preserved its social character (Chapter 5). We can hypothesise that the antinomy *Ego-Alter* has its origin in common sense thinking and that the grammar of the soul precedes, historically, the formal thinking of logic and linguistic grammar.

4.2   Dialogicality is more than I-Thou

The neo-Kantian philosophers did not all conceive the dialogical principle in the same way. Martin Buber expressed it in terms of I-Thou. He has become, today, the best known of all the neo-Kantians. However, his I-Thou remained basically at the level of dialogue between human individuals, that is, at an interpersonal level. In contrast, Rosenzweig's treatment of dialogue was much broader.

For Rosenzweig, the key to intersubjectivity was not only mutuality and reciprocity but, above all, dialogical asymmetry and tension. Moreover, I-Thou does not centre on two voices in a dialogue and their mutual relations. It centres on a multiple of voices in a broad community, in politics, ideology and in social institutions. He argued that one could not reduce the dialogical principle to intersubjectivity, reciprocity and mutual recognition. Being critical of Buber's narrow conception of I-Thou, Rosenzweig wrote to him: 'What would become of the I-Thou if they will have to swallow up the entire world and Creator as well? . . . For my and your sake, there has to be something else in this world besides me and you!' (cf Batnitzky, 2000, p. 253, note 44, letters of Martin Buber).

Rosenzweig did not treat dialogue simply as mutuality between the I-Thou but, above all, as the communal world with the prevalence of judgement, difference and conflict.[12] It is the impossibility of a total consensus that is the basis of all dialogues, indeed, the lack of consensus keeps the dialogue going. Rosenzweig's specific concern was the dialogue between Judaism and Christianity. Historically, religiously and politically, he viewed it as a difficult dialogue. The dialogical relation between these two religions strengthens and intensifies judgement of one another through tension. In Rosenzweig's religious treatment of these issues, tension and hostility nevertheless lead way to redemption.

Rosenzweig's treatment of dialogue has far reaching implications. It redirects the focus on thinking and communication not as something with a happy ending as Hegel conceived it or as something that always diminishes distances between people. Instead, dialogue is a communication in which the co-authors dispute, fight about ideas and negotiate their antinomies in thinking. In dialogue, the participants confirm one another as co-authors of their ideas and they also confirm their participation in social realities.

4.3   Living in the world of others

The Russian philosopher and a literary scholar Mikhail Bakhtin (1895–1975) was acquainted with neo-Kantian philosophy and with the German-Jewish Marburg School. While it is well established that Bakhtin was inspired by the neo-Kantians and that he particularly admired Buber's work, other scholars place a significant emphasis on the influence of the Russian Orthodox Church 'as a secret to all of Bakhtin's writing' (Mihailovic, 1997, p. 2).[13]

Mikhail Bakhtin lived, for much of his life, in an involuntary isolation from academic institutions in Soviet Russia, being saved from a more severe persecution thanks to his lifelong illness of osteomyelitis, which made him chronically disabled. His work was 'rediscovered' and started penetrating European and American scholarship during the later part of the last century. To the mysteries surrounding his life and work we may add the fact that in their attempt to 'discover' Bakhtin on the basis of insufficient knowledge and obscure sources, some Bakhtinian scholars made ill-informed shortcuts. These concerned in particular questions like what Bakhtin might have and might not have written under his own and under other names, the suppositions, which then led to further queries about him as a person and as a scholar. Was he a Marxist or a religious person? Or did he, throughout his life, practise a dialogical carnivalesque of the kind that he analysed in his masterpieces on Dostoyevsky (see later) (Bakhtin, 1984a) and Rabelais (Bakhtin, 1984b)?

Like Rosenzweig, so Bakhtin viewed dialogicality broadly, as a clash of ideas, as a heterogeneity of meanings in action and as multivoicedness (Wertsch, 1991). However, Bakhtin's originality and his influence on human and social sciences today does not lie primarily in his ideas on dialogicality or dialogism.[14] Many of these ideas had been developed by others before him. Instead, Bakthin's originality and force reside in the specific characteristics with which he impregnated dialogicality, and in the tenacity with which he pursued these ideas in their boundlessness. Dialogicality, for Bakhtin, offered infinite openings for new interpretations of language and thinking in the multifaceted and multivoiced world on which he insisted had no limits.

The Bakhtinian world consists of the phenomena that constitute monological objects on the one hand and the dialogical co-authors on the other. Objects are non-responsive, i.e. *monological,* while humans are by nature responsive, i.e. *dialogical.* This difference between the world of monological objects and the dialogical world of humans constitutes, for Bakhtin, also the division between natural sciences and human and social sciences. Natural sciences are concerned with the study of voiceless and reified objects, which need to be described accurately and explained. As Bakhtin said, natural sciences are monological because they examine things as if they existed only for the single human mind rather than for the mind in relation to other minds. Natural sciences are based on mathematical accuracy and on precision of measurement.

In contrast, the dialogically constructed and re-constructed social world is the world of multifaceted and multivoiced realities situated in culture. Any coherent system of signs, any text, a work of art, a piece of music, a historical interpretation, all of these have dialogical properties. They are products of human minds, which are orientated to other human minds and to their cognition. The human sciences, Bakhtin (1981) argued, are based on the epistemology of dialogism. Dialogism is an epistemology of the human cognition and communication and is, more generally, part of human sciences, which are concerned with the study of symbolic thoughts expressed in language. The social sciences and humanities study the social world of human dialogues, of texts and of polysemic and multifaceted meanings. Humanities and social sciences understand, transmit and interpret discourses of others (Bakhtin, 1981). Rather than examining accuracy and precision of the measurement, as do natural sciences, humans attempt to understand the ways of overcoming the strangeness of cognition of the other person. This is achieved through *active* understanding, through mastering the social environment, language and any object that the individual cognition appropriates. Understanding, precisely because it is active, is evaluative. Understanding and evaluation, Bakhtin (1979/1986, p. 142) argued, are part of an integral and unified action. The human and social sciences always involve the study of human cognition by another cognition. Cognitions are in tension, they clash, judge and evaluate one another. In other words, the human and social sciences are concerned with *dialogical cognition*. Bakhtin characterised dialogical cognition as a metacognition, as 'the reflection of a reflection' (1979/1986, p. 113). It always expresses different symbolic intentions, genres and different communication activities.

Bakhtin was one of the first to state clearly that dialogicality implies that every individual lives 'in a world of others' words' (1979/1986, p. 143). Humans make the world in terms of others and the entire existence of the self is orientated towards others' language and others' world. We begin life by learning others' words, the multifaceted world of others becomes part of our own consciousness and all aspects of culture fill our own life and orientate our existence towards others. In contrast, total death and non-existence, Bakhtin argued, is the state of being unheard, non-recognised and non-remembered. To be means to communicate and to communicate means to be for another, and through the other, for oneself. Bakhtin insists that a person has no internal sovereign territory and that he is wholly and always on the boundary with others. When he looks inside himself, he always looks *into the eyes of another* or *with the eyes of another* (Bakhtin, 1984b, p. 287). In other words, the limits of the self is not I, but I in interrelationship with other, '*I and thou*' (Bakhtin, 1979/1986, p. 167). All symbolic activity of humans is founded on 'dialogue' between different minds expressing multitudes of multivoiced meanings.

Bakhtin developed his ideas about dialogicality above all in literary analysis and he attributed a most profound mode of dialogicality to the Renaissance French writer Rabelais and to the nineteenth-century Russian writer Dostoyevsky. Despite the differences in their literary genres, the work of both is penetrated by oppositions, ambivalence, double-voicedness and hidden polemics. They are masters of human dialogue.

In his analysis of Rabelais, Bakhtin (1984b) showed, perhaps more than elsewhere, the power of notions of ambivalence and oppositions. We can hypothesise that Bakhtin chose the topic of the Renaissance carnival in order to exhibit his extravagance in the treatment of ambivalence and oppositions as dialogical concepts. He could hardly find another topic, which could give him the same opportunity and satisfaction to display the idea of double-voicedness. Ambivalence saturates language, daily life, culture, and the human body, simply everything that has some human relevance. All ambivalent images that Bakhtin displays are dual-bodied, dual-faced and pregnant with their oppositions. They integrate affirmation and negation, the top and the bottom, convergence and divergence not only as sequences of expressions but above all, as expressions in their simultaneity. Among them, the simultaneity of life and death figures as most prominent. Bakhtin dramatises his analysis to the extreme, presenting even dying as droll. He depicts an individual body in the throes of death and at the same time gives an image of another human body just being born. For him, where death is, there is also change and renewal (Bakhtin, 1984b, p. 409). The image of birth is also ambivalent, showing that where there is birth, there is also departure, these pictures culminating with the image of the birth-giving death (1984b, p. 352). Bakhtin presents variations of death in renewing the earth's fertility, the birth of Pantagruel which caused his mother's suffocation (1984b, p. 408), and even death from laughter.

4.4   Thinking through the mouth

Rosenzweig's (2001) essay on 'New thinking', expresses very clearly the spirit of the whole neo-Kantian movement that *thinking is essentially a dialogue*. 'New thinking' is directed both against the idea that thinking comes from the soliloquy and against the philosophical dialogues of the Platonic and Socratic kind. Rosenzweig argues that because these celebrated Platonic and Socratic dialogues are philosophical, they are not authentic dialogues. In these the speaker already knows what ideas he wants to communicate and argue about. They involve fictive interlocutors. In contrast, authentic dialogues are open. In a dialogue, we do not know beforehand what we shall say and how we shall express our thoughts to the other person. Moreover, we do not know beforehand what the other person will understand of our message, we learn that from his response. This idea, that we understand the meaning of our speech action from the response of the other, can also be found in the work of George Herbert Mead (1934). For Rosenzweig, thinking and communicating are active and mutual processes. The person with whom we talk and think, does not have only ears to listen as in the philosophical dialogues, but he also has a mouth and he *thinks through his mouth* (Rosenzweig, 2001, p. 159). 'New thinking' stems from reciprocity of the minds. It evolves from confrontation of ideas, includes passions and admiration as well as disappointment and misunderstanding resulting from this reciprocity.

I have taken a long journey to arrive at the first notion, *dialogicality*, in the title of this book. But in order to show that dialogicality is the fundamental capacity of the human mind to conceive, create and communicate about social realities in terms of the *Alter*, I needed to draw attention to the following questions. Could it be that human intelligence, based on making discrimination and on thinking in antinomies is, itself, an expression of dialogicality? Could it be that antinomies in language and communication, too, are hiding the dialogicality the mind?

It is only when we arrive at the antinomy *Ego-Alter* that the hypothesis that dialogicality could be so fundamental to human intelligence could be formulated. It is only now that our argument concerning the pervasive nature of thinking and communicating in antinomies can be turned upside down because now, antinomies can be viewed in terms of their dialogical significance.

If the *Ego-Alter* is ontology of communication and by implication, ontology of the human mind, then it is dialogicality that generates the manifold kinds of thinking and communication. Therefore, antinomies in thinking and language themselves, must be an expression of dialogicality. They are dialogical processes and products. Dialogicality, therefore, could provide grounds for the dialogical theory of social knowledge, i.e. for the dialogical epistemology.

Consequently, dialogicality would seem to be a good starting point for the making of social psychology.

NOTES

1. For Descartes there were 'no rules in mechanics which do not hold good in physics, of which mechanics forms a part of species [so that all that is artificial is also natural]' (Descartes, 1644/1911, pp. 299–300). Therefore, it was no less natural for a clock to indicate the hours than it is for a tree to produce fruit.
2. For a scholarly discussion of differences between Descartes and Vico see Hermans, H.J.M. and Kempen, H.J.G. *The Dialogical Self*, New York and London: Academic Press.
3. Johann Georg Hamann (1730–88), one of the largely forgotten German scholars who maintained that language was constitutive of cognition, pronounced very similar ideas. Although it still remains unclear as to what extent Hamann was influenced by Vico (cf. Berlin, 1976, p. 76n) his ideas are remarkably similar to those of Vico. Hamann argued that there is an underlying similarity between all languages due to the identical form of human nature. Just like Vico, he emphasised the role of poetry and Folk psychology in the development of language.
4. Taylor's analysis is pertinent to my argument because it underlines the features of Herder's thought, which pre-empt heterogeneity in language, thus opening

up the road towards the dialogicality of language and the mind (Chapter 4). Taylor's argument goes like this: there is an essential difference between operating with signals and using human language. This distinction was neither made, in general, by Herder's contemporaries and nor today, by those who claim that some animals can use language. Taylor is careful not to exclude the possibility that animals *may* use language, but, so far, it has not been shown. Responding to signals, Taylor points out, is an important achievement in the evolution of species and it enables solving a *non-linguistically-defined* purpose or task, for example, to go through the right hole in order to get cheese, to signal 'want banana', to learn to produce signals, to put together simple signs which produce a more complex message and so on. However, in all such cases of non-linguistically defined purposes or tasks, in which language is used as an instrument, 'to have it right' means to solve a non-linguistic problem. In order to perform such tasks, which in themselves are important, the individual, whether a human or an animal, can use the kind of language which does not necessarily require reflection on one's own and others' linguistic activities. In contrast, what characterises *human* language is its use in *linguistically defined* situations. In contrast to non-linguistic tasks or purposes, in which language serves designation, in linguistically defined situations language is multifaceted, polyphonic and heterogeneous. To respond correctly in linguistically defined situations requires sensitivity 'to irreducible issues of rightness' and it is 'a question of subjective understanding, of what rightness consists in for it, qua what word is right' (Taylor, 1995c, pp. 84 and 85).

5. I am grateful to Jim Wertsch for drawing my attention, on several occasions to the work of Gustav Shpet and specifically, in this context, to his analysis and interpretation of Humboldt.

6. John Locke (1632–1704), in his *Essay Concerning Human Understanding*, in book III, proposed the idea of the interdependence between knowledge and language. Here he raised many questions about the nature of reality and its relation to names, words, signs, and to language in general (see Chapter 1).

The second issue to which he contributed, makes Locke in a certain respect, an ancestor of Saussure. In the seventeenth century it was generally assumed that words are conventions. It was, however, also assumed, although it may seem paradoxical in the context of the previous assumption, that there is a correspondence between language and reality. This latter assumption was derived from Aristotle's philosophy according to which natural signs of reality are words or images, and these in turn stand for universals. Thus although words are conventional, they nevertheless stand for immutable ideas. These immutable ideas, some believed, are innate while others believed that they come from experience. In this way, it was assumed, there is correspondence between immutable ideas or universals and reality, which is mediated by words (cf. Formigary, 1988, for details). Locke claimed not only on the conventionality of words but also on their arbitrariness. Like Saussure in the twentieth century, he insisted that sounds have no connection with ideas, and that what they signify is arbitrary. For example, there is nothing common between the sound 'banana' and the object to which the sound refers. This is simply a convention. Locke emphasised that names and meanings do not refer to 'real Nature of

Things'. Instead, it is the propriety of speech that a word 'might be a Sun to one, which is a Star to another' (Locke, 1690/1975, III, VI, 1). What words do, however, is to record thoughts, communicate them to others, and make the self understood to others. Above all, words are signs or representations of reality and it is the mind's constructive power that generates these representations. In many of his examples about this constructive process, he drew attention to human experience. Thus it is experience that enables the mind to select the relevant aspects of reality for particular purposes.

7. Although originally it was primarily, though not exclusively, concerned with the study of language, in the late 1920s and in the 1930s this movement grew into a broadly based interdisciplinary and multidisciplinary semiotic orientation. It interpenetrated many spheres of cultural life, like the arts, literature, ethnography, aesthetics, film, theatre, as well as the social sciences and humanities. The main classical period of Prague linguistics and semiotics is usually placed between the years 1926, when the Prague Linguistic Circle was established, and 1939, when Czechoslovak Universities were closed by the Nazis (Vachek, 1964). The Circle was founded by Vilém Mathesius, following the model of the Moscow Linguistic Circle.

8. Jakobson particularly emphasised the interdependence between synchrony/diachrony in historical phonology. He showed that phonetic changes, i.e. changes in physical and physiological properties of sounds in the current linguistic system must be analysed in relation to the system of meanings to which these sounds refer, i.e. in relation to the phonemic system undergoing these mutations.

9. The emphasis on binary oppositions in structural linguistics is now more or less out of fashion. In my experience, Jakobson's emphasis on dialectically interdependent oppositions has never been understood and his work is usually interpreted in the traditional Saussurean sense.

10. Steiner observes (1982, p. 48), in his introductory notes to Karcevskij's chapter on dualistic asymmetry, that Karcevskij's notion of the dualistic asymmetry of the linguistic sign has its origin in the romanticist philosophy and linguistics of Humboldt and Hegel. Thus in the novel usage of language by an individual, there is always a potential for language change. Steiner points out that Hegel defined symbols as essentially ambiguous because while the *form of a symbol*, e.g. the word 'lion', contains meaning, when applied to reality, the form does not express that reality adequately. For example, the lion can symbolise strength but equally, strength can be symbolised by, say, a bull. And at the same time, 'a bull' itself has many other symbolic meanings, and so on.

11. This implies that if the Greeks had assumed that thinking starts from communication rather than from single individuals, the grammar would have obtained a different structure. It could have started with the Dative, asking first the question: To whom do I speak? It could have also started with the Vocative, the fifth grammatical case, by which we call others. Rosenstock insists that the Dative and the Vocative, are not derivations of the first grammatical case. Instead, Dative and Vocative constitute the grammar of the soul, and according to this grammar, the individuals and single entities

are secondary. The Dative is a communicative case by means of which we express our ideas to others. The Vocative, too is a communicative case. Through the Vocative we call to others and by calling we relate to others our ideas. In religions above all, humans call to God.

12. Batnitzky (2000, p. 113) argues that Rosenzweig's approach to dialogue stems from his understanding of the Jewish-Christian relationship which is 'never one of mutuality, but always one of absolute difference . . . judgement comes from difference, but without judgement, and thus difference, dialogue, and the potential for self-transformation, would not be possible.' (2000, p. 159). This idea of conflict between these two religions also constitutes the main feature of the letters between Rosenzweig and Rosenstock.

13. Mihailovic draws attention in painstaking detail to Bakhtin's life and writing, attempting to connect Bakhtin's work to the Johannine religious philosophy of the enfleshed and embodied word. The idea of dialogical struggle resulting in heterogeneity and multivoicedness in Bakhtin's work, Mihailovic argues, comes from christology (Mihailovic 1997, pp. 18ff.). Dialogue must be viewed as a human binding, as a contract, which provides a moral and ethical order of the religious kind. That religion, Mihailovic argues, for Bakhtin was above all the Russian Orthodox Church.

14. Bakhtin used the terms 'dialogicality' and 'dialogism' interchangeably, with both of them referring to the fundamental features of social and human knowledge, of human understanding, cognition and communication. Linell (1998) has recently made an important conceptual distinction between these terms. He implies on the basis of Bakhtin's work that dialogicality refers to the essential characteristics of human cognition and communication, while dialogism is an epistemology of human and social sciences.

4 Thinking through the mouth

Thinking takes many different forms and serves different purposes. Some philosophical and psychological traditions emphasise thinking in categories, e.g. time, space and quality, others focus on naming; still others pay attention to thinking in antinomies and polarities. Some kinds of thinking can be described as inductive and deductive, others as analogical and discrete. Some forms of thinking are scientific, others are artistic, religious, ideological, rhetorical or mystical. Different tasks are associated with different kinds of thinking. Thinking in order to flatter or manipulate someone is based on different presuppositions than thinking how to win in the lottery. Scientific thinking requires different premises than rhetoric.

But, 'what precisely, is "thinking"'? Albert Einstein, amongst others, pondered this time old question (1949, p. 7) when he was reflecting on his life and work. He answered it by noting the difference between sense-impressions, memory-pictures and a series of such pictures on the one hand, and mental processes, which are dominated by conceptual thought, on the other hand. Concepts are always connected with reproducible signs, e.g. words, and they differentiate, for Einstein, *non-thinking* mental phenomena from *thinking*. Thinking is conceptual and, most importantly, it is *communicable*.

Einstein was not the only one, or even the first one, for whom *communicability* or *speakability* was fundamentally interrelated with conceptual thinking. Hegel, Heidegger and Wittgenstein argued in a similar manner. Hegel (1807/1977), in the *Phenomenology of the Spirit*, analysing the nature of consciousness, drew a distinction between non-communicable mental processes like sensory and perceptual phenomena on the one hand, and communicable ones, which are social and conceptual processes, on the other. He discussed, among other things, the symbolic functions of thinking and language as reflected in the secret meaning of eating bread and drinking wine, which cannot be captured by the sensory aspects of eating and drinking. These symbolic functions, which are embedded in thinking, knowledge, believing and communication, all result from the representational capacities of language users (Marková, 1982).

Heidegger (1954/1968), in the series of his lectures entitled *What is Called Thinking*, focuses above all on different meanings of the word 'call'. Every call implies naming (hence the title of his lectures), he argues, and calling implies an approach towards the other. It is an invitation to someone, like welcoming a guest to one's home. Thus the question 'What is called thinking?' means that all thinking is directed at someone because the call 'is the directive which, in calling to and calling upon, in reaching out and inviting . . . a call has already gathered' (1954/1968, p. 124).

Wittgenstein (1953, pp. 327–41) answers the question 'What is thinking?' by arguing that language is the vehicle of thought. If language is the vehicle of thought, then thinking and speaking cannot be viewed as two parallel processes. The idea that we could translate thought into words into thoughts is senseless. Wittgenstein insists that thought cannot be comprehended as an immaterial process 'that lends life and sense to speaking' and that it is inconceivable that thinking could be separated from speaking. Speech without thought is an automatised process. Wittgenstein compares speech with and without thought to playing a piece of music with and without thought.

If thinking is by definition communicable and speakable, then making distinctions and thinking in antinomies must also be reflected in the vehicle of thought, i.e. in language as well as in the studies of language and in human dialogue. But then we need to turn the question round. Why do we think and speak in antinomies? Let us repeat our hypothesis that making distinctions and thinking and speaking in antinomies is already an expression of dialogicality, the capacity to conceive and comprehend the world in terms of the *Alter* and to create social realities in terms of the *Alter*. The *Ego-Alter* antinomy is multifaceted and is underpinned by heteroglossia in speech and polyphasia in thinking.

1   Dialogicality as ontology of humanity

Let us affirm with Bakhtin that '*To be* means *to communicate*' (Bakhtin, 1984a, p. 287). The *Ego-Alter* exists only within the realm of communication. Let us insist that the *Alter* stands for 'Others' rather than for 'Other'. This means that the *Ego-Alter* in terms of interpersonal dialogue, i.e. a dialogue between I and you, refers to only one kind of dialogue. The *Ego-Alter* equally refers to communication within and between groups, subgroups, communities, societies and cultures. The hypothesis of ontology based on the *Ego-Alter* dramatically changes the kinds of question that, in social psychology, we ask about individuals and groups in their communicative contexts.

If human existence is defined as the existence in communication, then questions that are often asked in social psychology about one dialogical participant but not about the other, would be inappropriate in the dialogical approach. Such questions, which bring into the focus only one dialogical participant, e.g. the group or the individual, ignore dialogicality, i.e. the mutual interdependence of participants and their mutual effect on one another. For example, they may bring into the focus the group that starts exerting pressure on the individual; or the individual who may choose to co-operate with others, defends his identity, and so on.

Examples of such inappropriate or misleading questions are the following:

• 'How and in what ways does the group influence the individual?'
• 'How does the individual perform, think or communicate in the social world or in social contexts?'

It is not that in dialogical approaches the individual and groups would be denied their existence *as* single entities. However, despite their physical, biological, physiological and social existence as entities, their dialogical existence is the communicative existence. They enter their dialogical relations as the specific *Ego-Alter*. Let us revisit, Hegel's example illustrating this point (Chapter 2). Before his son is born, a man exists in different kinds of dialogical relations: with his wife, with his family, with his friends, and so on. However, only when his son is born, does the dialogical unit father/son come into existence. Of course, the individual or the group does not transform by some magic their personal or individual characteristics. Yet, these characteristics reveal themselves in unique ways in specific dialogical relations – this is what makes for individuality. We do not perform as the 'same' entities in different dialogical relations. If we assumed their sameness, we would be denying individuals or groups their basic characteristic – the dialogical uniqueness. Paradoxically, it is dialogicality that identifies individuals *as* the individuals. Their dialogical uniqueness underlies their variation and creativity with respect to others.

Dialogicality, we must insist, is more than this or that concrete encounter of the *Ego-Alter*. We conceive of the concrete encounters of the *Ego-Alter* as instantiations of the ontology based on the *Ego-Alter*. This ontology, we have suggested, constitutes humans as symbolically communicating species.[1]

We can further presuppose that dialogicality, the capacity to conceive, create and communicate about social realities in terms of otherness, was implanted in the human mind during phylogeny and the socio-cultural history. Therefore, it is just as much part of human nature as are the biological and cognitive universals. It is dialogicality that makes it possible for concrete encounters to take place, enter into, interrupt, break off and re-start again.

If we accept the hypothesis that the dialogical relation is an existential relation, then our social psychological questions in theoretical and empirical research will be posed differently than those that are asked in non-dialogical approaches. Above all, such questions will not be about separate individuals and about separate groups. Instead they will be concerned with the varieties of the *Ego-Alter* relations which cannot be anything but communicative. Therefore, instead of asking questions *either* about the individual's performance in the group *or* about the influence of the group on the individual, we ask questions about the individual *and* group within their communicative interdependencies. For example:

- 'How and in what ways, within this or that dialogical relation do the *Ego* or the *Alter* preserve their uniqueness, e.g. their individual identities, activities, thoughts and language?'
- 'How do the *Ego* and the *Alter* influence one another or negotiate their positions as co-agents of a joint action or as co-authors of a discourse?'

Having made the conceptual difference between the individuals and groups as separate entities on the one hand and dialogicality of the *Ego-Alter* on the other, two remarks should be made.

First, the researcher working within the dialogical frame of reference may prefer using terms like the 'individual/social', 'minority/majority' and otherwise rather than the *Ego-Alter*. While terminology as such is not important, indeed, other chosen terms may express more precisely the researcher's intentions, it is the conceptual issue that is at stake. What matters is whether 'the individual' and 'the social' and 'the minority' and 'the majority' are treated as independent entities or whether they are conceptualised as the *Ego-Alter* in communication. For example, the functionalist models of social influence treat minorities and majorities as two independent entities. In contrast, the genetic model of social change (Moscovici, 1976) conceptualises minorities and majorities as mutually interdependent (Chapter 6).

Second, dialogicality of the *Ego-Alter*, we have implied, is embedded in history and culture. Dialogical practices are transmitted from generation to generation through collective memory, institutions and social practices. History and culture make demands on the dialogical styles of thinking and communicating and constrain them in specific directions. For example, there are different kinds of constraint on the past and the present, the individual and social, and tradition and novelty. These constraints and demands of the past and the present as well as the tremendous variety of situations in which thinking and communication take place result in the essential characteristic of dialogicality: its multifaceted, multivoiced and polyphasic nature.

2   Dialogicality and dialectic

Throughout this book the notion of *dialectic* has kept cropping up here and there and its relations to dialogicality cannot be passed over without some discussion. 'Dialectic' and 'dialogicality' are terms that scholars working within the tradition of dialogicality have sometimes used interchangeably. For example, the members of the Bakhtinian Circle like Voloshinov (1929/1973) and Medvedev (1934/1985), when they referred to antinomies and oppositions in various dynamic social systems like language, institutions, community, and so on, in addition to the term 'dialogicality', also used the term 'dialectic'. Thus Medvedev often talked in his study of literary history about the 'intrinsic' and the 'extrinsic' phenomena which are dialectically interdependent. Voloshinov (1929/1973) discussed dialectical generative processes in the context of language changes.

Dialectic permeates different philosophical traditions from ancient, e.g. Greek and Chinese, to contemporary philosophical thought. Consequently, there are different kinds of dialectic, ranging from 'materialist' to 'idealist' and from 'abstract' to 'concrete'. In a similar vein, the term 'dialogicality' is used today in many different ways. The multitude of meanings of dialogicality results not only from thinking with and rethinking Bakhtin (Morson and Emerson, 1989) and from pursuing other scholarly avenues, like the work of Levinas, Rosenzweig, Buber and Vygotsky among others, but also from denigrating dialogicality and dialogism as double-talks and clichés.

With regard to the objective of this book, I have characterised dialogicality as the capacity of the mind to conceive, create and communicate about social realities in terms of the *Ego-Alter* and I shall disregard other meanings of dialogicality. Equally, dialectic will be discussed only in terms of Hegelian/Marxist dialectic[2] because it is this kind of dialectic that often gets confused with dialogicality. The discussion of the relations between dialogicality and dialectic will be restricted accordingly.

Bakhtin was on the whole negatively disposed to dialectic (see e.g. Bakhtin, 1981). He viewed dialectic not as a dialogical process but instead, as a product, as he called it, of Hegel's monologism. Bakhtin objected to Hegel's attempt to systematise human social and spiritual phenomena and bring them under a single consciousness of the all-embracing Absolute Spirit. Dialectic, therefore, was for Bakhtin an abstract concept. It operated at the level of consciousness that is formalised and that is deprived of multivoicedness and multifaceted meanings. In contrast, Bakhtin argued, dialogicality is not abstract. Although it is the universal capacity of the mind, it operates only in concrete dialogues, i.e. in dialogues situated in specific encounters, whether interpersonal, intercultural or intergroup encounters. Only at a concrete level would the dialogical partners become co-authors of words or meanings in the true sense of the word 'dialogue', which they jointly co-author. Therefore, dialectic is secondary to dialogicality, in fact, it is 'born of dialogue' (Bakhtin, 1979/1986, p. 162).

But how can we understand this claim that dialectic is born from dialogue, i.e. that dialogicality is prior to dialectic?

Neither Hegel nor Marx conceived dialectic in relation to dialogicality or communication. Chapter 2 describes the two basic ways in which Hegel viewed dialectic.

First, both for Hegel and Marx, dialectic is the moving principle of reality. The world is seen as a system of mutually interdependent and organically interrelated forces. These are in constant movement, which arises from the struggle of opposite tendencies, e.g. stability and change, quality and quantity, determinism and free will. The resolution of conflict between oppositional tendencies at one stage of historical development leads to the next stage of the upward movement. Progress in nature and in human society is achieved through such upward movement. Universal laws that guide this struggle of opposite tendencies and the movement upward are common both in nature and in human society. Dialectic, in some Marxist interpretations, is a science enabling the study of the ways through which reality reveals or represents itself through praxis and critical thinking (e.g. Kosík, 1963). In other words, reality is something 'objective'. On the other hand consciousness, the capacity of the human mind to reflect this objective reality[3] through praxis and critical thinking, decreases the gap between objective reality and the ways that reality represents itself to the human mind. Specifically, Hegel's dialectic of nature of the late eighteenth and the early nineteenth centuries was an attempt to explain the logic of movement, the progress in development and change in the physical world and in nature. The concept of the dialectic of nature was also an essential part of Marxism and it became part of the doctrine of dialectical materialism, which studies the most general laws of the material existence on the one hand and of consciousness, as a product of the matter, on the other.

In contrast to dialectic, dialogicality is not concerned with logic, movement and change in the physical world and in non-human nature as such. It is concerned with human existence *as a communicative existence*. Physical and natural objects are not in communicative relations with humans and therefore they have nothing to do with dialogicality. Of course, they are objects about which the *Ego-Alter* communicates. In contrast to physical and natural objects, human social phenomena can be nothing but dialogical and they involve multiple variations of the *Ego-Alter* relations.

The second sense in which Hegel viewed dialectic, refers to *thought*. For him, dialectic is the essence of thought and the realisation of the spiritual development of the world. Here again, the thought in its very abstract form progresses in an upward movement to self-realisation. Dialectic in this second sense aims at achieving the Absolute Spirit. It embraces the idea of the systematic nature of human knowledge leading to an abstract and spiritual unification of all kinds of knowledge. For Hegel, the human mind has created itself through the historical process of self-education. It has undergone an upward progress, in which the mind has overcome lower stages in development in the progress upward. It has endured struggles and conflicts in its effort 'to know itself, to make itself objective to itself, to find itself, be for itself, and finally unite itself to itself' (Hegel, 1837/1956).

In this sense dialectic is a way of thinking about natural and social phenomena in their interdependence and movement. However, if dialectic is a form of thinking, then, pursuing our position outlined above, thinking is by definition communicable and this was Hegel's conviction (Chapter 3). Nevertheless, Hegel did not develop the communicative perspective with respect to dialectic.

If dialogicality is the capacity of the human mind to conceive, create and communicate about social realities in terms of 'otherness', then it must be prior to dialectic. It is dialogicality that makes possible dialectic as a form of thinking and indeed, as a formalised and an abstract form of thinking. A similar argument was put forward by Rosenstock (Chapter 3) when he argued that the grammar of the soul, which is dialogical, precedes formal grammar. Formal grammar could only be developed as an abstract form from dialogicality. It is in this sense that we can understand Bakhtin's claim that dialectic is born of dialogue.

There is yet another difference between dialogicality and dialectic.

Marx and Engels strongly objected to the very abstract, and 'idealist', form of dialectic. Contrary to Hegel, they regarded dialectic as existing in concrete social practices and in economic relations and they thought that higher forms of consciousness could arise from concrete practices. Marx and Engels claimed that it was necessary to turn Hegel on his head in order to make his dialectic applicable to the human condition.

However, what Marxists did not reject, was the idea of the upward progress in development, whether in nature or in society. In particular, the upward progress constituted an essential idea of the doctrine of historical materialism. According to this doctrine, throughout its history mankind has undergone the struggle through the upward stages of development, beginning from the primary classless through to class societies. Class societies are characterised by economic and political struggles, aiming towards higher and more progressive stages. The highest stage of this development is the classless society in communism. Communism no longer carries any negative features of the past but only develops the features that started during socialism, a stage that precedes communism.

The idea of an upward progress and of teleological explanation was much nourished in the Enlightenment and in the nineteenth century. The ideas, like the evolution in nature, the biological struggle for existence and the survival of the fittest, went hand in hand with technological innovations and public education. All these ideas and inventions seemed to support the aspiration for progress and they adopted the metaphors of 'lower' and 'higher' developmental stages (Gould, 1996). Hegel's dialectic aimed at its culmination in the Absolute Spirit. Similarly, the Marxist dialectics of nature and society was based on the idea of an upward progress. This was thought to be a scientific fact.[4]

Among those who debunked the idea of progress was Walter Benjamin in the early part of the twentieth century. Arguing specifically against dialectic as a myth of social evolution, in his *Theses on the Philosophy of History* (1955/1973) Benjamin expressed his 'non-dialectic' attitude arguing against the idea of 'progress'. For him, the twentieth century wars, the technological development and the mastery of nature were closely associated with retrogression of society, which resulted in catastrophes 'piling wreckage upon wreckage' (Benjamin, 1955/1973, p. 249).[5]

In contrast to Hegelian/Marxist dialectic, dialogicality is not goal-directed. The *Ego-Alter* interdependence is a communicative interdependence. Therefore, by definition it is open to different possibilities (Salazar-Orvig, 1999). Since dialogicality is open, multifaced and multivoiced, teleological explanation makes no sense. This does not mean that dialogues do not have established rules and norms. Indeed they do. Dialogical norms and rules are historically and culturally established and are carefully examined by students of conversation and dialogue (e.g. Linell, 1998). However, these norms and rules, that we discover backward, do not determine in what ways dialogues may develop and certainly they do not predict movement upward towards the progress. Conflicts and tensions of the *Ego-Alter* do not resolve themselves into a higher level unity, achieving, what one might call, a kind of 'happy communication' without asymmetries and tensions, or at least with reduced asymmetries and a decreased tension.

In contrast, dialogical antinomies both unite and divide, both estrange and appropriate, both orientate the self towards ideas and meanings of others as well as towards the self's own ideas.

3 Attempts to de-dialogise language

Pervasiveness of dialogicality in ordinary language and common thinking has proved to be a great nuisance for many who have tried to eradicate it in the name of objectivity, science, ideology or morality. Indeed, we could describe efforts to 'de-dialogise' language as one of the features of modern life. For a long time now, the attempt to clean language of its 'biases', ambiguities and polysemic features has been quite significant in scientific, ideological and professional communication. This section will give some examples of the 'problems' that dialogicality creates.

3.1 Achieving neutral language in science

In the early part of the twentieth century some philosophers, in their search for objectivity in science, argued that ordinary language, because it is filled with contradictions, heterogeneous meanings and emotions, is not suitable for scientific purposes. In psychology, the ideal of 'objective science' was connected with the effort for neutral observation. A neutral 'data language' was part of this aim. Turner (1967) comments on these efforts as follows:

Recall the cat in the Thorndike puzzle box. It claws, bites, struggles, strikes and finally escapes. Simple facts, it would seem. Yet to Thorndike it was a random trial and error sequence of responses supported by an initial, instinctive, response-repertory (Turner, 1967, p. 190).

For scientific purposes, in psychology words had to be carefully chosen to constitute the 'data language'. Words were restricted to 'neutral' expressions like 'reaction', 'habit', 'bar-pressing habit', 'threshold' and so on. Data language attempted to avoid words that were filled with 'redundant and biasing information' like 'to intend', 'to try' or 'to feel'. Some behaviourists like Hull, Skinner and Tolman were successful in using the data language and they received praise from their colleagues (Estes et al., 1954). In contrast, Kurt Lewin, whom Estes and his colleagues also labelled as a behavioural psychologist, was not praised for his use of language. His 'lack of any explicit consideration of the data language appears as a rather striking omission' and an apparent 'blind spot' in his work (Estes et al., 1954). The authors went on commenting that since Lewin neither defined nor used data language, his work did not provide a basis for adequate scientific communication.

3.2   A 'wooden language' of bureaucracy

Like science, so ideology and bureaucracy often view the use of a neutral language and an imposition of new words with very specific meanings as ideal solutions to the *problems of communication*, which arise from polysemy. Orwell's (1949) *Nineteen Eighty-Four* and Thom's (1987) *La Langue de Bois* (a wooden language, i.e. a non-flexible and impoverished language) presented, in different ways, vivid images of the attempts of totalitarian systems and bureaucracy to get rid of dialogicality. Orwell and Thom showed how totalitarian regimes and political powers, like governments or political parties, by imposing new words with specific meanings could destroy the existing social realities and substitute them with invented ones.

Orwell ridiculed and made parody of the 'beauty of destruction of words' in totalitarianism and of the effort of making the vocabulary smaller and the range of thought narrower. But Orwell's parodies had very real bases. For example, Stalin (1972), in discussing the questions of *Marxism and Linguistics*, drew attention to the changes in the Russian language during the Soviet rule. For instance, the new Russian words like 'kolchoz', 'kulak' and 'apparatchik' were not only new words in the Russian language during the Soviet rule; they reflected the totalitarian reality of the Soviet Union and they were exported to other languages of the Soviet bloc. The Soviet linguist Marr, whom Stalin first appreciated and then denounced, went even further. He claimed that, in communism, it would no longer be necessary to have languages with their unnecessary variations because a new, unique language, a one for all language of thought would be constituted (Marr, 1977, p. 24).

Thom described the linguistic characteristics of a 'wooden language' focusing on syntax, the type of vocabulary and style, e.g. rhetoric, euphemisms and hyperbole. This language contains little semantic information, few references to reality and it uses mostly impersonal types of sentences; it often expresses imperatives which indicate the will and power of bureaucracy. Thom pointed out that the traces of wooden language exist everywhere in modern society. For example, scientific language has its specific jargon in using nouns rather than verbs; bureaucratic and administrative language is characterised by impersonal style; and so on. However, he argued that it was the magnitude of wooden language and its penetration through all spheres of life in the Soviet mass media and in the French Communist Party, that the language, so created, became such a powerful tool of control.

Destruction of language in totalitarianism and the efforts to create a neutral language fascinated the Czech dramatist Václav Havel during the Soviet rule and in particular after the Soviet occupation of Czechoslovakia in 1968.[6] Many of Havel's dramas from that period were concerned with the efforts of bureaucracy to de-dialogise language and make it 'neutral' or non-communicative. Havel's persistent theme was the portrayal of language that lost its meaning and became empty: the language that did not speak to anybody specifically and for which nobody was responsible. In many of his dramas Havel's anti-heroes lost the ability to speak ordinary language.

Havel (1992) has shown that a totalitarian system, in order to continue its existence, *requires* the language of non-communication or in our terminology, it requires a non-dialogical language. The non-dialogical language is the language of non-commitment of speakers. It is the language of alibi. Words no longer carry meanings for which the speaker is responsible and they become signs of manipulation and obedience. Such language could be described as a system of rules, information and instructions. Like a set of orientation tables or travel information it carries messages with a minimum of content and it must be understood in the same way by everybody: do this, do not do that, go right or turn left. It is therefore a neutral language that does not require judgement or evaluation of information, but simply obeisance. It was a well-known guidance rule during totalitarianism that speakers should provide as little information as possible about themselves and others. The less information the message contained the less likely it was for the speaker to get into political trouble.

Individuals who have adapted to the totalitarian regime and more generally, to bureaucratic systems do not use words in their colourful plurality of meanings but they communicate only *as if.* They are no longer authors of what they say because they are not committed to words as actions. Indeed, they may not wish to be treated as authors because authorship implies responsibility and commitment. As a result, people may talk to one another only apparently: they say words but they say nothing: but 'the word that is not guaranteed by a life, loses its significance' (Havel, 1985, p. 359). What this means is that such apparent language in fact abolishes antinomy between the *Ego-Alter.* Apparent language, because it no longer involves tension between the *Ego-Alter,* turns into the language of non-communication. It is no longer dialogical.

Havel's drama *The Memorandum* is probably best known for the treatment of the language of non-communication. In this drama, a new official language is introduced into bureaucratic usage. It is designed to avoid confusion that normally occurs in an unscientific and a natural language. This artificial language, *Ptydepe,* is based on a ridiculous idea that *the differences between words should be maximised* so that meaning of one word cannot be mistaken for another. This leads to an introduction of non-sense words of extreme length. However, unfortunately, after a while this new language begins to acquire some of the characteristics of a natural language with its ambiguities and emotions. Therefore, it is replaced by another language, *Chorukor*, which is based on an equally ridiculous idea but, this time, it is *the resemblance between words that is to be maximised*. The more similar the words, the closer their meaning, so a possible error represents only a slight deviation from its proper meaning.

3.3   It is unethical to use language loaded with suggestions and emotions

In addition to scientific and ideological reasons for establishing a neutral language, there are also moral and ethical reasons for speaking 'neutrally'. For example, during the 1970s and 1980s, professionals explicitly argued on ethical grounds that patients and clients involved with various kinds of medical and social problems should be given 'neutral' information. 'Neutral' information gives them the chance to make their own choices, without professional advice, as to how to deal with their specific problems. For example, in genetic counselling a good practice prescribed that patients and clients should be given 'neutral' information about various kinds of treatment and about the kind of action they could take with respect to prevention or coping with a genetic disease. It was argued on perfectly well meant grounds that clients should be left free to decide which of the offered actions to choose. Thus, giving 'neutral' information was strictly separated from giving 'biased' advice or a recommendation.

For instance, it was thought that patients or prospective parents should decide on the basis of 'neutral' information provided by the professional, what kind of treatment they required or what options they could choose with respect to having or avoiding having an affected child (Marková, 1995). It was totally disregarded that communication between humans is dialogical and that it could not be reduced to something 'neutral'. In other words, it was ignored that humans actively listen and interpret the messages of their co-authors and that they read meanings into what is and what is not said. Our research (Marková *et al.*, 1984) has shown, however, that despite the fact that professionals were convinced that they provided 'neutral' information to their clients, the clients nevertheless interpreted 'neutral' information as advice to specific actions. Being uncertain and anxious to choose the right action, they expected to get advice, in one way or another, from professionals. Thus clients read between lines, searched for cues in nonverbal gestures, in the tone of voice, in the meanings of words that were expressed, as well as pondering why some other things were not said. Professionals could not avoid communication by tone of voice, by choosing particular terminology and a particular order of words which, in turn gave signals to clients who were looking for meanings in what was said. In one of our studies, while professionals claimed that they provided neutral information and not advice, 60 per cent of participants with haemophilia and their families that we examined in five countries thought that the professionals gave them 'advice' (Marková *et al.*, 1984).

In reflecting on a similar issue, Kessler (1980) discussed the idea of neutrality in counselling pregnant women at risk of having a child with Down's syndrome. The practice in counselling was to show the prospective mothers photographs of children with Down's syndrome, graphs, pictures and chromosomes. These were supposed to be educational practices consistent with neutral models of genetic counselling. However, Kessler pointed out, that these practices, magnified with pictorial images, focused the mothers' attention on disability rather than on normality. From such perspectives, Kessler maintained, 'the practice might be interpreted as an attempt to influence the counsellees to utilise the prenatal diagnostic procedure, violating professed values of neutrality and non-directiveness' (1980, p. 176).

These examples show that it is very difficult to turn dialogical language into neutral information. Since language is always loaded with diagnoses of events and actions as well as with prognoses for the future, one cannot abdicate responsibility by choosing presumably neutral words. Since participants in dialogue actively understand messages of others, any utterance carries already a germ of an answer (Voloshinov, 1929/1973; Rommetveit, 1974).

4   Dialogicality and the self

What can make communication non-communicative is non-commitment of the messenger to the recipient. Such communication is directed at 'everybody' and therefore at 'nobody'. In contrast, dialogical communication is an *Ego-Alter* communication. It would be a grave misunderstanding to think that dialogicality, because its point of departure is the *Ego-Alter*, de-emphasises the self. On the contrary, dialogicality brings into focus the features of the self that psychology has often neglected or ignored.

4.1   *Dialogicality and intersubjectivity*

Let us first turn attention to those aspects of dialogicality that social and developmental psychology has firmly established and abundantly explored both through theoretical and empirical research. For example, it has provided ample evidence, during the last century or so that the development of the self and personal identity goes hand in hand with the development of the concept of otherness.

Using terms like the 'dialectic of social growth', 'conversation of gestures' and 'inter- and intra-psychological processes', James Mark Baldwin, George Herbert Mead and Lev Vygotsky among many others, have proposed theories of self-consciousness built on the mutual co-development of the *Ego-Alter*.

Baldwin's concept of the 'dialectic of personal growth' views the process of the mutual interdependence between the *Ego-Alter* through give-and-take relationships in which 'the self meets self, so to speak' (Baldwin, 1895, p. 342). Baldwin postulated a theory according to which the self is originally crude, unreflective and largely organic and it is through interpersonal interaction that selves become 'purified and clarified'. He expressed this perspective, for example, in his studies of imitation, which were part of his theory of the self: 'My sense of myself grows by imitation of you, and my sense of yourself grows in terms of my sense of myself' (Baldwin, 1897, p. 15). Imitation for Baldwin, however, was not a passive process, it always involved creation and an idiosyncratic interpretation of the other person.

Mead's analysis of the development of self-consciousness and reflection was based on his presupposition that the self has an ability to call out in oneself a set of definite responses that the self acquires from others (Mead, 1934, p. 277). As the self develops this ability, it becomes an object to itself: it regards itself through the eyes of others. In his essay on 'The objective reality of perspectives' Mead (1927) develops this idea to include all environmental conditions around the self. Environmental conditions, he insists, exist only for concrete human agents who use them in their own idiosyncratic ways. Human agents, for their part, are never imprisoned in their own perspectives but are orientated towards others and their perspectives.

More recently, developmental psychologists like Newson (1979) and Trevarthen (e.g. 1979, 1992) have argued and provided empirical evidence that the child is born with a predisposition for intersubjectivity. In getting actively engaged with the environment, the child selects his own milieu. Parents, for their part, by providing a stimulating environment and indeed, by presupposing that young children already comprehend quite complex messages, further contribute to the intricate interplay between biological and cultural influences. Thus, by presupposing intersubjectivity they actually shorten the path to its achievement (Rommetveit, 1974). Trevarthen (1992, p. 102) maintains that understanding intersubjectivity can provide an explanation 'of how human social and cultural knowledge is created, how language serves a culture and how its transmission from generation to generation is secured'.

While social and developmental theories of Baldwin, Mead, Vygotsky and their contemporary followers have studied some aspects of the *Ego-Alter* dialogicality like role and perspective taking and intersubjectivity, equally important features of dialogicality, like authenticity and commitment have been largely neglected both in developmental and in social psychology. In order to develop the theory of social knowledge, we must extend the dialogical basis of the *Ego-Alter* to include these neglected features.

4.2   Dialogicality is not a fusion of the Ego-Alter

Despite running some risk of overgeneralising the case, let us insist on the following claim. Social and developmental theories based on perspective- and role-taking and on intersubjectivity assume that through communication and negotiation of meanings the differences between perspectives of the *Ego-Alter* come closer together. Do we not have enough evidence that diplomatic communication leads to a decrease of conflict? Should we not assume that dialogical participants arrive at a kind of fusion of their different perspectives preventing open conflicts and wars? Of course it would be foolish to deny that.

However, what is often neglected in these theories is that communication has two antinomic aspects, other-orientation and self-orientation. While Mead, and to some extent Baldwin and Vygotsky, focused on other-orientation in communication, i.e. perspective taking, Bakhtin focused above all on self-orientation. It was crucial for Bakhtin that the self does not fuse with the other in the process of dialogue. Reflecting on others' perspectives and accepting them is only one aspect of the development of self-concept. These processes determine the self only partly but they never lead to the fully developed self-concept. As Bakhtin expresses his position: 'What would I have to gain if another were to fuse with me? . . . let him rather remain outside me' (Bakhtin, 1979/1986, p. 78).

Already in his early work, but published only recently and entitled *Toward a Philosophy of the Act* (Bakhtin, 1986/1993), Bakhtin made a distinction between pure empathising and active empathising with the other. Pure empathising leads to submerging of the self in the other and viewing the world from the other's perspective. For Bakhtin, pure empathy erases the other, leads to annihilation and to loss of individuality and to non-being. In contrast, active empathising involves the struggle with the *Alter*, with the strange. What arises from this struggle is something productive and new. For Bakhtin, there is no communication unless the self lives through active understanding of the strange, of the *Alter*. The speech of others and their thoughts, all contains *strangeness*, which the self tries to overpower by imposing its own meaning on the other, or to appropriate it by making it part of its own thoughts and speech. The constant strife between the strangeness of others' thoughts and one's own thinking makes communication meaningful to the human condition. There could be no dialogue if participants were not opposed one to another through mutually experienced strangeness. Strangeness creates tension between them, tension, which is not bound to either of them, but actually exists between them (on the nature of the dramatic aspects of dialogue see also Mukařovský, 1940/1977).

But is there anything more that the self creates in overcoming the strange? In overcoming the strange the self confirms oneself as an agent. Bakhtin points out that when the self acts, it is because of some motives, goals and reasons. Acts are intentional and for them to be effective, they require personal commitment and responsibility. Words can be actions only to the extent that the co-authors give them the power to act through personal commitment and taking a stance. In contrast, the loss of commitment to one's words could result in one's loss of identity and authenticity.

4.3   Imposing one's own meaning on 'the strange'

Studies of 'difficult communication', e.g. studies of dialogues with people attempting to speak a foreign language or of people with impaired speech talking with their carers, often reveal dialogical features, which would not be observed in unproblematic communication. Such communication involves people with highly unequal communication resources. In order to get the message across, speakers must strategically and consistently impose their own meaning on the other or in Bakhtin's words, on the strange.

Our studies (e.g. Collins and Marková, 1995, 1999) have involved dialogues between people with cerebral palsy who had speech and communication problems, and their carers. In such situations, being consistent and innovative in imposing one's own meaning on the interlocutor is essential for the person with a speech problem in getting the message across. Such strategies of consistency and innovation have many similarities to those which minority groups apply in interacting with majorities in order to gain influence (Moscovici, 1976b). In 'difficult communication', just like in minority/majority influence studies, the interactional impact of any communication resource employed in action is dependent not only on the impaired speaker conveying it as integral to interaction, but, also, on the unimpaired speaker seeing it as such. Moreover, like in minority/majority interaction, so in 'difficult communication' no kind of communication resource employed by the impaired speaker can be considered as a discrete and isolated unit. Rather, each exists in a complementary relationship with other resources, as well as part of the total dialogical environment.

A person, who has a physical difficulty to voice words, uses any means available as a communication resource in order to impose his own meaning on the other. In order to illustrate this point, let us consider some examples from our research. The participants of the dialogue below are Guy and Mary. Guy has severe cerebral palsy and is in a wheelchair. He cannot talk and he uses an electronic communication system, which he operates by typing letters or words and the system can voice them. That morning Guy and other students in the college were writing letters to inform their families that they would be going out to dinner to the Italian Restaurant Maggios and then going bowling. These two events were to take place on the same day. Bowling is an important sports activity for people with cerebral palsy because in bowling they exercise their muscles to prevent atrophy.

At the start of the conversation Mary asked Guy what he was doing that morning. Guy tried to explain that they were writing the letters to their families informing them about those two events. In making his response to Mary, he used communication resources that were available to him, ranging from body movements to signing, typing single letters or single words. Here is the extract from the conversation between Guy and Mary:[7]

Extract 1: What are you doing here today?

Guy	Mary
// ↑M smiling	↓Talker ↑G
	well (.) // what are you doing (here) today
	(.) hmm=
= looks over his right shoulder presses keys	↓Talker ↑G
	(.)
//points and looks over at papers on table	//,,, follows point,,, looks over at papers
withdraws point	
	(↑G) ↓Talker
//moves finger to press keys	*what is it what's going on tod ay//* (.) hmm
,,, presses keys	
I live at	
gaze on papers	follows gaze holds gaze on paper
points over at papers	
65 Longbenton Avenue York	
	,,,↑G
	yes I kn ow you do but wha- (.)
	leans over G's chair

gaze on papers . . .

> *mm<what are you telling me that*
> ↓ paper, points at paper
> *for< oh   because of this*:
> *address her e* (.)
> ↑ and round at G

The conversation goes on for several minutes. Mary clearly does not understand that by typing 'I live at 65 Longbenton Avenue York', Guy is giving an answer to her question as to what he was doing that morning. From Guy's point of view, pressing a button, which speaks his address, can be considered an efficient communication resource that is available to him. He pursues with his response because Mary does not understand and one can say, that he is applying consistency as the behavioural style of an active minority (Moscovici, 1976b). He also looks round over his shoulder, gazes at papers and letters they were writing, which Mary views as 'being nosey', rather than interpreting his gaze as an answer to her question. Thus, rather than taking his looking around as a *communicative gesture* attempting to draw her attention to relevant objects, she interprets this as a *behaviour*, i.e. as 'being nosey'. Guy clearly expresses his ideas in dialogue by all communicative resources available to him but they are not taken as such by Mary. As the dialogue continues, Guy presses on his computer the word 'bowl'. Mary misunderstands because she interprets 'bowl' literally as a container and asks him whether he needs a bowl. Guy vocalises and mimes the action of bowling. At this stage she also disregards his gesture of miming the action of bowling. This gesture Guy uses repetitively from now on during the rest of the conversation.

Extract 2: Bowling

Guy	Mary
↓Talker, pressing keys	
bowl	
pressing keys	
bowl	
	a bow:l (.) *a bowl*
gesturing bowling	
	>or is it the < other kind of
	bowl >is it< bowling
nodding	
	nodding
//pulling at M's sleeve	*ye:es uh//right* ((laughing))
pressing keys	
pointing to himself	
((vocalisation))	
	is it ten pin *bowling*

In this extract Guy is systematic, building on what has been interactively achieved in order to help Mary to take his perspective. Finally, he is successful. Guy builds on this understanding, repeating again 'bowl' and gesturing a bowling action. The inventiveness of Guy and the rigidity of Mary clash in the dialogue because she takes his behaviour and communication in a literal sense.

When dialogical participants use communicative resources that are publicly available and publicly shared, they must be able to synchronise their meanings in time and space so that they can transmit them and make them part of the content of the message. These extracts show that synchronisation of meanings proceeds through two interdependent dialogical paths, first, through taking the perspective of the other and second, through imposing own meanings on the other. Their contrastive features are necessarily foregrounded in dependence on intention and motives for communication as well as on the nature of events of which the dialogue is part.

4.4   To pray or not to pray could be a grievous question

In his analysis of the emergence of the modern self in literature Trilling (1972) conceived of authenticity as the ability of humans to function *as* humans with respect to things that matter to them. For example, if in a culture, privacy is a value that matters, to be deprived of it would mean living an inauthentic existence. Or, if having a job means having human dignity, then being unemployed means living an inauthentic existence. Authenticity therefore is an expression of the *Ego-Alter* dialogicality. It presupposes a triadic relation: the self-respect, respect from others and respecting others. These aspects of dialogicality, however, may be in conflict, if the self-respect and respect from others require different kinds of action. Take the following example from James Joyce's *Ulysses*. It concerns the conflict between self-respect and respecting others.

Joyce's novel *Ulysses* starts with an authenticity problem of one of the heroes, Stephen Dedalus. Stephen's mother was at her deathbed and she begged her son to kneel and pray for her. However, the young Irishman educated in Oxford was no longer a religious man. He refused and his mother died without the comfort of his prayers. Why he did not do it, asked another hero of the novel, Buck Mulligan, 'there is something sinister in you' because 'you crossed her last wish', but 'I did not mean to offend the memory of your mother'. For Stephen, however, this grievous event was not an offence to his mother. Being caught between two communication actions, either to kneel and pray and betray his authenticity or not to pray and cause grief to his mother, he chose the former. Commenting on Stephen's action, Budgen (1972) points out that there is no right solution, if Stephen is the person he is. If he was an indifferent rationalist, he could pray and come to no harm. However, he knew the mysterious potency of words and gestures that have cumulated during centuries. Therefore, for him, 'to pray and not to pray is a grievous question. If he refuses he must be tortured; if he consents he is lost' (Budgen, 1972, pp. 40–1).

Dialogically speaking, Stephen faced the problem of two kinds of commitment: first to authenticity based on self-respect, and second to his mother, based on respect for her; but saying what she requested would have destroyed his respect for himself. His sense of self-identity was not based on 'I am I' or 'My identity is determined by my past experience'. His sense of self-identity stemmed from conflicting actions due to the *Ego-Alter* encounter.

4.5   To obey and not to obey may not be a grievous question

Stephen's problem may not be shared by many of those who live in totalitarian regimes where language has lost its potency and where words have no longer any author and therefore, any meaning.

One of the main messages in Havel's plays is that the loss of ordinary language leads to the loss of moral principles and identity. The main anti-hero of Havel's *The Garden Party*, Hugo, has lost the ability to use ordinary language. He has learnt, however, to use bureaucratic languages and to use them at the right time and in the right places. This enabled him to achieve his political success. In the end, being able to speak only bureaucratic languages and having lost the ability to use ordinary language, he loses his personal identity, does not recognise himself and equally, his family no longer knows who he is. Without actually expressing that explicitly, Havel shows in his dramas that dialogicality is essential for personal identity and that the loss of dialogicality also means the loss of personal identity.

Havel (1992) illustrates this fact with an example which has become classic. It refers to the period in Czechoslovakia after the Russian invasion in 1968, known as 'normalisation'. The manager of a grocery shop places in the window of his shop, amongst the onions and carrots, the slogan 'Proletarians of the whole world – unite!' The slogan arrived in his shop from the store together with those vegetables. The display of slogans like that one was part of the routine the grocer had been doing for years: one of those little things that one does in order to secure a relatively quiet and peaceful life in a totalitarian (or a post-totalitarian, in this case) regime. In contrast to Stephen, the grocer did not care about the potency of language and the semantic meaning of the slogan. He knew that those who bought his carrots and onions would not care about it either. The function of the slogan was to make a sign, addressed to those in authority and to others who might disrupt his rather peaceful life, in case he did not display the slogan.

Havel was showing the power of a sign, which masks its real meaning. It is an alibi that can be used by everybody, from a grocer to someone very important. It creates a world with a mystified appearance and non-authenticity, in which everything seems to have its order and its logic. It is not that language here speaks in double voices. Language always speaks in double or more voices but that does not matter in this case. What matters here is that the printed words have no relation to the meaning of the ritual of displaying them. Nevertheless the meaning of this ritual is clear to everybody. By adopting the appearance as reality, the grocer accepted ritualised communication.

The single sentence, like the slogan displayed in the grocer's shop window, 'Proletarians of the whole world – unite!' of course, has a meaning on its own. In fact, linguists and psycholinguists in the 1970s were busy analysing meanings and presuppositions of such single linguistic units in terms of truth-conditional semantics. The slogan presupposes that the proletarians of the whole world have not yet united. Yet, obviously, from the grocer's point of view, it was not the truth-value of the statement about which he cared when he displayed the slogan.

In one sense, the slogan 'Proletarians of the whole world – unite' pretends to be just as neutral as a word in the dictionary. It is nobody's sentence, it flows in time and space on its own without an author. It is typed on a poster as a slogan and without stating explicitly who is responsible for its content. It appears to have been disappropriated by the speaker, should there be one. Yet, in another sense, the sentence has an author, but his identity is hidden. Havel pointed out that while the *semantic meaning* of the slogan, in this particular context, is irrelevant with respect to the belief or commitment of the grocer, the *action* in which it is embedded, nevertheless expresses some meaning, though different from its semantic meaning. It is the meaning of an action which functions as *a sign* that could be clearly spelled out as follows: 'I the grocer XY, I am here and I know what I should do. I behave in a way that is expected of me, I am reliable and cannot be blamed. I am obedient and I have a right to live peacefully'. Thus, while the display of the slogan is non-communicative with respect to its semantic meaning, as an action, i.e. as a gesture of obedience, it is clearly communicative. It communicates the grocer's obedience to the ideology of the dominant political regime.

This case shows that the communication power of a sentence on its own does not indicate whether it is an expression of an ideology, of a social representation or whether it simply does not carry out any pragmatic meaning. In order to identify its specific meanings, we must address the question as to what kind of commitment the individuals, who express that sentence, actually have: whether they authenticate that sentence or not. Thus, the grocer in the above example appeared not to authenticate the slogan. The slogan functions as an alibi for the whole of society, from the grocer with his alleged concern for the unity of the workers of the whole world, to those in power who express clichés about serving the working class.

For Stephen Dedalus in *Ulysses*, like for Bakhtin and Havel, there is no alibi in communication and one cannot abdicate one's responsibility. Bakhtin insisted, that one cannot, as easily as the grocer appeared to be doing that, denunciate one's own responsibility because 'there is no alibi in being' (Bakhtin, 1986/1993). He maintained that, of course, there are many cases in which we behave as if this were possible. The consequence of such alibistic existence is depriving one's subjectivity of the *Ego-Alter* interdependence, i.e. of authenticity. Inauthenticity implies stripping dialogicality of every possible link with living language in its multifaceted nature. The persistent denunciation of responsibility in communication led to what Central and Eastern European scholars and writers have described as the crisis of identity.

Social scientists have dealt with similar distortions of the *Ego-Alter* dialogicality in less threatening contexts of Western democracy. Such distortions came partly from what Tocqueville (1835/1945) coined as a 'soft despotism' when he analysed threats to democracy in America. According to him, it is not direct force that is a threat to democracy, but apparent choices that those in power offer to fragmented and lonely individuals of the modern era who have deprived themselves of communities and of the authentic *Ego-Alter* relations. As a result, in order to secure a relatively comfortable life and petty pleasures, these modern strangers, all equal and alike, deprived of traditional communities that had held people together, are prepared to give up their identities for some trivial rewards. Moreover, Tocqueville argued, for such fragmented individuals, only immediate social environment has any value, it leaves aside the concerns of any wider interest.

Concepts of the crisis of identity and threats to identity, if conceived from the point of view of this discussion, are concerned with different kinds of issue than those studied in current social psychology. Current social psychology views self-identity either as already given or as something that the self possesses. It assumes that identity has a structure. Individuals may try to cope with the identity that is threatened or that they desire to be recognised by others. In such cases, identities are conceived as products of previous interactions and past experiences. The idea that identities are or could be threatened presupposes a danger from outside, e.g. by ideologies or groups in power.

In contrast, dialogicality does not conceive of identity as something given that can be threatened from outside but as a relation between the *Ego-Alter*. As shown above, the loss of self-identity can result from a lack of commitment and responsibility and from inauthenticity. This could be due both to inability of the self to resist the direct external force from the specific *Alter* or/and from the *Ego* subjecting itself more or less voluntarily, to a soft or hard despotism. I suggest therefore, that in view of dialogical relations concerning both self- and social identity, the concept of identity as something given and as something threatened from outside needs to be replaced by a dialogical concept of identity. Only then could we ask meaningfully the question to which many social psychologists today seek an answer: What are the relations between the theory of social representations and identity?

5 Diversified styles of dialogical thinking and speaking

Different cognitive goals employ heterogeneous modes of thinking and communicating, ranging from scientific to religious, metaphorical, ideological and so on. To think means to attempt different routes. In his analysis of the products of thinking the French philosopher Meyerson (1934, p. 137) emphasises that human thinking is never completely logical and never entirely rational. If it were, it would not be thinking. Thinking means taking diversions. Rigorous rationality would mean nothing but identity of thought from one moment to the next and consequently, no progress in thinking would ever be achieved. The secret of the excellence of the mind is to penetrate diversities of thinking and communicating.

5.1 Cognitive polyphasia and heteroglossia

Dialogicality displays cognitive polyphasia, i.e. the 'diverse and even opposite ways of thinking' (Moscovici and Marková, 2000, p. 245), which are suited to and articulated in different contexts, of which they are parts. These diverse and multifaceted ways of thinking and communicating can be, so to speak, 'out-of-phase' with one another, in opposition and in conflict and striving for dominance. This is what is expressed in Moscovici's (1961, 1976a) hypothesis of the cognitive polyphasia (la polyphasie cognitive). The term 'polyphasia' comes from the physics of electricity where the adjective 'polyphasic' refers to the existence of alternative and simultaneous currents which, however, can be out of phase with one another. The hypothesis of cognitive polyphasia refers to the possibility of using different and sometimes diverse ways of thinking and knowing, like scientific, common sense, religious, metaphorical and so on. For example, when Newton saw the falling apple, he had a choice to apply various kinds of knowledge in order to account for the fall of the apple. He might have thought that the fall could have been due to the wind, to the fact that the apple was ripe or perhaps that it had rotted and was easily detached from the tree, or that Newton, indeed, was thinking of his mechanistic laws (Moscovici and Marková, 2000, p. 246).

In social psychology Fritz Heider (1958), too, was concerned with different descriptions of a single event in common sense thinking and in ordinary language, e.g. 'a man rowing the boat across the lake'. Such a relatively simple event could be viewed as the man's ability and competence to row, or alternatively, as the result of weather conditions facilitating or mitigating against rowing. One can see different things. One can think about them in different ways and express them in language according to circumstances, experience, motives and intentions. Thinking, therefore, rather than being homogeneous or monological, is normally antinomic and dialogical. We are able to combine and use our intellectual capacities in multiple manners and we can express our ideas in different ways using specific words, gestures and symbols.

It has been recognised for a long time that dialogical participants may perform several different things – or functions – in speech at the same time (e.g. Bühler, 1932; Jakobson, 1960/1981). For instance, a single speech action may, at the same time, provide information, flatter and express emotions. These functions, by co-existing together have usually been described as having an additive impact on the meaning of communication.

The notion of different functions co-existing in speech actions must not be confused with Bakhtin's dialogical notion of 'heteroglossia' or 'multivoicedness'. Just as cognitive polyphasia refers to different modes of thinking, so 'heteroglossia' refers to divergent styles of speech arising from the infinite openness of languages in different concrete situations. The *Ego-Alter* relations are by definition unique and in each case they are filled with judgement and evaluation. Any thought and any word is undetermined in the sense that it can be interpreted in different ways depending on who the *Ego-Alter* are. For Bakhtin, '[N]othing conclusive has yet been spoken, the world is open and free, everything is still in the future, and will always be in the future' (1984, p. 166).

In his analysis of carnival in Rabelais Bakhtin (1984, p. 420) shows a specific case of heteroglossia, that between unofficial and official cultures represented by the folk and vulgar language on the one hand and the Latin and polished language on the other. In his analysis of carnival heteroglossia breaks down the borderline between these two cultures. Bakhtin shows how Renaissance discovers different dialects and employs them as linguistic masks – as the *commedia dell'arte*. In carnival heteroglossia sets free 'forbidden' and comical meanings and meanings from the established dogma. Similarly, Bakhtin's analysis of Dostoyevsky's novels shows that heteroglossia saturates all aspects of dialogicality: ambivalence, hidden and open polemics, parody, irony, hidden dialogicality, open and hidden rejoinders, collisions and quarrelling. All of these are ridden with tension in which different points of view clash and languages overlap exposing them to new interpretations.

5.2   Hidden polemics

Polyphasia and heteroglossia open up for social psychology the whole range of as yet unexplored features of social thinking and language. Above all, polyphasia, heteroglossia and heterogeneity in meanings detract attention from the study of speech actions which are seen as transparent and unitary. They also detract from conceiving words and sentences as having literary meanings and easily identifiable references. Instead, polyphasia, heteroglossia and heterogeneity show that these transparent linguistic and cognitive phenomena are no more than the tip of the iceberg hiding an infinite openness of dialogicality (Salazar-Orvig, 1999, 2000). For example, the *Ego-Alter* often expresses their relations indirectly either to be polite or to hide tensions, repress conflicts and conceal meanings. These styles of *thinking through the mouth* (Moscovici, 1984b) display themselves in syntax, grammar, voice or even in discussing an idea that is outside the main topic. While great literature and the daily discourse overflow to bursting point with these dialogical styles, for social psychology they remain an enigma awaiting to be explored, whether through communication genres, in focus groups, or in dialogues and narratives.

Bakhtin coined the term 'hidden polemics' to refer to a specific manner of expressing an indirect attack, evaluation or criticism of the other person. While open polemics is directed at the interlocutor, hidden polemics is indirect, focusing, for example, on the object of discourse. Rommetveit's (1991) analysis of Ibsen's *A Doll's House* shows the work of hidden polemics. The drama starts with a discussion of Nora and her husband Helmer of Christmas gifts that Nora has bought for the family. As the conversation unfolds it becomes more and more apparent that the talk is not about Christmas gifts but about Nora's behaving irresponsibly by spending money and about the family's economic affairs. While talking about the Christmas gifts that Nora has bought, Helmer, employing semantics, syntax, intonation and grammar to make a 'sideward glance', to use Bakhtin's term, judges and criticises his wife. A sideward glance towards objects serves as a hiding place that, however, they both understand, at least implicitly.

Aronsson's (1991) study of multiparty-medical dialogues involving the doctor, the parent and the child shows that the child, the weakest participant in the dialogue, could be turned into an 'object' of talk while the intended receiver of the message is the parent. By talking to the child, the doctor can express criticism and warning to the parent and indicate the parent's negligence of the child's health without talking to the parent directly, which could be openly polemical and face threatening. Hidden polemics can take different forms. For example, it could transform someone's statement into a question and thus make it problematic; and it could be reflected in grammar or in intonation without being directed at the interlocutor.

5.3   External and internal dialogue

Experimental studies of social influence and attitude change usually examine the direct effect of communication and persuasion as manifested by the participants' responses in questionnaires or in attitude scales. If the participants' responses do not overtly show the change of opinion, the researcher concludes that the message was not effective. For example, in a typical experimental paradigm the participants first express their opinion about the subject matter individually, then they are subjected to the influence of a minority as a group. Subsequently, they are re-tested individually. The re-tested individuals may or may not overtly change their attitudes, i.e. they may or may not show the manifest effect of minorities' influence. Yet, Moscovici argues, even if the manifest effect does not show up, it does not mean that there is no effect at all. Latent effect, which is often ignored in social psychology, is equally important. Dialogically speaking, latent effect suggests that messages may produce hidden conflicts in the individual that will perhaps manifest themselves later.

In a series of studies Moscovici and his students have explored latent effects in laboratory experiments on minority/majority influence. The essence of these experiments has been to give evidence that although no manifest change in opinion is shown experimentally, nevertheless, changes in attitudes, perceptions, content of responses and the ways of thinking have nevertheless taken place. Latent effects work through tension, conflict and through unconscious change of opinions and attitudes. Moscovici refers to latent effect as conversion:

The conversion produced by a minority implies a real change of judgements of opinions, not just an individual's assuming in private a response he has given in public. This is why we are often unaware of the profound modification in our perceptions or our ideas from contact with deviants (Moscovici, 1980, p. 217).

A number of ingenious laboratory studies based on the concept of conversion have shown several different latent effects. The essence of these experiments was to give evidence that although no manifest changes are shown, these may, nevertheless, be found in the apparently *'unrelated'* experiments, e.g. in changes in attitudes with respect to 'unrelated' issues, in perceptions, content of responses and the ways of thinking. This effect, it is argued, results from the conflict in the minds of respondents. For example, Moscovici and his collaborators have shown the shift in the perceptual threshold (Moscovici, Lage and Neffrechoux, 1969, Moscovici and Personnaz, 1991); differences between conscious and unconscious influences (Moscovici and Personnaz, 1980); indirect influence (Pérez and Mugny, 1986) and influence on the way of thinking (Butera *et al.*, 1991–92).

We can suggest that what goes on in the individual's mind during the process of conversion, is an *internal dialogue*. What originally was externally discussed when the issues were presented and problems created, has now transformed itself into an internal and a hidden conflict. When the internal conflict is resolved, an internal dialogue will again turn into an *external dialogue*, and subsequently, into a social action.

We can suggest that Rommetveit's (1991) analysis of dialogue in Ibsen's *A Doll's House* also shows the latent effects of the internal dialogue. Being a 'doll' first in her father's house and then in the house of her husband Helmer, at the beginning of the play Nora behaves obediently, accepting her role as a 'doll', a co-operative and submissive partner who lets herself be controlled. She is largely deprived, as Rommetveit terms it, of 'epistemic responsibility'. Epistemic responsibility is 'responsibility for making sense of the talked about state of affairs and bringing it into language' (Rommetveit, 1990, p. 98) and of 'control of intersubjectively endorsed perspectives on things and states of affairs [the partners] . . . talk about' (Rommetveit, 1991, p. 195). In her dialogue in the first act of the play she seems to be happy, hiding her little pleasures, like eating macaroons, humming to herself and going along with her husband's perspective of herself as 'a little pet'. She does not have much to contribute to the thematisation of issues that are spoken about but this does not seem to be a real problem. However, as in conversion studies, we can observe changes in Nora's thinking in the final act of the drama. She now takes the initiative and controls words and expressions which they both use to topicalise those states of affairs and which transform them into potentially shared social realities. The polemic is no longer hidden, it is now open and it results in Nora's action. She is no longer a doll to be played with and leaves her husband.

If we accept the hypothesis of ontology based on the *Ego-Alter* and if we accept that dialogical communication is a fundamental characteristic of humans as social beings, we are committed to far reaching implications. A science that is based on ontology of the *Ego-Alter* and that studies human social phenomena in dialogical communication is not – and cannot be – a science concerned with disengaged phenomena that are 'objective' and 'neutral'. On the contrary, it is concerned with phenomena that matter to humans, whether they concern health and illness, the breakdown of communities, political agendas and environmental polution. Such science cannot be modelled on the sciences that study physical, physiological reactions or structures in neural nets. Neither can it be modelled on psychology or indeed on social psychology that carries out its business with clearly defined variables, whether they concern social cognition, decontextualised language or dissected gestures.

Instead, the laboratory of dialogically based social psychology is human life with all its passions, myths and diversities of thinking and communication. In such a laboratory, political, environmental, community or health issues cannot be ignored.

Moreover, dialogicality is not about 'a happy end' resulting in reducing tension and conflict, achieving intersubjectivity and taking the perspective of the other. In contrast, dialogicality is both about lack of tension and tension, about acknowledgement of the other and the struggle for self-recognition. Its concern is both commitment and alibi, questions that remain unanswered and desires that are ignored. It is antinomies of the *Ego-Alter* that make dialogicality a plausible basis for the theory of social knowledge.

NOTES

1. It would be superfluous to repeat that symbolic communication in humans is the *Ego-Alter* communication, which means, it is communication of dialogically unique species. This distinguishes symbolic communication in humans from symbolic communication of bees and other species that communicate symbolically (cf. Luckman, 1990).
2. While the experts will rightly claim that the Hegelian and the Marxist dialectics should be differentiated one from another, such differentiation is, nevertheless, irrelevant in the context of this chapter. It is only the general principles of dialectic that Marx borrowed from Hegel that are of interest in our discussion of dialogicality and dialectic.
3. Matter is the fundamental philosophical category of Marxism and of Marxist materialism, i.e. scientific conception of the objective world. Matter is the primary category and it is always contrasted with consciousness, the capacity of the mind to reflect (mirror) the objective reality. Scientific materialism is contrasted to non-scientific idealism, in particular to religions that claim

the priority of God or spirit over matter. However, Marxist materialism also rejected what was called a vulgar materialism of the nineteenth century (e.g. L. Büchner, K. Vogt and J. Moleschott). Vulgar materialism would transfer knowledge from physiology to the sphere of mental processes, e.g. 'the brain produces thoughts in the same manner as liver produces bile'. Chomsky's comparison of the bodily organs, e.g. vision to the operations of organs in the mind/brain, would presumably fit the ideas of vulgar materialism of the nineteenth century.

4. Darwin did not accept the idea of progress in his theory of natural selection (Gould, 1996). Rejecting this idea, he always referred to variation as a feature of natural selection.

5. In this context Benjamin refers to Paul Klee's painting 'Angelus Novus' which shows that 'angel of history' 'does not dialectically move forward into the future, but has his face turned toward the past' (Arendt, 1955/1973, p. 18). Benjamin describes Klee's painting 'Angelus Novus' in Theses IX as follows: 'A Klee painting named "Angelus Novus" shows an angel looking as though he is about to move away from something he is fixedly contemplating. His eyes are staring, his mouth is open, his wings are spread. This is how one pictures the angel of history. His face is turned toward the past. Where he perceives a chain of events, he sees one single catastrophe, which keeps piling wreckage upon wreckage and hurls it in front of his feet. The angel would like to stay, awaken the dead, and make whole what has been smashed. But a storm is blowing from Paradise; it has got caught in his wings with such violence that the angel can no longer close them. This storm irresistibly propels him into the future to which his back is turned, while the pile of debris before him grows skyward. This storm is what we call progress' (Benjamin, 1955/1973, p. 249).

6. For the analysis of Havel's dramas, see R. Pynsent (1994).

7. Transcripts were made by Sarah Collins, using the transcription notation system developed by Jefferson and outlined in Atkinson and Heritage (1984, ix–xvi) with some modifications to accommodate the use of gesture and the system of alternative and augmentative communication that the non-speakers used. The layout of the transcription is such that the actions of each participant are transcribed in two parallel columns, with the non-verbal/non-vocal actions described in the upper line of each row, and the verbal/vocal actions in the lower. Overlap between two participants' actions (e.g. between gesture and speech) is demoted by the use of a square bracket. The sign '−' is used to denote that one action follows on immediately from another (this is used both within one participant's actions, and across both participants). Italic script is used to record verbal/vocal actions. Standard script is used in the description of non-vocal/non-verbal actions. Gross motor activity, gestures, head orientation and facial expressions are verbally described, in as much detail as seems relevant and appropriate. Eye gaze direction is described by means of an upward and downward arrow, e.g. ↓Talker ↑G.

5   Social representations: old and new

1   From mental to collective and social representations

Every concept of lasting importance is couched in history and displays duration. Nevertheless, concepts of lasting importance radically change. For example, the concepts of atom and continuum in Greek philosophy and in modern quantum physics display both a duration and a radical transformation in human thinking regarding the phenomena to which they refer. Similarly, the concepts of democracy in ancient Greece and in contemporary society reflect both the permanence and variation in human condition.

Equally, let us consider the concept of social representation. One can hardly write a book that has in its title the term 'social representations' without discussing the concept of collective or social representation[1] of the French sociologist Emile Durkheim (1858–1917). Yet Durkheim's explicitly proposed concept of collective representations was already implicit in the moral philosophy of Charles Renouvier. And Renouvier stood on the shoulders of Immanuel Kant. And Kant – but one cannot always go back to the beginning of the world.

It was Durkheim who put the concept of collective representation at the centre of the theory of sociological knowledge. Durkheim presupposed that knowledge of the external world could be established only through collective representations and he was convinced that the sociology of knowledge must be built on this concept. Having put forward such an argument, he then proposed that sociology should be instituted as an independent science based on the study of collective representations.

Durkheim's concept can be viewed as being at a cross-road between the *mental representation* of the static foundational epistemology (Chapter 1) on the one hand, and the *social representation* of the dynamic and dialogical epistemology (see below and Chapter 6), on the other. These epistemologies imply different theories about the origin of representations, different perspectives on science and common sense, on communication and the change of representations. In order to bring home the continuity and the dramatic difference between Durkheim's *sociological* concept of representation and Moscovici's *social psychological* concept, we need to reflect on both.

1.1   'Représentation' *and* 'representation'

While collective representation was a fundamental concept of Durkheim's sociology of knowledge, apparently, he never defined the term *'représentation'* (Pickering, 2000a). The term *'représentation'* was, in his time, commonly used and understood in various spheres of intellectual life in France, ranging from philosophy, social science, arts and literature on the one hand, to professional fields, e.g. law, on the other. Thus, there was no urge for Durkheim to define the term *'représentation'* and it appears that he was not criticised for this 'negligence'. On the basis of his writing we can safely infer that for Durkheim, collective representations referred to various activities of the mind, rather than to specifically defined phenomena. As Pickering (2000c, pp. 98–9) maintains, Durkheim spoke about *représentations* in different senses, referring to scientific, collective or social, individual and religious *représentations*, the *représentations* of feelings as well as other kinds of *représentations*. For him, everything could be represented and this view was shared by other French scholars of his time.

The word *'représentation'* was already known in the French language in the thirteenth century. It has always been a highly polysemic term, referring to various activities of the mind, like the production of images, symbols and signs, as well as graphic demonstrations, e.g. Cartesian coordinates and imitation. Most importantly, however, the first meaning, listed in the French Dictionary Robert, characterises *'représentation'* as an action of placing something in front of the eyes of another or in front of the mind of another. This indicates that the French *'représentation'* displays, above all, social and dialogical characteristics. One of the earliest meanings refers to a theatrical *représentation*. Acting is by definition communicative and is directed at others. In a play, the actor communicates to others her images of an absent object. An absent object is made meaningful to others by means of an image or a sign or by discourse. In a dramatic dialogue the actor never repeats or mirrors an absent event but through *représentation* he creates a new interpretation. We also need to emphasise in this context that the prefix *re-* in *représentation* has nothing to do with repetition but, linguistically speaking, it is an intensifying prefix.

In contemporary French *'représentation'* maintains its dynamic meaning (cf. Pickering, 2000a; Prendergast, 2000). It refers to various kinds of activities and is widely used in anthropology, sociology, arts and literature as well as in daily discourse. In the same way, *'représentation'* in the philosophical and psychological sense retains its dynamic and communicative characteristics. Moscovici (1976a), in the Preface to the second edition of *La Psychanalyse* draws attention to this fundamental characteristic of *représentation*. *Représentation* is always directed at others: through pointing out something to someone, it speaks; and through expressing something to someone, it communicates (1976a, p. 26).

The word *'représentation'* was exported into English and it is already found in the fourteenth century. However, the meaning of 'representation' in the two languages has never been the same. Although in English the term is also polysemic and dictionaries display a range of meanings, it is the emphasis on these different meanings that directs attention to their diversities in the two languages. English meanings emphasise representation as likeliness, a picture, a model or a reproduction, imitation and mirroring. It evokes static rather than dynamic meanings. Today, the meaning of representation in human sciences is largely associated with individual cognition, with the mechanistic and computational approaches in the study of the mind/brain and with the idea of internal mirroring of the external world (cf. Chapter 1). In the history of philosophy, from Locke to Kant, representations have been conceived usually as signs of reality and as appearances that the mind accepts from the external world or constructs from sensations and perceptions. In modern cognitive science, representations have become formalisations, processes and rules, symbols, images and pictures produced by the mind of the individual.

1.2   To represent means to think

Philosophers and researchers in natural and social sciences have different choices when approaching the study of mental phenomena. For some, the starting point of inquiry could be sense-impressions or individual perceptions, for others it could be cognition; still some others choose thinking, concepts, ideas – or representations – as a point of departure.

Yet whatever the choice, we find one pervasive tendency both in philosophy and science. It is the tendency to conceive such mental phenomena in a similar manner as we conceive the physical matter or material. For example, ideas are often considered as coming from inside the brain or the outside world; representations are discussed as constructs that mirror reality, or are defined as social facts. Cognition can be treated as a mechanism, a tool, an organ, a device or a computer. In other words, these metaphors tend to treat mental phenomena as entities to which you can point in the same way as you point to material things and which you can define with the same precision as you define material objects like hammers or bananas. Such images or metaphors, although they do not say very much on their own, may fashion our understanding of mental phenomena. Perhaps then it is not surprising that the question 'how do you define social representations?' is posed in the same manner as if, when talking about social representations, one was dealing with objects like a banana, a hammer and so on. What is more surprising is the frequently posed question 'how do you operationalise representations?' This request is still made not only by those who subscribe to some versions of empiricism and positivism or at least to their residuals, but also by those who would never perceive themselves as being associated in any way with these approaches.

In contrast, let us make an alternative choice in the study of social representations. Following the French meaning of the word, let us consider representations as thoughts in movement. And thought, we have argued earlier, is conceptual and communicable. If we insist on this proposition then the question of operationalisation of social representations, which invites defining them as something finished and complete becomes meaningless. Social representations are dynamic and open phenomena and the concept of social representation is formed and re-transformed together with the transformation of its theory.[2] The theory and the concept of social representations both develop as long as there are researchers who make significant contributions to their study. This is why concepts of lasting importance both display duration and radically change. In order to understand Moscovici's concept of social representation, let us reflect on the historical transformation of the concept of collective representation into social representation.

2   The sociological theory of collective or social representations

2.1   From Kant to Durkheim

According to the eighteenth century German philosopher Immanuel Kant, representations are formed through perception and cognition of the external world as it exists independently of the mind. However, according to Kant's epistemology, the mind does not have direct access to the real world or *the world-in-itself*. Kant perpetuated the belief of earlier philosophers about dualism between the objective world and the subjective mind. Kant believed that the mind cognises the world only indirectly. It combines the sensory data into representations of objects and thus it constructs appearances of the world. These appearances are regular and orderly but they exist *only* in the mind, in our sensibility (Kant, 1787/1929, A 127) and *not* in the real world, which remains unknown. By producing appearances or representations, Kant claimed, the mind gives laws to nature. One can interpret Kant's claim concerning the law-giving capacity of the mind in a *psychological* sense. It is the constitution of human cognition that determines *what* we comprehend about the world behind appearances (Marková, 1982).

Although Kant followed in principle Cartesian thought, his position with respect to representation constitutes an interesting twist, which contrasts with earlier philosophy. According to Kant, representations are not the passively produced mirrors of nature, but are actively constructed by the mind through experience. The constitution of the mind makes representations *a priori* possible, but they can be constructed only through experience. Although the mind does not have access to the world as it is, its constitution enables it to give meanings to reality and to form representations. The law-giving capacity makes the mind active.

This Kantian twist eventually led to an important question: do these representations belong to the single mind or are they commonly shared experiences?[3] While it is unlikely that Kant himself was preoccupied with this question, the issue, as to whether representations belong to the individual mind or whether they are commonly shared, became a subject of debate for the neo-Kantians in France (Paoletti, 2000). Among them, the French philosopher Charles Renouvier (1815–1903), following Kant, was concerned with establishing morality as a scientific field. Today, Renouvier is largely a forgotten philosopher, but it was he who went beyond Kant in a revolutionary manner. In particular, he built on Kant's point of view, which had already established the centrality of representation in the theory of knowledge.

Renouvier rejected the Kantian idea of the *thing-in-itself*, i.e. the idea that we can have no knowledge of objects and of the selves as they really exist and that we can only acquire knowledge of appearances. He argued that the general sense of the concept of Kantian representation was possible only because representations are socially shared. It seems thus that it was Renouvier who made the first explicit proposal for the social, rather than mental origin of representations. The logic, on which Renouvier built his argument, underlined the authority of collective representations (Stedman Jones, 2000, p. 47). With respect to morality, in contrast to Kant, for whom morality was *a priori* mode of knowledge, Renouvier argued that morality is socially determined. He maintained that it is based on co-operation and solidarity and that human society, in order to exist and progress, must establish legitimate social relations.

2.2　Durkheim's sociology of knowledge

When Durkheim came on the scene, the ground had already been well prepared for him. Strongly influenced by Renouvier, Durkheim was much preoccupied with the sociology of knowledge. His main question was the following: 'how does one acquire knowledge of the external world'? Durkheim followed Renouvier in his post-Kantian and social direction. Like Renouvier, Durkheim rejected the Kantian thing-in-itself and adopted the point of view that the world can be understood not through *a priori* representations of single minds, but through social experience. Having made his position clear, he went beyond Renouvier in giving to the concept of representation an explicitly social meaning. Representations are generated collectively in social life. They are the key to the knowledge, logic and understanding of mankind (Pickering, 2000b, p. 12). We can comprehend things because we can imagine, visualise and feel them. We experience things, they live in us in the form of the representations that express them.

Durkheim's sociology of knowledge has a number of specific characteristics of which I shall emphasise the following:

- duality of human nature
- stability of collective representations
- institutional and constraining nature of collective representations
- collective monologism of representations
- continuous genesis of collective representations from religion to science.

2.3　Duality of human nature

For Durkheim (1914/1970), the constitutional, or one could say, the *ontological* specificity of human nature was a dualism and it appeared in at least two forms (Moscovici, 2002a). First, Durkheim conceptualised dualism in a manner similar to that of philosophers before him: as dualism between body and mind. He considered body and mind as the two components of human nature that are not only different but also mutually opposed to one another. They are largely independent from one another and often in conflict (1914/1970, p. 315). He ontologised this kind of dualism and consequently, this had direct implications for his epistemology. According to Durkheim, psychological activities of the body inhered in sensations and emotive tendencies. Activities of the mind, on the other hand, consisted of conceptual thinking and morality.

Durkheim extended this traditional dualism of body and mind to the second kind of dualism, that between the individual and society. On the basis of these kinds of dualism he postulated two different kinds of psychology: individual and social. Accordingly, he sharply distinguished between individual representations and social representations. The former representations are studied in individual psychology and the latter should be studied by social psychology. Durkheim restricted individual representations to physiological and neurological phenomena (Durkheim, 1898). Consequently, he insisted that if perceptions and knowledge were to be based only on individual representations, people would not be different from animals, whose behaviour is guided by sensations. Individual representations, according to Durkheim, do not have much to do with knowledge. They result from the physical and biological nature of the individual and therefore, they are variable and personal.

While degrading the epistemological status of individual representations, Durkheim at the same time elevated the epistemological status of collective representations. He made them the basis of the sociological theory of knowledge.

Collective representations, e.g. images, beliefs, symbols and concepts, arise directly from social structures. They include all socially produced phenomena that circulate and are shared in society, like religions, myths, science and language. Collective representations are social facts and they form social reality in the same way that physical facts form physical reality. They are external to the individual who does not contribute towards their formation. Instead, they impose irresistible pressure on individuals. Yielding to their coercion, individuals internalise and perpetuate these social forms of acting, thinking and feeling. Collective representations are above the individual and they have the power to generate new representations.

Despite the fact that Durkheim repeatedly proclaimed the dual nature of humanity and representations, in the second preface (1901) to *The Rules of Sociological Method* he raised the question about the relations between individual and social representations 'since both are equally representations' (1901, p. 41). He was aware that the question of the relations between these two kinds of representation should not be trivialised. Society constitutes individuals and sociology cannot understand group activities without paying attention to the individual. He maintained that little was known, at the time, about the theory of ideas of the individual and he thought that, apart from hypotheses about the association of ideas with one another, there was no other knowledge available about individual representations.

Durkheim thought that even less was known about the formation of collective ideas, a subject, which, according to him, should be studied by social psychology. However, he pointed out that current, 'social psychology' was no more than 'a term which covers all kinds of general questions, various and imprecise, without any defined object' (1901, p. 41). According to Durkheim, social psychology should explore how collective or social representations attract and amalgamate, and repel and exclude one another. However, neither the sociology nor the social psychology of his day tackled this problem in a satisfactory manner.

Durkheim himself did not pursue the question about the relations between individual and collective representations. Having made the decision about the differences in the epistemological status between individual and collective representations, and having proclaimed that the relations between individual and collective representations should be studied more adequately, he did not go any further.

2.3.1   Culture and society

While nowadays cultural and social sciences pertain to different fields of enquiry and belong to separate university departments, 'society' and 'culture' were not so distinguished in Durkheim's time. Cultural and social phenomena were viewed as being intertwined and the idea of collective representations, as proposed by Durkheim, formed an interface between culture and society. Durkheim's collective representations concerned cultural phenomena, like religion and systems of beliefs and knowledge, as well as social phenomena, like normative constraints of society, moral order and social solidarity.

Durkheim developed this idea, integrating the cultural systems of representations and the structure of society, through the study of primitive societies, in which society and culture are less differentiated (Parsons, 1974) than they are in modern societies. He used the term 'social' both for social and cultural systems and did not distinguish between them. One can hypothesise that in pre-modern societies people shared their experiences more intimately and therefore, they also held more similar representations than in modern societies. In other words, through collective representations in pre-modern societies, Durkheim was able to study collective representations in the forms that were more transparent to his observation. In these societies, interpersonal and institutional relations appeared less complex than in Durkheim's own time.

Let us consider the following question: in what ways, according to Durkheim, do collective representations form social reality? Social reality, which is created by social facts, like collective representations, language, morality, myths, and so on, has above all an institutional and coercive role. Society imposes constraints on the individual through norms and through sets of standards for goals and actions. If the individual does not fulfil these standards, society enforces sanctions. Originally, Durkheim's focus was primarily on legal and moral norms. Later he came to emphasise more general aspects of institutionalised norms and values. These social facts and constraints constituted essential parts both of culture and society. Durkheim considered them to be external to the individual and he argued that the individual adopted them through the process of internalisation. Social facts grew into the individual's thinking and personality.

With these presuppositions concerning social reality, Durkheim conceived of the sociology of knowledge as being firmly based on the concept of stable collective representations that reproduce themselves through the process of internalisation in single individuals. His view of societal sanction and guilt arising from deviation from norms is not too distant from George Herbert Mead's concept of the 'generalised other' and from Freud's 'super-ego'. However, careful analysis of these different concepts is required before one makes a direct comparison between them on the basis of a superficial similarity (Marková, 1987a).

Like collective representations, for Durkheim language is a social fact. Language is a system of signs and symbols, something above sensations. It circulates in society and imposes its power on individuals. The power of a word is particularly important in religion where the word can attribute certain characteristics to objects that those objects do not have. When we acquire language, we also acquire a whole system of ideas that have already been classified and differentiated from one another in collective thought. There would be no general ideas without language; words fix ideas and transmit them from generation to generation. Language therefore is a social 'thing' (Durkheim, 1915).

However, language is not merely an external expression of thoughts, it is also internalised. Moreover, not only does it express thoughts, but it also creates them. Durkheim assumed, however, that the laws of thought and the laws guiding language are different and that, therefore, words can deform and violate thinking. In particular, 'It is a deformation of this sort which is said to have created the special characteristic of religious thought' (Durkheim, 1915, p. 75). Language forms the individual's social environment, imposing on him or her irresistible pressure. As words always have an influence on the ways in which phenomena are classified and thought about, they also affect collective representations. Durkheim sometimes goes even further. He claims that the ideas, which correspond to various elements of language, are actually themselves collective representations (1915, p. 434).

Although one can find references to the power of language exerted on thought throughout Durkheim's work, these references did not play any significant role in his study of collective representations. Durkheim's account of language as a social fact corresponds to his static view of collective representations. Of course, Durkheim knew that neither collective representations nor language are totally stable. He assumed that they change slowly over time. In his sociological analysis, nevertheless, he ignored their change. While his rival, the sociologist Gustav Tarde studied conversation as an inter-psychological fact and proposed that the study of conversation should be part of social psychology, Durkheim did not take this proposal on board as something relevant to the theory of collective representations.[4]

We can conclude that social facts are facts of collective solipsism and of a collective monologue. Being impersonal constraints on the individual, they do not allow for dialogue between individual and society.

2.4   From religion to science

In his analysis of Durkheim's sociology, Piaget (1965) emphasised the concept of a continuous genesis in Durkheim's work on collective representations, which connects contemporary society with the past, including most pre-historical societies. Durkheim sought to explain rationality, logic, morality, legal and religious institutions in terms of the past, showing systematically the origin of collective representations in religion and myth. Durkheim, however, did acknowledge both the diachronic and synchronic character of social representations. Piaget, nevertheless, appreciated above all Durkheim's diachronic approach, i.e. the socio-genetic method in sociology, but he pointed out that Durkheim's socio-genetic method ran into problems because it did not deal with synchronic structures.[5] One cannot explain new representations solely by references to history and past culture, argued Piaget, one also needs to study the contemporary, i.e. the synchronic structures of society.

Piaget's theory of child development is well informed by Durkheim's ideas. In particular, and as Moscovici (1998a/2000) shows, Durkheim's ideas of rationality and of an uninterrupted continuity of development from primitive to modern societies are reformulated in Piaget's genetic method. Like Durkheim, Piaget adopts the idea of 'an uninterrupted continuity from child to adult' (Moscovici, 1998a/2000, p. 219). However, Piaget reverses the Durkheimian process from thought to action and instead, 'makes action or ritual the principal agent endowing people with stable and shared representations' (Moscovici, 1998a/2000, p. 219). Moreover, in order to grasp synchronic structures, which Durkheim omitted, Piaget proposes the mechanisms of accommodation and assimilation. Through these two mechanisms the existing elements in synchronic structures are rearranged and through them equilibrium in the developmental process is achieved. However, despite its sophistication, the concept of equilibrium does not resolve the epistemological problem

of change (Chapter 1). That will be achieved only through tension between the *Ego-Alter* in the dialogically conceived concept of social representations (Chapters 6 and 7).

Durkheim thought that there was a direct relation between religion and
scientific knowledge. According to him, both religion and science are
based on collective representations. Religion is the product of society
and the ideas of God, myth and magic became collective fixations or collective representations through socially shared beliefs and commitment
to beliefs (Durkheim, 1915). Beliefs[6] originate in religion and from religion they enter into the field of science. Starting from beliefs, slowly
and gradually, humans approximate knowledge. In this position of a continuous progress in the acquisition of knowledge we can see clearly why
Durkheim rejected the Kantian 'unknowable thing-in-itself'. The world
becomes knowable through the development of science and education.
For Durkheim, the difference between religion and science is a matter
of degree. Scientific knowledge is built slowly, systematically, piece by
piece and surely, with all steps being subjected to verification. Science,
for Durkheim, is the surest of all kinds of knowledge. Scientific representations are therefore closer to the truth and more perfect than religious
representations. Religious representations are contaminated by symbolic
meanings and by language. Moreover, religious representations distort
reality by attributing to objects characteristics that they might not have,
like for example, being sacred.

These thoughts about science and religion have another important consequence in Durkheim's theory of collective representations. Like many
of his time, Durkheim privileged scientific knowledge to common knowledge. He went even further and argued that common thinking is erro-
neous and usually trivial. Collective representations are often based on
religious beliefs and despite being rational, they thwart reality. Scientific
knowledge, according to Durkheim, must therefore be superior to the
knowledge of an ignorant layman (Pickering, 2000c, p. 113). This kind
of reasoning also assumes that the scientist does know reality, whereas a
non-scientist does not. Therefore, the scientist has a better representation of reality than a non-scientist. Pickering points out that this elitist
view of knowledge Durkheim also applied to other mental activities, like
morality. Throughout his entire life Durkheim upheld the view that the
professionals' representations were closer to objective reality than lay representations. This view he applied both in science and morality.

Durkheim was convinced that beliefs were fundamental to the well-
being of society. Society has to believe in something in order to live.
He argued that a long-term Cartesian scepticism about reality is unten-
able. If society has no available knowledge about reality, belief is the

best substitute. Beliefs assure an escape from scepticism because they are fixations of the mind, they are certain. As Durkheim (1955, p. 184) maintains, 'Society cannot wait for problems to be solved scientifically' (Durkheim, 1955, p. 184). In fact, he was not the only one who expressed the point of view that beliefs are an indispensable part of life. While he argued this point as a social scientist, the famous French writer, Balzac, expressed the same point of view in one of his novels some decades before him. Thus Balzac writes in *Une Ténébreuse Affaire*: 'The absolute doubt which Descartes demands of human thinking is no more possible to come by than is the emptiness in nature. The mental operation by which this doubt could be achieved would be like an effect of the pneumatic machine, an exceptional and hideous event. Whatever is the matter, one must believe in something'.

Durkheim thought that beliefs were necessary to compensate for the limitations of science. To that extent, his sociology of knowledge, Paoletti (2000) maintains, responds to fundamental human concerns.

2.5   Durkheim's realist position

Let us now probe into the following questions: What kind of science did Durkheim celebrate? What was the Durkheimian vision of science? Despite the fact that in the history of philosophy of science one often talks about the origins of science in ancient Greece, China and Babylonia, European science has its 'true' origin in the seventeenth century (Lloyd, 2000). The concept of seventeenth century science was initially based on mechanistic principles. Later on, both mechanistic and organic principles constituted the basis of the realist theory of knowledge. According to this view, science aims to discover 'true' characteristics and 'the natures' of the objects of knowledge, and in this effort it gradually approximates the understanding of objective reality. This concept further presupposes that, in order to approximate understanding of phenomena in the world, science must proceed systematically from the corpus of evidence, from rules and scientific methods and it relies on what it considers to be facts. Science represents continuity in its struggle of the mind to make sense of the physical and social world. Its method is to constantly doubt 'evidence' and to question the accepted 'truths'.

Durkheim's vision of science basically fitted this point of view. Since reality cannot be grasped immediately, society creates collective representations, which contain some truth, some beliefs and some false convictions. This also means that as sciences progress, representations approximate reality more adequately and this view expressed Durkheim's realist conception of knowledge (Pickering, 2000c, p. 103).[7]

However, during Durkheim's life in the second half of the nineteenth century, science was dramatically changing. It was turning, in various aspects, from a mechanistic to a relativistic science. While mechanistic science was based on the idea that scientific progress was a continuous process, relativistic science came up with the ideas of discontinuity and instability. In this new science, reality was no longer something concrete. Durkheim's theory of sociological knowledge, however, remained unaffected by these new ideas of science that were taking place at the time. While he was very interested in science, Durkheim stuck to the perspective of continuity in the scientific progress. Yet, despite his interest in science, Durkheim studied collective representations in the context of religion rather than in the context of science. Moscovici has drawn to my attention yet another reason why Durkheim studied representations in the context of religion. Durkheim was committed to the collective and social nature of representations and it could not be disputed that religion is 'social'. In contrast, scientific knowledge, while it does have social bases, also accentuates the leading role of individual scientists or small groups of researchers in the scientific enterprise. It is not social movements that produce scientific knowledge.

2.6   An unfinished task

Durkheim's separation of the individual and the social was a crucial step in the further development of psychology and social sciences. Psychology has established itself as a science concerned with the mind and actions of the individual. Sociology has become a science concerned with collective mental processes and collective activities.

Having moved the pendulum from the focus on individual mental representations towards that on social and collective representations, Durkheim nevertheless remained Kantian and even Cartesian in his theory of knowledge. He insisted that knowledge must be certain and stable, otherwise, it would not be knowledge; therefore, collective representations, in order to have the status of knowledge, must be stable. Or if they change, they change very slowly (Pickering, 2000b, p. 16). As he studied collective representations as more or less *stable* concepts, the question of *change* of representations arose for him only as an empirical problem. It seems that it did not occur to him that change of representations raised an epistemological problem. Since collective representations change very slowly, Durkheim granted them the prestige of being constitutive of objective reality. They should be studied by social psychology in a comparative manner in mythical themes, popular legends, traditions and languages.

Durkheim holds a firm intellectual position in sociology in most of the areas he examined, e.g. religion, ethics, institutions and the rules of sociological method. However, it is significant that sociology on the whole has remained unmoved by Durkheim's theory of knowledge generally and by his concept of collective or social representation specifically. With the benefit of hindsight we can hypothesise why Durkheim's concept of collective or social representation has been passed over. First, both his proposed theory of social knowledge and the concept of collective representation are static. Modern sociology is concerned with phenomena in change and with phenomena that tend to turn society upside down. Therefore, from this perspective Durkheim's theory of knowledge could be seen, today, as irrelevant and outmoded. Second, Durkheim developed his concept of collective representations in the study of pre-modern societies. Therefore, sociologists might have ignored the compelling relevance of collective representations for complex modern societies in rapid change. Durkheim, of course, viewed collective representations as pertinent to any society and his choice to study them in pre-modern societies could be viewed as a strategic decision in an attempt to clarify his theory in more 'pure' human conditions. Parsons (1974) pointed out that because Durkheim studied social representations only in less differentiated societies, he could not touch on the explanation of the relations between collective representations and complex social structures in modern societies. Thus, while his concept of collective representation could have become very fruitful, Durkheim left, one could say, an unfinished task.

3   The social psychological theory of social representations and communication

If Durkheim's *sociological* theory of collective representations has not succeeded in gaining primary consideration as a sociological theory of knowledge, we need to answer the following question.

What it is that makes the *social psychological* theory of social representations and communication the most plausible candidate for being the social psychological theory of social knowledge and consequently, the theory that should re-define the field of social psychology? The answer to this twofold question lies in four issues:
- common sense as a resource for social representations
- dialogical triads the *Ego-Alter-Object*
- cultural embeddedness and dynamics of social representations
- communicative genres

In the remainder of this chapter I shall discuss the first issue, i.e. common sense in relation to science. Dialogical triads will form the basis of

Chapter 6. The cultural embeddedness and dynamics of social representations and communicative genres will be discussed in Chapter 7.

3.1   The concept that got lost

Although Durkheim was a very influential social scientist during his life, after the end of the First World War new trends were coming to the fore, for example, Marxism and structuralism, among others. Durkheim's work lost its impetus and his concept of collective representation more or less disappeared from French sociology. In fact, and as we have already commented, it has never come back to sociology with any force. Nevertheless, the concept of collective representation continued to have some impact in other social sciences. In anthropology, it was adopted by Lévy-Bruhl, who used the notion of collective representation with reference to the modes of thought of 'primitive mentality'. Like Durkheim, Lévy-Bruhl claimed that collective representations are social facts. People are born into collective representations and therefore, through them their mentality becomes objectively defined (Evans-Pritchard, 1981, p. 123). However, while Evans-Pritchard drew attention primarily to commonality of the social modes of thought in Lévy-Bruhl's work, he left out another, and an equally important defining feature of collective representations: that they are not only common, but that, above all, they have an institutional and coercive power. They have a constraining effect on thinking and on language meanings.

In developmental psychology the notion of collective representation strongly influenced Piaget both in his genetic epistemology and in his studies of child thinking. Equally, the concept of collective and social representation played a significant role in the work of Vygotsky and Luria in their research in Uzbekistan in the early 1930s (Luria, 1976). In developmental psychopathology, Janet (1926) found the notion of collective representation applicable to his studies of psychopathy and pathological beliefs.

It was only after the Second World War, throughout the 1950s and 1960s, that the concept of collective or social representation was re-instituted in the social psychological studies of Serge Moscovici. Since the concept had disappeared from sociology, Moscovici (1961) referred to social representation in the first chapter of La Psychanalyse as the lost concept. He recognised its significance for the study of thinking and language as genuinely social and dynamic phenomena.

Inspired by Piaget's studies of common sense knowledge in children, Moscovici turned his attention to common sense knowledge in adults. Thus he declares (Moscovici and Marková, 2000) that his interest in social representations originated from Piaget's work rather than directly from Durkheim. Via Piaget's child psychology Moscovici then proposed a transformed concept of social representation based on common sense thinking, knowledge and communication.

3.2   The science of discontinuities and instabilities

Every scientist is a child of his epoch. Durkheim's sociology of knowledge was deeply rooted in the image of science that was informed by the Newtonian-Kantian philosophy. It was guided by the idea of science as accumulating knowledge, progressing and providing humans with more adequate approximations of realities. Within this context, Durkheim's primary concern was to follow the route from religious to scientific representations. However, during the second half of the nineteenth century science took a dramatic turn.

Above all, the scientific discoveries of the nineteenth and twentieth centuries undermined the realist conception of 'the world out there' that could be reached more adequately with the accumulation of already existing knowledge, like a jigsaw puzzle that would come to completion when all the pieces were properly assembled. The image that science traditionally provided of the world of continuities and equilibria, has disappeared. Science no longer satisfied the notion that reality is something concrete. Instead, science has become preoccupied with discontinuities, disequilibria and relativities. Moreover, in contrast to the past, science was becoming more of a public property due to the growth of educational institutions and concern with public education.

Discoveries of new phenomena like X-rays, radioactivity, wireless telegraphy and the theory of evolution, were not secrets hidden in laboratories but they were publicly discussed. They were producing images that were not thinkable before. For example, the discovery by Roentgen in 1895 of what has become known as X-rays fascinated not only the science world but also the art world and the general public. The possibilities of seeing the human body through clothes and even through skin and flesh inspired a multitude of images and new representations. These images of X-rays ranged from those that were something like an extension of photography, to those that invoked extrasensory reality and occult phenomena (Henderson, 1998).

The discovery of X-rays also became a strong argument against positivism relying on the sense data. Sensation and reality were now clearly recognised as being two different things and this recognition contradicted everything that had been previously considered as certain. Artists of the time, like the Czech mystic painter František Kupka and the French painter Marcel Duchamp, were fascinated by X-ray imagery. Duchamp's paintings of the time, specifically, represented X-ray images of demate-rialised forms, transparent figures and the fourth dimension of figures. Both Duchamp and Kupka were exploring X-ray plates in order to rep-resent invisible realities in their paintings (Henderson, 1998).

This science not only revolutionalised laboratories and arts but it also had a profound influence on literature, public education and public com-mon sense. Popular art, songs, cartoons and advertisements presented abundant images of the invisible possibilities of the world that exists beyond senses and which the senses cannot capture: the extrasensory world. Science of the twentieth century has become a major source of occult ideas, it supplied images of immortality as well as images of the imminent death of the universe.

In her brilliant analysis of the effect of this science on literature and more generally, on public education, Beer (1993) draws attention to its conflicting epistemologies, relativism and the cerebration of disequilibria as the conditions of life. It was thought important that this science would also reach the general public. Beer comments that the physicist Clerk Maxwell hoped that thanks to this new science 'the intelligent public' would be weaned from determinism. Instead, he expected that the public would pursue 'the study of the singularities and instabilities, rather than the continuities and stabilities of things' (Campbell and Garnett, 1882, p. 444). We could speculate that transformation of this scientific knowl-edge into common sense knowledge, with its new images of far reaching possibilities, might require more varied, and indeed, different forms of thinking than those necessitated by the earlier science.

3.3   Against the point of view that 'le peuple ne pense pas'

In contrast to Durkheim, Moscovici has lived through the science of dis-continuities, instabilities and relativities. Equally important, he has lived through the age of social sciences that have been profoundly shaped by two world wars and by totalitarian regimes like Nazism and Soviet com-munism. Thus, when he asks questions like 'How is scientific knowledge transformed into common or spontaneous knowledge?' (Moscovici and Marková, 2000, p. 228), and, more specifically, 'how are scientific dis-coveries transformed into social representations?', the meanings of these questions are very different from Durkheim's epistemological concerns.

The question of science and its meaning, Moscovici (Moscovici and Marková, 2000) comments, was an attractive topic for the young gener-ation in the late 1940s and early 1950s, when he was a political refugee in Paris and a student at the Sorbonne University. He says about that:

There was a problem that my generation widely debated: the problem of science. It was after all the problem of modernity. We were all interested in understanding in what ways science had an impact on historical change, on our thinking or our social prospects. All young people who were attracted by Marxism, communism and socialism were preoccupied by the question of science, technology and such matters (Moscovici and Marková, 2000, p. 227).

He was not, at that time, interested in how science affects everyday thinking and how scientific ideas could become part of common beliefs. However, to move from an issue like 'in what ways science had an impact on historical change' and 'on our thinking' was an easy step to the question as to what happens to scientific ideas when they spread to community. This question became important for him after he had initiated the study of social representations of psychoanalysis in the late 1950s. For him, specifically, that question has had a life-long significance. Even at the beginning of the Second World War (cf. Moscovici and Marková, 2000, p. 227) he was critical of the Marxist and Lenin's point of view that spontaneous and common knowledge is inferior because people cannot think rationally, that 'le peuple ne pense pas'. Marxists insisted that spontaneous knowledge contains many irrational ideas like folk myths, religious beliefs and reactionary and idealistic views. The Marxist, materialistic and scientific view of humans and of history and nature should substitute this irrationality in the process of the development of a socialist man and woman. Moscovici comments: 'Marxists did not believe that the diffusion of scientific knowledge could improve common knowledge or thinking. The former had to eradicate the latter' (Moscovici and Marková, 2000, p. 227).

3.4   *Common sense as a social sense*

One cannot understand the concept of social representation without taking a fresh look at common sense knowledge. Humans are born into symbolic and cultural phenomena and they do not invent everything by themselves in their individual experiences. These facts do not need to be laboured. Cultural phenomena, into which we are born, like the modes of social thinking, collective ceremonies, social practices and language, are transmitted from generation to generation through daily experience, communication, collective memory and institutions, often without much individual effort and without much cognisable change. These phenomena form the large panorama of our social realities and become imprinted in our common sense knowledge.

Thus, through common sense knowledge we intuitively know what kinds of things are and are not edible, we use moral categories like

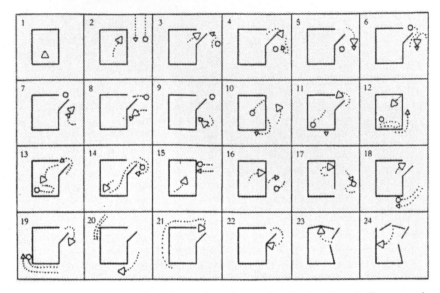

Figure 5.1 Outline of story in a picture film. Broken lines indicate a path of movement. From Heider (1967). Copyright © 1967 by the American Psychological Association. Reprinted with permission.

good/bad, we treat people as agents who are responsible for their actions and we learn to understand specific meanings of words. For instance, in interpersonal interaction we treat others as agents who have intentions, goals and motives. We spontaneously understand their bodily movements as intentional actions. We perceive activities as meaningful wholes rather than as disconnected movements. Classic examples of these facts come from experimental demonstrations of Heider and Simmel's (1944) cartoon film (Figure 5.1), showing movements of three geometric figures in time and space. 'Objectively' speaking, the cartoon shows no more than the changing positions of triangles and a circle in a sequential order.

Despite that, individuals who take part in these demonstrations have no difficulty in seeing directly these changing positions of geometrical figures as meaningful actions guided by goals, intentions, reasons and motives. They use words attributing the meanings to interactions and diagnosing them as chasing, following, pursuing, being in love, being jealous, and so on.

In a similar manner, From's (1971) filmed demonstrations of simple activities such as a man moving his hand down his thigh, then up under the bottom of his jacket and so on, have shown that such movements are spontaneously interpreted as meaningful and connected actions. Observers of these filmed demonstrations did not see simple movements of a man's hand in time and space. Instead, they saw a man lighting his pipe, a man leaving a room, a man sitting, writing or a man smoking his pipe. Such results, of course, are not at all surprising to anybody who shares, in general terms, the same culture as did the participants of From's and Heider and Simmel's demonstrations. Indeed, our perceptions and cognitions of others are so ingrained in our minds that we abstain from questioning to whether what we 'see' is correct and thus, we relinquish alternative explanations of others' actions and of the contexts within which they operate. Common sense knowledge is a kind of knowledge that is taken as certain and that does not leave any space for doubt. It is socially established. Common sense, Moscovici argues, is a social sense (Moscovici, 1998b/2000; also Bergson, 1932/1935). Common sense knowledge constitutes a fundamental resource for the theory of social representations as a theory of social knowledge.

3.5   *Common sense knowledge and scientific knowledge*

Philosophically, interest in common sense knowledge goes back to Aristotle. Historically, common sense knowledge has been one of the main resources for the development of scientific knowledge. Despite this, throughout the development of civilisation, common sense knowledge has been treated, implicitly or explicitly, as inferior to scientific knowledge. More specifically, natural science has become associated with the power of reason and rationality. In contrast, folk knowledge, beliefs and myths of common sense knowledge have been affiliated with lack of rationality or even with irrationality. This perspective dominated rationalism of the seventeenth and eighteenth centuries, Enlightenment, Marxism, and more generally, the generations of philosophers and social scientists defending Cartesian rationalism. Let us consider the views of some rationalists that have had a significant influence in social sciences.

Chomsky argues that the study of common sense knowledge could be of interest only to the extent that it is based on 'naturalistic inquiry', i.e. on its study from the perspective of natural sciences. Since in his study of the mind/brain he always likens organs of the body to the organs of the mind/brain and considers that they are localised in the mind/brain, he also transposes this metaphor to the faculty of common sense. More specifically, Chomsky even refers to a science-forming faculty on the one hand and to a faculty that yields common sense on the other. While the products of the science-forming faculty constitute fragments of scientific understanding, the common sense faculty grows and penetrates into the semantics of language and into belief systems. For him, it is 'a commonplace that any similarities to common sense notions [in science] are of no consequence for science' and he believes that with progress in understanding, scientific theories will become 'divested of the distorting residues of common-sense understanding' (Chomsky, 2000, pp. 22 and 23). His perspective degrades common sense thinking to something that is of no scientific interest and that is conceptually inferior.

Ernest Gellner, the important sociologist and philosopher, held similar views on common sense knowledge to those of Chomsky. In his influential book *Reason and Culture* Gellner (1992) claimed, in the Cartesian spirit that human rationality is innate, universal and that it exists independently of cultures. Although all humans have a *potential* for rationality, it is culture and common sense knowledge, which may hinder this potential. While 'reason is latent in us all', 'most cultures fail to promote it' (1992, p. 53). As a result, the universal potential for rationality that exists in all humans results in two kinds of knowledge. The first kind of knowledge is universal. It originates from the universal rationality and therefore, it is knowledge that comes from the mind of the individual. The individual achieves it on his own: 'we discover truth alone, we err in groups' (Gellner, 1998, p. 3). This kind of knowledge is superior and it is entirely rational. The laws of physics and mathematics, for example, must be universally valid in order to count as scientific laws. Scientific rationality follows the principle that concepts must subscribe to the same rules in relation to evidence; rationality rejects contradiction and the logic of the argument must be seen through. The ideals of scientific knowledge are universal truths.

The second kind of knowledge, Gellner argued, is communitarian and cultural. It is less rational and therefore, it is inferior. This knowledge is a product of the collective. Gellner points out that this kind of knowledge endorses the hypothesis that no individual can achieve knowledge on his own, but that knowledge is essentially 'a team game'. Individuals interpret and understand the world in terms of concepts, which have been transmitted to them from generation to generation through culture and language.[8]

While the former kind of knowledge is universalistic, the latter is relativistic; the former represents rationality and reason, whereas the latter represents irrationality and culture.

For rationalists, the capacity to think rationally has emerged in the process of anthropogenesis involving cognitive, innate and universal capacities of *the individual*. During ontogenesis, this capacity unfolds throughout the development of the individual's cognition.

In contrast to rationalism, dialogicality is based on the hypothesis that rational thinking has emerged in anthropogenesis due to the *Ego-Alter* dialogical relation. Therefore, *the cognitive capacity to think rationally is by definition the capacity to communicate.* The capacity to think rationally and to communicate constitutes the potential for common sense thinking. Rationality, we can say therefore, is not an *individual rationality* but a *dialogical rationality.* Thinking and language originate from the *Ego-Alter* antinomy and consequently, common sense knowledge is both the source and the product of dialogical rationality.

When we are born into society and culture, we are also born into common sense knowledge. It is all around us and we adopt it for better or worse. For example, we learn unwittingly to eat certain kinds of things and to avoid others, we adopt cultural criteria of beauty and ugliness, morality and immorality and we are socialised into common sense physics. We learn these things through communication, through daily activities and through our own activities. Common sense knowledge is also interwoven with diverse forms of thinking, knowing and communicating. For example, it guides us in conversations, it structures our daily routines and organises social encounters. It also comprises manifold kinds of knowing like beliefs, myths, understanding interpersonal relations, experiential knowing and practical skills. Since common sense knowledge guides humankind through living, directs attention to danger as well as to the extension and satisfaction of life and is the source of scientific knowledge – where do we have evidence that it is inferior? As Moscovici argues, common sense knowledge is accompanied by a variety of cognitive goals ranging from 'a search for truth, persuasion and exerting power, to seduction and the enjoyment of life' (Moscovici and Marková, 2000, p. 246). For a social psychologist, therefore, common sense knowledge forms an enormous source of ideas, imagination and of social scientific research.

Before pursuing the ideas about common sense further let us not forget the following point. The two alternative perspectives, the one concerning *individual rationality* and the one concerning *dialogical rationality* are two different hypotheses about what it is to be human. Scientifically, neither of these hypotheses can claim that they provide conclusive evidence about the nature of rationality, i.e. that it emerges in the mind of the individual or that it emerges from *Ego-Alter* interdependence. All we can claim is that they are two competing hypotheses and they should be treated *as* hypotheses, despite the fact that the former, the one based on individual rationality, has dominated European thought for centuries. This of course does not prevent us, in this book, from treating dialogicality as the more plausible of the two hypotheses.

Rationalists like Chomsky and Gellner are explicitly outspoken about the unequal status of the two kinds of knowledge, i.e. scientific and common sense knowledge. However, even those who accept the parity between common sense and scientific knowledge, often make allusions that send similar signals concerning the unequal status of these two kinds of knowledge. For example, in psychology, there are well-established points of view that compare knowledge based on common sense and scientific knowledge.

Fritz Heider (1958), in discussing common sense psychology, recognises its significance in everyday life. He defends the point of view that scientific psychology has a great deal to learn from common sense psychology. He points out that all psychologists use common sense ideas in developing their scientific theories. Nevertheless, despite the fact that Heider aims to support the significance of common sense knowledge, unfortunately, he blurs the matter. When discussing common sense psychological knowledge, Heider calls it *naïve* knowledge and he compares it to a naïve physics, which relies on non-scientific ways of understanding of simple mechanical laws in everyday life. In other words, Heider implies that even naivety can be useful in scientific thinking!

Psychologists often present the image depending on whether scientific and common sense thinking are similar to one another. Gruber (1973), in discussing Darwin's scientific work, describes creative activities of children and likens them to those of scientists. He argues that just like children are born into the already existing world, so creative scientists find themselves in the world of existing social, scientific and semi-scientific ideas. In order to develop their own ideas, both children and scientists must depart from those ideas that are commonly accepted by their culture. They have to cope with pressure from others and with fear of punishment for non-conformity.

More recently, again in developmental psychology, Gopnik and Meltzoff (1997) suggest that our ordinary and everyday thinking should be viewed as being analogous to scientific thinking because these two kinds of thinking have similar qualities. While the authors do not say that children actually make science, they insist that the cognitive processes that underlie scientific thinking are identical to the cognitive processes that underlie cognitive development: 'Scientific progress is possible because scientists employ cognitive processes that are first seen in very young children' (1997, p. 32).

All these metaphors, that either turn naïve people into scientists or that liken scientific thinking to cognitive processes of young children, are seductive. Their authors not only present arguments showing that common sense knowledge and scientific knowledge are underlined by similar cognitive processes; they also pinpoint some common problems shared by children and scientists, like pressure towards conformity and fear of punishment. Nevertheless, these metaphors hide some essential differences between the logic of science and the scientific method on the one hand, and the logic of common sense and the method of common sense, on the other.

3.6   Studying the products of knowledge

Throughout his academic career Moscovici has argued that common sense knowledge and scientific knowledge are two essentially different yet complementary kinds of knowledge. They are based on different kinds of rationality. Through history and culture, scientific and common sense knowledge have each developed their specific kind of logic and different methods of thinking. Accordingly, these two kinds of knowledge, scientific and common sense knowledge are irreducible to one another and one cannot replace the other. Moscovici's argument, which is essential to the theory of social representations, is often misunderstood and therefore, we must consider it in some detail.

We have already presented the hypothesis that humans are *born with dialogical rationality* (cf. also Newson, 1979, Trevarthen, 1979, 1992). We claim, at the same time, that they are *not* born with *scientific rationality*. They are born into common sense knowledge but they are *not* born into scientific knowledge. Moscovici brings to our attention the fact that scientific rationality and scientific knowledge is something that humans acquire in the process of education (Moscovici and Marková, 2000). Those who present us with metaphors concerning children's and scientists' thinking (see above) ignore the following important point.

Scientific knowledge is a specialised knowledge. In order to become a scientist, the individual is educated in a specialised way. She needs to acquire a specific intellectual discipline in order to pursue scientific tasks, as well as the ways of thinking that enable scientists to continue work that others have been unable to complete. The scientist needs to be able to build on other people's knowledge and reach beyond. This means to evaluate critically and consciously build on the work of previous scientists. Whether the scientist chooses to continue working on something that others carried out before him or to originate something 'totally' new, he must acquire scientific ways of reasoning. Science formalises theoretical reasoning; its ideal is universal knowledge independent of the content of the phenomena it examines. It constantly doubts the products of his knowledge.

Scientific knowledge, although it is generated from social knowledge, acquires, to a considerable extent, an individualised and a monologised character. Although we must not be too dogmatic about it, this means that the scientist develops above all his own scientific perspective, often independently of others and sometimes in spite of others. Scientific creation is a largely individualised process despite its implicit social nature.

Scientific knowledge, Moscovici observes (Moscovici and Marková, 2000, pp. 246–7), is studied from the point of view of its *products*. In order to explore the nature of scientific knowledge, a researcher or a practitioner comes to analyse scientific theories, to examine the relevant experiments and to review research articles or written documents. He may also observe how research is carried out in the laboratory or in the field. Hardly ever is scientific thinking examined through psychological tests of reasoning, memory tasks, syllogism, statistical inferences and information processing tasks in order to find out how scientists think, and whether or not they are 'biased'.

In contrast to scientific knowledge common sense knowledge is not usually studied through its products, but it is studied in psychological laboratories from information on how ordinary people 'think'. Experimental subjects are given artificial tasks of syllogism, anagrams, nonsense syllables and so on, so that their 'distortions' in thinking process and their 'biases' in thinking are exposed. For example, the notion of error has always been crucial to studies in deductive reasoning. In these studies, the standards of thinking have been the Aristotelian logic of syllogisms and the formal logic of propositional and predicate calculus. An error of thinking in such reasoning tasks has been defined as an arrival at a conclusion that differs from the one determined by the rules of syllogistic inference or by the logical calculus (Marková, 1982, p. 33).

Such experiments sometimes acknowledge that the content of the task has an effect on subjects' thinking or that it may 'bias' the ways in which subjects approach the problem. However, *the content of the task* has rarely been the subject of study despite the fact that common sense thinking is embedded in common sense knowledge of phenomena around us. Therefore, scientific knowledge on the one hand and common sense knowledge on the other, have been studied in very different manners. The products of common sense knowledge exist everywhere around us, in discourse, human activities, texts, language, folklore, and in literature. These products are based on and developed from, what I have called above, a dialogical rationality. These products include different kinds of knowing. Some of them concern interpersonal relations, others involve daily routines, yet others concern common sense knowledge of specific objects and phenomena like an animal, a human, France, the United Kingdom, and so on. Common sense knowledge never concerns the knowledge of objects and phenomena in isolation but of objects and phenomena in relation to one another.

At this point the reader may pose the question: 'You have discussed these two kinds of knowledge, scientific and common sense, but you have not operationalised common sense knowledge. What is common sense knowledge?' I have argued throughout this book that we cannot define social phenomena in the way that we define physical objects like bananas or hammers. Social phenomena are dialogical phenomena in relations. It is meaningless to define them as independent entities. We can only define or characterise them with respect to other social phenomena. In this chapter I have presented common sense knowledge *in relation to*, or in antinomy to, scientific knowledge. Common sense knowledge of course could be in antinomy to other kinds of knowledge, e.g. professional knowledge, knowing how, knowledge of rules and norms. These different kinds of antinomy all foreground different features of common sense knowledge because they are parts of different kinds of relation. The human mind always sees phenomena in relations.

The choice, in this chapter, to oppose scientific knowledge and common sense knowledge, has been determined, in the study of social representations, by historical and epistemological reasons. Moscovici started studying social representations by drawing a distinction between these two kinds of knowledge. He was concerned with the traditional argument that 'le peuple ne pense pas'; that common knowledge is inferior to scientific knowledge. This has also given him an opportunity to reflect on the fact that scientific knowledge, despite being social in its origin, is usually produced by individuals or by small groups of scientists. Common sense knowledge, in contrast, retains its genuinely dialogical character.

3.7   From common sense knowledge to social representations

The relations between common sense knowledge and social representations now need to be characterised.

Any object or phenomenon, whether physical (e.g. a kitchen), interpersonal (e.g. friendship), imaginary (e.g. a Loch Ness monster) or socio-political (e.g. democracy), can become an object of a social representation. However, this does not mean that the theory of social representations studies 'just anything'.[9] Despite the fact that we can 'know' and 'represent' any conceivable phenomena, *the theory of social representations and communication* studies very specific kinds of representations. It studies and builds the theory about those social phenomena that have become, for one reason or other, the subject of public concern. These phenomena that are thought about and discussed, they are phenomena that cause tension and provoke actions. Such phenomena in public discourse can pertain to different kinds of *Ego-Alter*, i.e. to individuals, groups or societies that *actively engage in thinking and communicating* about such phenomena.

Let us explain. Psychoanalysis became the subject of Moscovici's study of social representations in the late 1950s. At that time, psychoanalysis was the subject of intense public interest. Notions that were part of the professional vocabulary on psychoanalysis proliferated into daily language and became subjects of metaphors and puns. They diagnosed relationships and personal activities. This, however, did not happen by a peaceful transfer of scientific vocabulary into daily language. Moscovici (Moscovici and Marková, 2000, p. 239) described the penetration of psychoanalysis into public life as a cultural fight and an intellectual polemic between different ideologies.

Social representations of such specific phenomena, like psychoanalysis, are embedded in, or interrelate with, various social practices and with professional and scientific discourses. This means that social representations must be extracted, by social scientific methods, e.g. by observation, analytical methods or by thought (*Gedanke*) experiments, from common sense knowledge, from practices, and from discourses in which they are embedded or with which they interrelate. In other words, while for Durkheim collective representations referred to different activities of the mind, social representations are concerned with specifically defined phenomena that must be analytically discovered. Not 'everything' is a social representation. Let us consider a concrete example.

In hospitals for people with learning disabilities, for instance, we can find different kinds of discourses and social practices. These may include:
- medical and social routines and activities, e.g. those arising from attempts to improve the quality of life and independence of residents;
- practices and discourses determined by economic constraints. For example, economic conditions of the country determine the proportion of resources assigned to learning disability;
- political demands of self-help groups;
- practices resulting from various kinds of social problems like overcrowding, low motivation of staff, insufficient number of trained staff;
- historically rooted social practices, e.g. of a religious nature. For example, Andrew Jahoda (1995) has analysed social practices in mental handicap hospitals throughout history. He has shown that many hospitals for people with learning disabilities in the nineteenth century were prompted by Christian principles. At the same time some people believed that learning disability was a divine punishment for parental immorality. Still others believed that learning disability was a throwback to primitive stages of man. Such differences in beliefs instill different communicative and behavioural patterns among those involved in the daily activities of residents in hospitals.

- totalitarian or democratic routines in political systems of the country as a whole, which reflect themselves in daily life and which also manifest themselves in hospital practices. For example, authoritarian practices based on obedience outside hospital may have a strong projection inside hospital.

Thus we see that social practices and the ways they are spoken about, involve a variety of heterogeneous phenomena, some of which might involve social representations, while others could reflect political, economic and institutional issues. It is not always easy to distinguish between these different discourses and practices on the one hand and social representations on the other. The task of the researcher is to extract social representations from these discourses, practices and common sense knowledge, using analytical procedures and theoretical concepts. This task constitutes and will continue to constitute a challenge for the theory of social representations for years to come.

NOTES

1. Durkheim used the concept 'collective representation' and 'social representation' interchangeably, although he used 'collective representation' more often.
2. In contrast to Durkheim, who, as Pickering observes, did not change his theory of collective representations throughout his life, Moscovici has substantially developed the theory of social representations and communication over the years. At the beginning his theory was more informed by Piaget and later more by Durkheim. Today, the theory of social representations and communication stands much on its own as a theory of social knowledge clearly grounded in dialogical epistemology.
3. In his analysis of Kant's metaphysics, Walsh (1975, p. 89) comments that this question cannot be easily answered. It is not clear from Kant's expressions, whether appearances (and therefore representations) belong to a private or to a common experience. It is not clear whether it is the structure of the mind that produces representations or whether representations are socially constructed.

   In this ambiguity, however, we can already see an impending problem: individual representation versus collective representation. This problem, however, was not just a problem of Kantian philosophy. It was the problem of the time. Antinomies between the individual and society were felt everywhere in economic and political changes, in struggles for democratisation, equality, rights and for social recognition in general (Chapter 7). Antinomy between the individual and the social also emerged in new concepts of language. Among others, Kant's contemporary, Wilhelm von Humbold, was preoccupied with the nature of the social and individual in language.
4. It is only when Durkheim was concerned with ethics and morals that he explicitly treated language as action that binds society together by contractual relations and solidarity. The declarations of moral significance are carried out by means of words which have 'power to bind and compel those who pronounce

them' (Durkheim, 1957, p. 186). In particular, when specific words are expressed in specific rituals, they assume a sacred quality and impose respect or a contract. A contract has a meaning only if both parties in communication accept it as binding. If the will of fulfilling contract is missing on either side, the contract is empty: 'All that is pronounced is words devoid of meaning and so, devoid of value' (1957, p. 203). One could interpret Durkheim's ideas as pre-empting the analytic Oxford speech act theory and specifically, Austin's perlocutionary act 'I promise' (cf. also Nerlich and Clark, 1996). This is probably the closest point where Durkheim approached the notion of interaction and communication, which he saw as an exchange, as placing someone in obligation. This particular subject of exchange, and of gift as an exchange, later developed Durkheim's nephew Marcel Mauss.

5. In other words, new representations cannot be explained only through recombination of past representations but through the study of contemporary social structures. Piaget applauds this genetic method and in fact, this is something which he himself adopted from Durkheim (Moscovici, 1998). Piaget continues with Durkheim's rationalism. While Durkheim starts with thought and representations as social facts and from these he derives action, Moscovici shows that Piaget reversed this process. Piaget starts from action and arrives at thought. Like Durkheim, he hypothesised an uninterrupted continuity, in his case from child to adult.

6. Although Durkheim did not study beliefs systematically, Pickering (2000d) and his colleagues argue that the theory of collective representations is in fact a theory of belief and that, indeed, belief is a synonym for collective representation (Paoletti, 2000, p. 129).

7. As we noted in Chapter 4, the Marxist point of view also emphasised the idea of continuity in progress.

8. To illustrate ways of life, Gellner refers to the well-known distinction between *Gesellschaft* and *Gemeinschaft*, society and community, respectively. *Gesellschaft* consists of a society of anonymous individuals, liberalism, free markets and 'open' society. In contrast, as a way of life, *Gemeinschaft* binds together members of a community with romantic ideas of cultural closeness, of uniqueness and distinctiveness of culture. Gellner applies these two conceptions of knowledge specifically to Central Europe where these two styles were present in the nineteenth and twentieth centuries. In particular, they were characteristic of the Habsburg empire but one can find them also in other socio-historical contexts. In discussing *Gesellschaft* versus *Gemeinschaft*, Gellner does not define analytically the distinction between the two kinds of knowledge, but presents them descriptively. In the former case he characterises knowledge as a relationship between the sole individual and nature and in the latter case as a team or collective game (Gellner, 1998, p. 6).

9. We have pointed out earlier in this chapter that for Durkheim *any mental activity* was a representation.

6 Dialogical triads and three-component processes

1 Thinking in triads

1.1 The magic number three

Let us recapitulate. Traditional epistemologies require *two separate elements* to explain the process of knowing: first, monological and solipsistic knowers, either individuals or collectives; and second, the objects of knowledge.

In Platonic/Cartesian theories of knowledge the knower is an *individual*. Continuing on this tradition, modern cognitive-computational theories often reduce the knower to the mind/brain (Chapter 1), which contains specialised computational devices enabling the process of knowing. These devices analyse information or translate information from one specific form into another one. The process of knowing involves the formation and reproduction of *mental representations*.

Alternatively, the knower is a *collective*. The idea of a collective knower, collective consciousness or a crowd soul was quite common in sociology in the nineteenth century. The collective knower also figures in the sociological theory of knowledge of Emile Durkheim. The collective knower, i.e. society, observes and interprets social facts, which exist *a priori* as a given social reality. Society regulates and sanctions activities of individuals who, as a result, reproduce social facts. In this case, the process of knowing involves the formation and reproduction of *collective representations*.

In both cases, traditional theories of knowledge provide descriptions and causal explanations surrounding the object of knowledge. They are both depicted in Figures 6.1 and 6.2.

In contrast to solipsistic and monological knowers of traditional epistemologies, be they individual mind/brains or collectives, the knower in a dialogically based theory of knowledge is the *Ego-Alter*. Therefore, a dialogically based theory of knowledge requires the *Ego-Alter* and the object of knowledge to be the starting point of enquiry.

If the *theory of social knowledge* starts from the *Ego-Alter* and from the object of knowledge, we are faced with the following question. What kinds

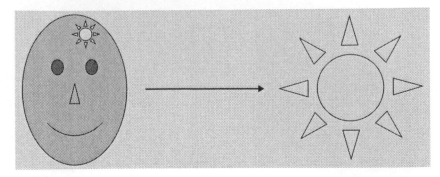

Figure 6.1 Mental representation

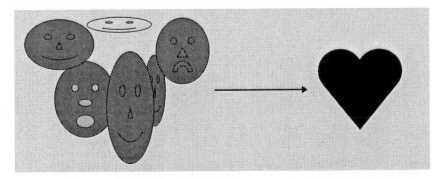

Figure 6.2 Collective representation

of conceptual tool do we need in this theory of social knowledge? We need to find out how to proceed from *dialogicality of the Ego-Alter*, which we have already hypothesised as *ontology* of humanity, to *dialogical theory of social knowledge* based on the *Ego-Alter-Object*. How do we conceptualise this magic three?

The magic number three comes not only from fairy-tales, from the three wishes, the three trials and the three wonder words. Triadic models of various kinds have pervaded the whole history of humankind. Triads represent religious images of God, we can find them in the mediaeval magic (cf. Chapter 2) and in different kinds of dialectic that are based on the resolution of two conflicting components into the third component. Fichte's and Hegel's dialectics, based on the thesis-antithesis-synthesis, are but examples, among many others, of thinking in triads. Semiotic relations, too, have been commonly modelled as triadic. Above all, Peirce's semiotic theory of the growth of knowledge[1] attempted to explain communication and knowledge by means of triadic signs.

More recently, the triangles of representations have become incarnated in literary theory, politics, history and philosophy (e.g. Prendergast,

2000). These various triadic semiotic conceptions and the underlying triangles of representations are based on heterogeneous theoretical presuppositions that serve different purposes. These semiotic conceptions all argue that human symbolic functions cannot be captured on the basis of a single element or two elements because symbols are constructed socially. In order to account for a social construction you need an individual, a society and an object. Nevertheless, not all of these triangles of representation are pertinent to our case. We cannot make magic simply because we have found three elements that can be juggled together.

1.2   Bühler's triadic organon model of communication and representation

Let us start with Karl Bühler's triangle of representation, which is perhaps more relevant to our case than other triangles of representation. In the early part of the twentieth century Karl Bühler (1982) argued that in order to understand the nature of knowledge and language, we must not look for it in the cognition of the individual. Analysing the social nature of the mind, this anti-Cartesian philosopher, psychologist and linguist assumed that what constitutes the mind is 'the social matrix of language' rather than 'the individual-related speech act'.

Bühler studied signs and meanings in communication. For him, signs and meanings were socially constructed through an irreducible mutuality between the sign-giver and the sign-receiver.[2] All languages have their own grammatical, semantic and pragmatic means to serve their representational or symbolic functions. They thematise social reality in the manner that is specific to each language (Bühler, 1934/1990). All linguistic signs are related to specific fields of practice and each field of practice requires specific symbols or representations to make communication possible.

The concept of representation figures in Bühler's organon model. This model is based on the idea that language accomplishes three functions: expressive, appealing and representational. Representation does not refer to the mind as mirroring the external world. The conception of mirroring would imply, again, the separation of the object of knowledge from the mind, a kind of Kantian thing-in-itself and its cognitive representation. Rather, a representation in Bühler's sense is the capacity of the mind to imagine, to fantasise and to create something new, using symbols in the field to which they apply.

It was on these grounds that Bühler postulated triad *Ego-Alter-Object* (representation) as the basis of his semiotic theory of knowledge (Figure 6.3). This figure clearly shows that knowledge of an object is co-constructed by the *Ego* and the *Alter*. The *Alter* is not just another person but a group or a society. It is the triad *Ego-Alter-Object* that, for Bühler, is the unit producing knowledge.

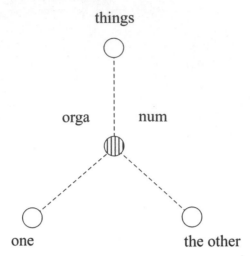

Figure 6.3 Bühler's organon model. From Bühler (1934). Copyright © 1990 John Benjamins B.V., reproduced by permission

With the triadic relation *Ego-Alter-Object* we now have a unit of knowledge, which radically differs from the unit constituted by the knower-object of traditional epistemologies. This unit cannot be decomposed into its constituents, the *Ego*, the *Alter* and the *Object*. The *Ego-Alter-Object* can function only as a whole. If we decomposed this unit into its constituents and if we treated them separately from one another, we would be back to the traditional epistemology.

Although we now have a different unit of knowledge, we have not resolved the essential question. The triad *Ego-Alter-Object is not intrinsically dynamic* and therefore, it could still refer to knowledge as a stable relation rather than to *knowledge as a dynamic relation*. Despite Bühler's claim that the *Ego*, the *Alter* and the *Object* are interdependent, he did not show what it is that makes their interdependence dynamic. In fact, he was not concerned with that issue.

If the frame of reference in traditional epistemologies was *stability*, the frame of reference in the theory of social knowledge is *change*. Therefore, we need to face Moscovici's question: How can static epistemologies be transformed into dynamic epistemologies? How can we transform Karl Bühler's unit the *Ego-Alter-Object* in order to make it dynamic?

1.3   Dialogical tension

The term 'tension' is not the one, which social sciences in general, and psychology specifically, enthusiastically incorporate in their scientific terminologies, despite the fact that 'tension' has been used for centuries in medical, biological and physical sciences. In medicine and in the natural sciences 'tension' refers to strain, pressure or to being stretched.

Tension arises from activities of different forces. For example, it comes from conflicting powers within a single entity, like attraction and repulsion in electricity and magnetism, or between the organism and its environment. However, sewing machines also have 'tension devices' as a dictionary explains: 'By adjustment of the pressure at the tension device, the required tightness of stitch is obtained' because 'a loose tension will produce a flabby, ill-fitting garment' (*The Oxford Modern English Dictionary*, 1992). Nevertheless, while low tension will produce a flabby garment, low-tension systems of electricity are safer and cheaper than high-tension systems! High tension can lead to nervous exhaustion, anger, violence or a sudden collapse.

Terms like 'distension', 'extension', and 'pretension' all accord with 'tension' and the variant 'tention' agrees with 'attention', 'intention' and 'contention'. These dictionary meanings all show that the notion of tension is polysemic and that it has different applications both in daily language and in sciences. Yet these meanings have one sense in common: the notion of tension expresses impetus to an action or to a change.

The study of tension in psychology has been very limited and apart from the work of Kurt Lewin and Sigmund Freud, there is not much to be found. However, in the work of these two psychologists, tension is viewed either as a force to solve conflicts or as a negative and a damaging force. Kurt Lewin beautifully depicted tension in behavioural activities of young children and captured them in his films[3] in the late 1920s. These films show in great detail that it is tension that motivates the child to resolve problems and to achieve goals he sets for himself. Both Lewin and Freud considered tension as a force to resolve the individual's problem arising from the choice between conflicting alternatives or between own goals and obstacles posed by the environment. The balance of the organism is re-established through the reduction of tension.

However, tension is implicit in all life situations although it may not be explicitly regarded as such. For example, in everyday life and in professional contexts we often hear that in order to instigate individuals or groups to action, we need to increase their awareness of the main issue. Thus, health campaigns attempt to increase public awareness of risks attached to smoking, drugs or lack of exercise. Or, training courses attempt to increase professionals' awareness of the difficulties involved in communication with people with a disability. These well-meant practices, however, often ignore the fact that knowledge and awareness as such are insufficient to instigate action. We can have as much knowledge and awareness about the issue in question as we like, but unless that knowledge creates tension and conflict in the self and groups, action is unlikely to be taken.

The experience of contradiction, to which Hegel already drew attention and which he called 'the root of all movement and vitality' is not enough to instigate action. It is not contradiction that living organisms must endure in order to live, but it is tension and conflict arising from contradiction that is the source of action and vitality. The concept of tension is *implicit* in Hegel's master/slave parable (see Chapter 7, note 2).

In Karcevskij's theory of meaning (Chapter 3) and the change of meaning, the concept of tension is indispensable. Similarly, in Rosenzweig's and Bakhtin's dialogical theory tension is the source of dialogical change. Tension is inherent in the relation *Ego-Alter* and, by implication, in the theory of social representations and communication. There can be no communication unless the participants are drawn together by tension. There can be no social action – unless oppositions in tension confront one another, are negotiated, evaluated and judged.

We can suggest that the attempts to achieve goals and to reduce tension are no more than specific instances of the dialogical tension.

2   Dialogical triad

Throughout his whole academic career Moscovici has always placed emphasis on tension as the force of change. In contrast to Bühler's *Ego-Alter-Object*, what makes Moscovici's (1984a) semiotic triangle *Ego-Alter-Object* (Figure 6.4) dynamic, is the presence of tension.

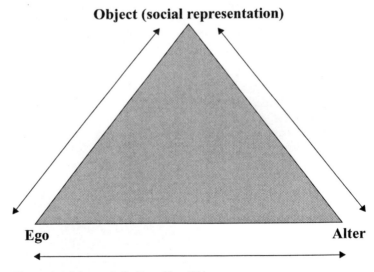

Object (social representation)

Ego   **Alter**

Figure 6.4 Moscovici's *Ego-Alter-Object*

With tension we have a *dialogical triad*, the dynamic unit of the theory of social knowledge. The *Ego-Alter-Object* is a triad within which the components are internally related. As in Bühler's triad, if the components are internally related the unit can function only as an organic whole that cannot be decomposed into its parts.

2.1 Components in dialogical triads are bound together by internal relations

In order to explain the meaning of internal relations between the *Ego-Alter-Object* let us consider two examples from rather different spheres of social science.

Our first example comes from the extract of a conversation between two individuals. One of them has cerebral palsy and his speech is severely impaired. The other person is a carer in the day-centre, which the participant with impaired speech attends on a daily basis. In the extract below the impaired speaker tries to explain to his carer that on Monday, at 8 o'clock in the morning, he watches a television programme called 'Wheel of fortune'. The dialogical triad is constituted of the *Ego* (impaired speaker)-the *Alter* (carer)-*Object* (the television programme 'Wheel of Fortune'). The *Ego-Alter* dyad is in a dialogical and collaborative relation. What is problematic in their dialogue is to identify the *Object*. The person with unimpaired speech could say 'I watch *Wheel of Fortune* on Monday at 8 o'clock in the morning' using a single sentence. In contrast, someone with a speech disorder will need to apply a strategy in which each part of the message must be well understood by the other participant so that he can piece the parts together into a meaningful whole.

The sequence starts with the impaired speaker's gaze directed to the wall, while pointing his finger at the carer and at the same time vocalising 'omu'ay'.[4] The carer watches the impaired speaker in his attempt to comprehend 'omu'ay'. The impaired speaker consistently redraws the circle with his fingers and points to the chart and to the carer. Both participants are simultaneously directed to one another and their vocal, verbal and non-verbal gestures could be only artificially decomposed into independent components. Instead, their vocal, verbal and non-verbal gestures are integrated and synchronised. The carer needs to discover several things in order to identify the *Object*. He must interpret the impaired speaker's dialogical contributions
- 'omu'ay' as 'on Monday',
- the circle drawn with fingers as a wheel
- the connection between the expression 'omu'ay' and the drawn circle

- the gesture of pointing at a chart on the wall as the object showing television programmes
- the impaired speaker's pointing to the watch as a reference to time at which the programme takes place
- and all these parts must then be combined together to express 'I watch *Wheel of Fortune* on Monday at 8 o'clock in the morning'.

In this conversation the *Ego-Alter* are co-authors of each gesture that takes place in a seamless and uninterrupted fashion. In addition to simultaneous co-authorship of gestures the process of knowing take places in time and is sequentially organised. Interactional meaning of dialogical contributions is intrinsically determined by their position in sequences (Linell, 1998). Sense-making activities are orientated both towards past and towards retrospective interpretation as well as anticipating which possible directions knowledge and communication could take (Linell and Marková, 1993).

Extract: *Wheel of fortune*   (NS = nonspeaker; S = speaker)

NS: (*looking and pointing at wall behind partner*)
    uuh omu'ay
    (*draws a circle in the air with his finger*)
    er'l

  S: (*leaning forward*)
    circle

NS: (*pointing insistently at wall behind partner*) (vocalises)

  S: (*looking at the wall*)
    what in the work?

NS: (*holds up one finger*)

  S: one

NS: (*points to himself, draws a circle in the air with his finger*)
    aah omu'ay

  S: (*scratching his head and looking confused*)
    *Mon*day?

NS: (*lifts up his wrist as if to look at his watch*)
    uu' ay clo'

  S: (*looking confused*)
    three o'clock?

NS: (*holding up eight fingers*)
    ay clo'

  S: eight o'clock

NS: (*nods*)
    mmmm:

  S: eight o'clock on Monday (*smiles*) circle (.) eight o'clock in the *morning* (*smiles*)

NS: (*shaking head*)
    no

  S: (*turning round to look at wall*)
    oo::hh right

The microanalysis of the video of this dialogue shows that the participants' co-actions are synchronised and that they appear to be seamless to the extent that it is difficult to subdivide them into the actions of two persons. Nevertheless, despite their dialogical interdependence, the *Ego* and the *Alter* retain their independence as individuals. In other words, they do not 'fuse' with one another. Due to tension, each individual firmly retains his individuality *as* individuality. Terms like 'mutually constituted' or a 'seamless' relation do not imply a fusion of the two components and a loss of their individuality.[6] Dialogical tension manifests itself in both participants. With respect to the non-speaker, he assiduously attempts to redraw the circles (the wheel) and to revocalise 'omu'ay'. Concerning the speaker, he pays careful attention (see: tension – attention, in English) to the non-speaker's gestures and vocalisations in order to piece the message together.

As another example, let us imagine a dialogical triad consisting of an artist (the *Ego*), viewers of art (the *Alter*) and a modern collage painting (*Object to be represented*). The collage painting could include a conglomeration of different entities, like a piece of rock, a flag, a wire and a rose. It could have a title *The bride of Jesus*. We can pose the question that is by no means original (cf. e.g. Mukařovský, 1936/1970). How is it possible for a material object, in our case a conglomeration of heterogeneous entities like a rock, a flag, a wire and a rose, to rise to the status of an aesthetic object in the eyes of viewers? Such transformation depends on several factors, for example, on content, extra-artistic circumstances, the taste of viewers, historical contexts, to mention but a few. Above all, the piece of art must provoke, it must cause tension (or attention!), and it must create a challenge for the viewers. However, if the challenge is too easy, if viewers do not perceive much that is new, they will say that the artist has produced no more than a cliché. This could be like an ill-fitted garment produced by 'a loose tension' (see section 1.3 above). On the other hand, if the problem is incomprehensible and if the artist distances himself too much from accepted norms, then the viewers will not understand the painting and will reject it.

Acceptance or rejection of a painting therefore may depend on the perceived continuity and discontinuity in artistic traditions. Modern art frequently heightens the antinomy between continuity and discontinuity and invites the viewer to share the meaning of this antinomy, i.e., continuity/discontinuity, with the artist. For instance, a surrealistic painting can be composed from totally heterogeneous objects. Or in a cubist painting, an object, say a musical instrument, can be completely decomposed into its parts and thus deprived of its unity as a well-recognised object. On the other hand, surrealist or cubist objects are reorganised in new ways and they propose themselves to viewers as objects with new meanings. For example, they propose themselves as objects of the de-humanised world. Thus the artist creates a special kind of tension for the viewer, a tension based on collisions between known and unknown, old and new, discontinuous and continuous, among other things. More generally, art presents the viewer with several kinds of antinomy at the same time, creating perceptual, emotional and representational tensions. Such antinomies are created not only in visual art. Similarly, the theatre of small and fringe avant-gard groups change the existing norms, attract new audiences by creating new kinds of tension. From the fringe, avant-gard groups move to the centre of attention.

In literature, too, the relationship of the aesthetic norm of the time and shift of the work away from the norms institutes a dynamic tension (Vodička, 1976, p. 198). The tension leads to the reconstruction and innovation of literary norm of a given period and thus to a 'change in the literary viability of individual works and authors' (1976, pp. 203–4). Every artistic and literary work represents in one way or other the existing social realities of the time. Simultaneously, they communicate something new that violates these realities. The study of changes in readers' representations of literary work, of their taste, of political and other kinds of tension, Vodička argues, are essential features of the study of the evolution of literature.

Clashes between the past and the present and between conventions and innovations create the history of art (Gombrich, 1968). They also create the history of social psychological phenomena. They are, therefore, of urgent concern to social psychology and specifically, to the theory of social representations. These clashes, of course, have a different strength and oscillate between periods in which adherence to norms predominates violation of norms. Tension, we have seen, is not a yes-no concept. There could be a low tension in a system that hardly produces any effect. In contrast, there could be a high tension leading to conflict and revolution. Sometimes tension manifests itself only internally as an internal polemics without any apparent external effect (Chapter 4) at the time, but preparing its effect for the future.

2.2   Multiple facets of the Ego-Alter-Object

Each dialogical situation involves different kinds of the *Ego-Alter*. For example, the *Ego-Alter* could be made up of I-specific group; I-another person; I-nation; group-community, and so on. During a single encounter several dialogical *Ego-Alter* relations may simultaneously compete and clash one with another. Dialogical participants bring into dialogue their present experiences and past traditions as well as expectations about their futures. They may choose to change their priorities. They may perpetuate continuities and create discontinuities. They can focus on themselves and above all express their own interests. Alternatively, they may orientate themselves toward their *Alter*.

Let us consider a case from our research (Collins and Marková, 1999). This case illustrates multiple facets of the *Ego-Alter-Object*. Participants' communicative choices produce different kinds of tension and this in turn has implications for the process of knowing.

Imagine two participants, one with cerebral palsy, which presents a speech and communication disorder, and the other without any speech and communication disorder. They play a well known guessing game. The participant with cerebral palsy has a picture of a kitchen, which is hidden from the view of the other participant, who by asking suitable questions has to reconstruct the kitchen.

The picture we used in the actual study was *The Far Side* cartoon by Gary Larson of the kitchen (Collins and Marková, 1999; this picture was reproduced with permission on p. 344). This picture displays common features of a kitchen in industrialised countries. There is a sink, running water, cupboards and so on. The picture of the kitchen also shows features that are specific to this particular kitchen: there is a little dog on the picture making a cup of coffee. Using the concept of dialogical triad, we can think about different *Ego-Alter-Object* relations that enter into the reconstruction of the picture of the kitchen. The manner in which the dialogue takes place is determined by the presuppositions for communication of the two participants. We can imagine different dialogical triads of *Ego-Alter-Object* co-existing at the same time and clashing with one another. This may facilitate or impede the reconstruction of the picture.

One communicative possibility may involve the two participants focusing on the fact that there is asymmetric knowledge between them in terms of the specific game which they play. The participant with the speech and communication disorder has knowledge of the picture of the kitchen, while the other does not. We can depict it as a dialogical triad consisting of:

- *Ego*: the first participant's knowledge of the picture
- *Alter*: the second participant's lack of knowledge of the picture
- *Object*: the picture of the kitchen to be reconstructed.

This specific triad creates several kinds of tension. For example, one kind of tension arises from asymmetry in the participants' knowledge, from the necessity to ask relevant questions and to provide appropriate responses. Another kind of tension is created by the difficulties in co-constructing mutual understanding due to the specific speech and communication disorder of one participant. Tension of this kind can be diminished by negotiation of meanings, by self-repairs in talk and by mutual repairs.

We can depict another dialogical triad consisting of:

- *Ego*: the first and the second participant's commonalities in their respective images of the kitchen in question, e.g. due to commonalities in their personal experiences
- *Alter*: schematic or collective knowledge of kitchens in the participants' common culture, e.g. knowledge that kitchens have tables, chairs, refrigerators, cupboards, and so on
- *Object*: the picture of the kitchen to be reconstructed.

This kind of triad generates other kinds of tension, e.g. between what is taken for granted in the reconstruction of the picture and what therefore does not enter into the conversation; or in contrast, what is thematised in the conversation.

Third, we can depict yet another kind of triad. In this case we can focus on the two participants' own specific images of the kitchen containing specific features, e.g. the kinds of kitchen in their own homes, kitchens they have seen in shops and advertisements, their neighbours' kitchens and so on. Thus we can dream up another kind of dialogical triad:

- *Ego*: the first participant's idiosyncratic image of the kitchen
- *Alter*: the second participant's idiosyncratic image of the kitchen
- *Object*: schemata of kitchens in their common culture

This triad may generate communicative tension with respect to what is and is not taken for granted with respect to the two differing idiosyncratic images. It may lead to misunderstandings between the two participants and to negotiation and thematisation of their respective meanings.

These different dialogical triads may, moreover, compete with one another and clash in the process of the game and in the construction of knowing. They may become part of the game through the kinds of question that the participants ask one another and through the responses that they obtain. They may be reflected in drawings; and in the seriousness or lightness with which the participants play the game.

We cannot explain the existence of these and possibly other dialogical triads in terms of choices that the two participants make here-and-now. Their presence or absence can be related to social representations that the participants hold. For instance, the participant without a communication disorder may hold a certain social representation of disability, which the other, by having direct experience of the disability, will not share. For example, the participant without a communication disorder may hold a social representation of people with cerebral palsy as having not only a muscular disability but also an intellectual disability. Therefore, even if the able-bodied participant asks questions relevant to the game, she

Figure 6.5 A reconstruction of the kitchen in drawings: little resemblance to the original picture

may not await the response from her co-participant whom she considers to be intellectually disabled. Instead, she may venture to reconstruct the picture of the kitchen largely on the basis of schematic, culturally shared knowledge rather than on the basis of information given by her co-participant. Such social representation could instigate the formation of the following dialogical (or indeed a monological!) triad:

- *Ego*: schematic or collective knowledge of kitchens in the participants' common culture, e.g. knowledge that kitchens have tables, chairs, refrigerators, cupboards, and so on
- *Alter*: schematic or collective knowledge of kitchens in the participants' common culture, e.g. knowledge that kitchens have tables, chairs, refrigerators, cupboards, and so on
- *Object*: schemata of kitchens in their common culture

In this fake triad, the *Ego* and the *Alter* represent only the carer's voice. It is a monologue that excludes the voice of the person with impaired speech. This is what actually happened in our study. As a result, reconstructions of the kitchen in drawings were of a poor quality because they did not contain relevant features of the original picture that could be provided by the impaired speaker. One can see that these drawings (Figures 6.5 and 6.6) show no more than schematic features and that they have little resemblance to the original picture. In contrast, when the able-bodied

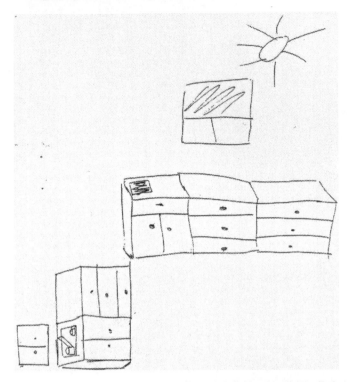

Figure 6.6 A reconstruction of the kitchen in drawings: little resemblance to the original picture

participant did not make assumptions about the intellectual disability of her partner, or if she seriously considered information provided by her dialogical partner, the reconstructed picture bore a great deal of similarity to the original picture. The drawing in Figure 6.7 results from the latter case. It includes details of the original picture, e.g. it shows the little dog making a cup of coffee, the details of the taps and even a chequered tablecloth.

This example from our research shows cognitive polyphasia and heteroglossia at work. The reconstructions of the picture by different dyads were regulated by more or less permanent styles of thinking and communication. These styles were partly due to social representations that participants held. In addition, they were partly determined by temporary motives, goals and situational contexts. In our concrete cases, the participants employed different kinds of knowledge, e.g. schematic, specific to the task or knowledge based on experience. Their choices were also influenced by the kinds of questions they asked or avoided asking; the kinds

Figure 6.7 A reconstruction of the kitchen resembling the original picture

of responses they gave or did not give; the kinds of issues they raised and thematised. In addition, their communicative choices were dependent on the quality of dialogicality they displayed with respect to one another: whether they treated one another as dialogical partners or whether they pursued monologically their own goals and perspectives.

A final point: the aim of the above considerations concerning different kinds of *Ego-Alter-Object* is *theoretical* and not *empirical*. This analysis shows that in any dialogue we must presuppose polyphasia and heteroglossia. Moreover, we must also presuppose *co-existence* of different styles of thinking and the *co-presence* of different voices in communication. It would be a misunderstanding if these considerations evoked the idea that we could discover, *empirically*, dialogical triads as a mechanism of generating data resulting, for example, in specifying different kinds of dialogical triads and their quantification.

A dialogical triad is not an empirical datum but it is a conceptual construct enabling the researcher to consider the problem from its theoretical perspectives. It is a construct for generating ideas. It could be used as a *Gedanke experiment* (thought experiment) to enable questions to be asked which otherwise are likely to be ignored. Examples of such questions are the following. Which aspects of culturally shared knowledge are taken for granted in the given case? Which aspects of culturally shared knowledge are thematised? What characteristics of objects do participants presuppose? A theoretical analysis and the relevant theoretical questions will enable the choice of research methods to answer those questions.

3   Object in the dialogical triad

3.1   *From stable to transient objects*

No theory of knowledge can ignore the object of knowledge. Objects, however, could mean very different things in different theories of knowledge. For example, for philosophers of the seventeenth century like Descartes and Locke, the starting points of enquiry were objects, which they could perceive clearly and distinctly. These objects were mechanisms that had unchangeable qualities, like 'an orange beak', 'whiteness', 'a long neck', and 'black legs' of a swan.

The ways in which objects are represented is not only a prerogative of philosophers. Representations of objects are cultural representations and they penetrate all spheres of life. There is a similarity between Descartes' and Locke's representations of objects with clear and distinct qualities and the artistic representations of objects at that time. It is because we recognise such representations as pertaining to particular historical epochs that the history of art could develop as a scholarly discipline.

In order to illustrate this point let us consider the painting of Hans Holbein the younger from the sixteenth century entitled *The Meyer Madonna*. On this painting there is a detail of the two wives of one of the friends of Holbein, Jacob Meyer, who was at the time an important person in the City Council in Basle. This beautiful painting of the two serene faces, like a photograph, mirrors the expressions of these two women. It captures minute details of their emotions as well as of their scarves and dresses as if the painter wanted to grasp reality in its entirety and truth. These faces of the two wives of Jacob Meyer are a detail from a religious painting, in which several pious women encircle the Virgin Mary. Holbein's image of these 'objects' corresponds to the representation of an ideal aristocratic woman of his time: stable, elegant, reliant, pious and aware of her duty.

The modern world and its technology hardly ever deal with objects that merely impinge on our senses and present themselves as the reason for contemplation and reflection. Instead, objects are conceived as transient.

In the early part of the twentieth century the French painter Marcel Duchamp was fascinated by X-ray imagery (Chapter 5) of objects and by the possibilities created by X-rays to penetrate invisible realities. He displayed his fascination with transient objects in many of his paintings. Like Hans Holbein, he painted the faces of two women, in this case his two younger sisters (Figure 6.8). He entitled his painting *Yvonne and*

Figure 6.8 Duchamp's painting of Yvonne and Magdaleine torn in tatters

Magdaleine in Tatters. The paintings of Hans Holbein on the one hand and that of Marcel Duchamp on the other represent contrasting perspectives of objects and their respective social realities. While the former shows stability, continuity and serenity of the objects in their visible reality, the latter shows the objects with their life histories, discontinuities and movement in their invisible realities. The latter painting shows four profiled heads of the two women, showing their motion in time as they progress from youth to old age. The painting is a study of the modes of representation with the nose as a focus. The dark nose or Magdeleine links Duchamp's image specifically to X-rays. X-rays pass through the cartilage of the nose and are resisted by bone (darker blots). Duchamp related X-rays to the idea of transparency and cutting (Henderson,1998).

It is not that the world of the sixteenth and the seventeenth centuries was the world of stable objects. Hans Holbein, René Descartes and John Locke all lived in the world of transient objects just like we do, although they might not have experienced changes so rapidly as we experience them today. Clearly, Descartes and Locke could have focused in their epistemologies on phenomena in change, because such phenomena were around them. Objects, which they perceived as stable, were those existing naturally in the physical world like rocks, artefacts and physical characteristics of animals and plants. These also included their images of pious and serene women.

Objects of symbolic power, like, for example, *money*, have hardly ever been in the focus of attention in the traditional theories of knowledge. Moscovici (1988/1993), in discussing society as a machine for making Gods, analyses *money* as passion throughout the history of mankind, showing stabilities and changes in their social representations. The magical power of money was shared by most cultures from early antiquity. Money has always created powerful images in all spheres of life. It has had a profound influence on economy, it has been a ubiquitous theme in world literatures and it has always led to gruesome murders and horrific wars. Nevertheless, until the nineteenth century money was hardly an object of social scientific exploration. Liu (2002) shows how money has become an obsession in China's current transition to a market economy, where material possessions have become closely linked with a lay representation of a market economy. This obsession sharply contrasts with the previous socialist system and its promised goal, a communist state in which money would be abolished.

The modern world and its technology present us more and more often with objects that are fluid and transient. We can hypothesise that their fluidity is one of the reasons why, today, various relativistic epistemologies proliferate in social sciences.[7] Think of an object like *food*, something essential for survival, the source of pleasure and life, or of illness, poison and death. What today is considered as *food* constantly changes its boundaries and these boundaries are dialogically formed and transformed. We might consider a beautiful looking vegetable, which is genetically modified, as *inedible*. We might eat meat and wonder whether or not it is *contaminated*. Social knowledge cannot ignore conceiving objects of daily life as being in transition.

The changing nature of the object of knowledge gives rise to scientific and public disputes. It also affects the kinds of tension in communication between the *Ego-Alter*. For example, if the object does not present itself to senses or is difficult to comprehend, e.g. the AIDS virus, it gives rise to myths and beliefs and it alters the ways in which we communicate about it.

3.2   *A baby as a virtual object*

Let us consider an example of the transient object in the study by Middleton *et al.* (2001). Middleton *et al.* (2001) explored a prematurely born baby as an 'object' in the neonatal care unit. The neonatal care unit can be described as a complex social practice, which involves a multidisciplinary team of professionals, parents, technologies and medical services, all working together to safeguard the healthy development of the baby. The authors explain that the prematurely born baby is ambiguously thought of as being placed between a 'social' and a 'biological' entity, his life being dependent on technology, medical care and the knowledge of professionals. The boundaries of the neonatal care unit constantly change and are often ambiguous. As new patients come, new parents get involved in the functioning of the unit, different staff members are employed and new technologies are used.

In their study, the authors make an explicit assumption about *change of the unit*, its boundaries and practices. In contrast, if a *relative stability* of social practices in the unit is observed, it is something that requires explanation. Moreover, 'ambiguity and uncertainty rather than clarity and procedure are important features of neonatal care' (Middleton *et al.*, p. 6). Working in the face of radical uncertainty, the participants in the neonatal care unit orientate themselves 'to the production of stabilities in practice', adapting their knowledge and actions to the changing circumstances.

The 'object' is a baby who is an agent and therefore, is in a constant state of change both because of his activities and because he develops. This 'object-baby' also transforms the relations between each of the co-acting individuals and other participants because his needs for medical care change and he requires different kinds of care and professionals. Through their involvement, as well as the involvement of the baby's parents who take a more active role in his care, the baby gets better. This is why the authors refer to *the baby as a virtual object*, i.e. as something, which stabilises the dynamic relationships between the social order, action and technology. In this example, the authors' analysis of the case continuously balances on the verge between realities and potential realities.

This virtual object and the authors' focus on shifts between realities and potential realities cannot be conceived in mechanistic terms but in dialogical relations. Introducing the concept of virtual object raises new questions about the dialogicality of realities and potential realities, which constantly shift their boundaries. What is supposed to be real and what is potentially real is dialogically determined within the multitude of relations between the *Ego-Alter-Object*.

In what ways the changing object takes part in the formation of social knowledge and social representations will necessarily become an intriguing subject of study in social representations in years to come. For example, modern technology, like computers, changes not only the nature of communication in general but, more specifically, the relations between the *Ego-Alter*. Moreover, the dynamic object can take on different functions. For example, the object could be something of what the knowers may try to make sense, e.g. medical knowledge, democracy and the functions of institutions. Alternatively, the knowers may themselves create the object of knowledge or they may transform it, e.g. democracy, genetic modifications or virtual objects.

3.3   Belief-based and knowledge-based social representations

In the discussion of dialogical triads I have so far ignored one important issue: the relative strength of relations between the three components in the dialogical triad. This means that I have not raised the question as to whether there could be, for example, strong relations between the *Ego-Alter* on the one hand, but relatively weak relations between the *Ego-Object* on the other hand. Alternatively, whether there could be strong relations between the *Ego-Object* but weaker relations between the *Ego-Alter*.

If we consider relations between the *Ego-Alter-Object* in science, we can assume that the relation between the *Ego-Object* is foregrounded. The scientist focuses above all on the object of knowledge, on evidence concerning the nature of that object and on scientific explanations relating to that object. We can also assume that while she does not ignore, whether implicitly or explicitly, the community of communication with other scientists, these relations could be less important in scientific work.

In contrast, if we consider the relations between the *Ego-Alter-Object* in social representations, we can hypothesise two possibilities involving the strengths of relations between the *Ego-Alter-Object*. We can make a very tentative suggestion about these two possibilities that follows from Moscovici's (Moscovici, 1998b/2000, p. 136) ideas about beliefs and knowledge in social representations.

Some kinds of social representations are predominantly belief-based. In the theory of social representations beliefs are considered to be mental states of some considerable duration. Beliefs are usually rooted in culture, tradition and language. They are characterised by firmness and rigidity of conviction and they are often bound with passions. Beliefs are of social origin and the fixation on the object of belief comes from the *Alter* rather than from the *Object* as such. This means that the believer neither searches for proof, nor for evidence relating to the object. For example, if one believes that AIDS is transmitted through a handshake, one will not look for facts to prove this belief. The hardness of this belief will lie in its attachment to other beliefs, for example, to the belief that AIDS is a dirty disease, or that AIDS is associated with the punishment of the perpetrator and that punishment is linked with death. Such beliefs may implicitly live in a community for generations. They may be unconsciously transmitted through collective memory, implicit communication and traditions.[8]

Beliefs are also built on 'the reciprocity of perspectives' (Schutz, 1970). Sharing cultural schemata and taking part in actions jointly with others produces similar experiences in individuals who are part of that culture. Cultural schemata get re-cycled and become part of routines that consequently affect our motivational, topical and interpretational 'relevances'. We see what we are motivated to see: in view of these motives, paradoxically, things lose their particular significances and they become, to use Schutz's words, 'topics in hands'. In such cases, interpretation, too, loses its relevance because motives have already determined our interpretation. Sharing cultural schemata and motives, values and topics resulting from them also means that our *Ego-Alter* relations are in the foreground while the relations between the *Ego-Object* are in the background. Culturally shared beliefs, which lie behind these schemata of 'topics in hands', make us oblivious of differences and of inconsistencies in perception and experience.

When something like an outbreak of AIDS takes place, beliefs become invigorated and, being expressions of conviction and commitment, they make social representations salient and powerful. In the case of strong beliefs, even logical contradiction or sensory contradiction is ineffective for the believer. Beliefs can be effectively replaced only by another belief. In order to deny the belief, Moscovici argues, we must present a powerful image that evokes commitment to passions (Moscovici, 2000, p. 252). Beliefs, therefore, while they are fixations on an idea or on an object, paradoxically, are also expressions of a social commitment. They differ in durability, strength and the degree of engagement. Some beliefs are more easily changed than others.

Other kinds of social representations are predominantly knowledge-based. Common knowledge involves different kinds of knowing. It can involve transformed scientific knowledge or knowledge based on the experience of interpersonal relations, conversations, daily routines and so on. To know, just like to believe, means to hold something true. Knowledge-based social representations foreground the relation between the knower and the object of knowledge, i.e. the *Ego-Object*. To know is to examine, as far as possible independently of others, the nature of the phenomena in question. Of course, the notion 'independently' has a relative meaning because we can hardly totally ignore knowledge circulating in public discourse. Knowledge in social representations is always social and the *Alter* remains part of the dialogical triad. However, the relation between the knower and the object of knowledge is not fixed but is open. In contrast to the believer, the knower is ready to enter into the argument, proof and criticism. If someone 'knows' that 'AIDS can be caught from a hand-shake' such 'knowledge' will be based on the search for evidence. For example, the individual may present personal experience or argue on the basis of observation. He will negate his knowledge if he finds evidence against it. In the case of knowledge, the *Ego* may go against the *Alter*, whether it is common opinion or the ruling majority or otherwise.

The difference between knowledge and beliefs does not concern the content of propositions expressing one or the other (Moscovici, 1998b/2000, p. 136). Propositions expressing knowledge and beliefs can have the same content. However, whether such propositions are ascribed the status of beliefs or knowledge rests in the style of thinking and the method of searching for 'truth'. If individuals or groups search for evidence of the truth concerning that object, the resulting social representations are knowledge-based. If, on the other hand, representations are formed and maintained through the consensus with others, representations are belief-based.

In reality, social representations always involve both knowledge and beliefs[9] and it is unlikely that we could find a system of thought that would be based purely on one or the other, whether it is science or religion. The question as to whether a social representation is knowledge-based or belief-based, is a matter of prevalence of one or the other style of thinking and reasoning.

However, the question as to whether social representations are based predominantly on knowledge or on beliefs could have important implications for social practices. For example, belief-based social representations may inspire social categorisation and exclusion of groups and individuals. This is why self-help groups, just like governmental campaigns, attempt to change belief-based social representations into knowledge-based representations and thus reduce or eliminate exclusion and discrimination (Farr, 1995).

4   The three-component process

4.1   *Simultaneity and sequentiality in a three-component process*[10]

The *Ego-Alter-Object* is the dynamic unit of social knowledge and the relations within that unit are both simultaneously and sequentially dynamic. It is the co-existence of simultaneous and sequential relations in the three-component processes that defines the concept of social change.

We have already characterised the simultaneous relation in the *Ego-Alter* as a figure-ground relation and we have illustrated it with respect to the Moscovici concept of minorities/majorities. Minorities are defined in terms of majorities and dialogically speaking, a group could constitute the majority *only* in terms of the specific minority (Moscovici, 1976b, 1979). A particular minority and majority come into being together like figure-and-ground not because of a characteristic that is *a priori* important in some sense but because, for one reason or other, that specific characteristic becomes significant for their emergence as the minority/majority. This characteristic defines their *internal* relations and therefore, is also a defining characteristic of that specific majority/minority. Such an internally significant characteristic could be anything, whether it is having black eyes or holding a specific political view. Importantly, that characteristic creates a dialogical tension within the *Ego-Alter*: it becomes a subject matter for their communicative relations, that is it becomes an *Object*.

In contrast, no characteristic, however important it may seem to an observer, e.g. power, discrimination or exploitation, can define two groups as the minority and majority, if that characteristic is *outside* their relations, i.e. if it is not in their discourse. In other words, however dominant one group could be with respect to another group, if the two groups do not define themselves in terms of dominance and submission, *vis à vis* that characteristic, they do not form the majority/minority. They simply remain two independent groups. They could be dependent in some other sense but not as the minority/majority with respect to dominance/submission.

The fact that the *Ego* and the *Alter* enter into existence simultaneously gives rise to their *sequential* relations. Sequential relations are *internal* relations and must be contrasted with *external* sequentiality. External sequentiality is constituted of a series of static states which, when quickly projected, lead to the image of the change as we have seen in Saussure's case or as we can find today in many linguistic and cognitive models (for criticism see Marková, 1990; Rommetveit, 1990; Linell and Marková, 1993; Linell, 1998). Sequentiality in these models is *external* to the *Ego-Alter* because each dialogical contribution is conceived as an independent act, one contribution following the other. For example, the teacher asks a question, the pupil responds, the teacher provides a positive remark and so on. External sequentiality treats change as a linear sequence of moments in time.

In contrast, internal sequentiality is implied by simultaneous changes in *Ego-Alter* even if these may not be immediately apparent as we have seen in the case of conversion in minority/majority experiments. For example, internal sequentiality may work as an internal dialogue and may have latent effects on dialogical participants. These effects produce tension, conflict and unconscious dialogical changes. Internal sequentiality is intrinsically contingent. Actions derive their meanings from their place in the communicative project or genre of which they are part (Linell and Marková, 1993).

Internal sequentiality, therefore, implies both apparent continuity and discontinuity of dialogical contributions of actions. Any dialogue is constituted of different kinds of the *Ego-Alter* (e.g. I-group, group-culture, I-you) that clash with one another and create different kinds of tensions which may result in discontinuities (Salazar-Orvig, 1999), abrupt changes like Mukařovský's (1940/1977) semantic reversals or hidden polemics discussed above. In other words, internal sequentiality treats change as non-linear and multifaceted.

We need to understand, above all, that simultaneity and sequentiality are theoretical and not empirical concepts. This means that they are conceptual tools enabling questions to be asked rather than answers to be given to empirically defined problems.

For example, the presupposition of simultaneity and internal sequentiality directs attention to the formulation of questions about the interdependence of the *Ego-Alter* rather than questions about a single communicative participant. A majority may try to impose its norms and rules on a minority. However, in doing so, the majority is under pressure from the minority, which tries to make itself understood and establish its visibility. It attempts to create its own rules and norms and make them accepted by the majority.

4.2   La Dissidence d'un Seul

Simultaneity and sequentiality of the relations between the *Ego-Alter-Object*, are theoretical concepts developed by Moscovici in *the genetic model of social change* (Moscovici, 1976b, 1979). The genetic model treats minority/majority as a simultaneous and internally interdependent relation with respect to a specific object, e.g. social recognition. The genetic model of social change is based on the dynamic three-component processes of the *Ego-Alter-Object*.

Let us explain this genetic model of social change by relying heavily on Moscovici's (1979) brilliant essay on *La Dissidence d'un Seul*.[11] The essay is an observation, a description and an analysis of a single man in 'minority', of the dissident Russian writer and the Nobel Prize winner Alexander Solzenitzyn and of his conflict with the 'majority', the authorities of the Politburo (Political bureau) in the Soviet regime. Thus Solzenitzyn and the Politburo are in *Ego-Alter* relations. What was the *Object* in this situation? The *Object* in the three-component process is Solzenitzyn's novel *One day in the life of Ivan Denisovitch*. Thus we have a three-component process *Solzenitzyn (Ego)-Politburo(Alter)-One day in the life of Ivan Denisovitch (Object)*.

The dyad Solzenitzyn-Politburo (the *Ego-Alter*) came into being simultaneously. Of course, the person, i.e. Solzenitzyn as well as the Politburo that came to constitute this dyad had existed before both as an individual (Solzenitzyn) and an institution (Politburo). Alexander Solzenitzyn had his life as a husband, as a writer and as a friend to various people. The Soviet political bureaucracy, i.e. the Politburo, existed too, carrying out its various political activities like persecuting dissidents, cleansing the Communist Party of traitors, and so on. Despite the fact that the Politburo persecuted other dissidents and groups, the dialogical dyad Solzenitzyn-Politburo came to existence when Alexander Solzenitzyn and the Politburo defined one another in a specific conflict. From that moment on, their activities within that dyad were meaningful with respect to one another: as the *Ego-Alter*.

Let us consider the emergence of another *Ego-Alter*. The Czech writer and dramatist Václav Havel (1979) refers to an event describing the beginning of the Czechoslovak dissident movement known as the Charta 77. After the Soviet invasion of Czechoslovakia in 1968, various intellectual groups attempted to express some form of independent thinking but there was no uniting impulse to bring them together. The crucial moment arose in a totally different context: the regime found itself in the situation in which it challenged an a-politically-orientated generation of young people. The regime forbade public performances of a nonconformist group of young rock musicians called *The Plastic People of the Universe*. When the musicians resisted this pressure, they were arrested. The action of the regime led to the emergence of the *Ego-Alter*, the regime versus the young rock musicians. As an avalanche, this situation provoked to action various isolated groups of discontented citizens. When the regime arrested the nonconformist young men with long hair and when it performed a political trial with them, it did not realise, Havel points out, the consequences of their action. The regime never wished that to happen. The attack against an unknown group of young people was suddenly felt as an attack against freedom in general. It was felt as an attack against everybody. In other words, the established totalitarian regime created its own political oppositions from which yet another *Ego-Alter*, i.e. the regime versus the Charta 77 emerged shortly afterwards.

These two events, Solzenitzyn-Politburo-*One day in the life of Ivan Denisovitch* and the regime-Charta 77-freedom show the emergence of the simultaneous *Ego-Alter-Object* relations.

The dialogical situation described in Moscovici's essay *La Dissidence d'un Seul* also displays sequential effects. Moscovici describes events from 1962 when Solzenitzyn published his novel *One day in the life of Ivan Denisovitch* to 1974, when he was expelled from the Soviet Union. The novel was first published in the journal *Novyj Mir* after Solzenitzyn had consistently refused to make any changes in his writing. This bothered the Soviet authorities and the situation created a conflict between him and the Politburo. The Politburo, despite the attempts to become more liberal in the early 1960s, could not cope with Solzenitzyn's exposing the taboo of the Soviet totalitarian practices. The publication of the novel led to a dialogue of intensified judgement of one dialogical participant by the other, in which no compromise was possible.

Tension and conflict so created were both manifest and latent, expressing themselves in hidden and open polemic, internal and external dialogues and other means of polyphasic and heteroglossic thinking and language. On the part of the Politburo, for example, Solzenitzyn was manifestly and satirically called the Father of Justice, and he became someone who was visible in the eyes of the general public and of intellectuals. Latently, there was a newly created problem for the redaction of the *Novyj Mir* as to how to cope with censorship and with dissidents of Solzenitzyn's type. The Politburo used to deal with such individuals privately at the personal level whether by interrogation, threats or by producing fear in order to prevent public dramatisation of the problem.

Solzenitzyn's and the Politburo's co-actions had both a personal effect on the writer and a boomerang effect on the Politburo. In order to understand this, we need to consider several related effects.

First, how did Solzenitzyn's actions affect him as a person? To answer this question we need to bear in mind the peculiar way of living that occurs in a totalitarian regime. This is living a divided life – one private and one public – and this double-existence in order to survive, is an essential moral problem for many. Moscovici has reminded me that the dissidents, by sticking to their consistent behavioural style, destroyed the double-existence, which the totalitarian regime forced upon them. By rejecting compromise they could live their own single life, or as the Czech dissident Václav Havel called it, 'the life in truth'. Living their authentic life was a reward for the problems they experienced, like persecution, interrogation and censorship.

Second, how was the regime affected? Moscovici shows in his essay that the dissident movement produced a boomerang effect on the majority in political power because, what was aimed at dissidents in terms of threat and anguish, turned back on the communist authorities in terms of public and international disrepute. In whatever way they treated the stubborn dissidents, that treatment affected them. If the regime expelled dissidents from their own country, the dissidents influenced the public opinion from the outside, from abroad. If they were persecuted in the country, they negatively influenced public opinion from the inside.

Havel (1992) raised the question as to why the Soviet regime decided to expel a single man like Solzenitzyn and why a thousand chartists in Czechoslovakia were perceived as dangerous to the totalitarian regime. He pointed out that neither of them, i.e. Solzenitzyn and the chartists, presented themselves as a threat to the regime, nor did they present themselves as an alternative power. They did not even fight for power. However, the regime perceived them as threat because they insisted on living in truth and in freedom. The regime that was corrupt and that was profoundly distrusted by its citizens had no choice but to define them as an opposition. Consequently, it had to bear all the consequences for the confrontation so created. By acting on the world individuals not only change the world, but they also change themselves. They then act on the basis of their changed selves. Thus we have a full three-component process *Ego-Alter-Altered Ego*.

Neither Solzenitzyn nor Havel succumbed to the regime's effort to monologise, by imposing rules and not giving them the possibility to respond, the dialogical relationship on which they both insisted. Instead, they both continued their difficult dialogues. As well-known writers, they were highly regarded outside the Soviet bloc, received prestigious prizes and rewards in the West for their literary works and any action of the totalitarian regime against them was immediately widely publicised in the West. The regime found it very difficult to cope with such individuals. Solzenitzyn was expelled from the country so that the regime could avoid putting him into prison. Havel, instead, was imprisoned on several occasions. He was even given an opportunity to ask for release from prison and the regime might have gladly given him pardon. However, Havel rejected that offer and created even more embarrassment for the regime.

Other dissidents did not have such high international prestige and they could hardly carry out such a dramatic dialogue with the totalitarian and post-totalitarian regimes. They often disappeared in prisons and in hard labour camps without being noticed by anybody. For them, 'the life in truth' was too costly. A Czech dissident Milan Šimečka expressed how he, like many others, conformed to the regime rather than had the courage to take an uncompromising moral stand. He pointed out that he would employ words that were not his own words, but simply an expression of hypocrisy. He would search for excuses and would try to deceive himself by sifting through cases of justice, injustice and violence, in order to avoid taking risks and shouting that the Emperor was without clothes (Šimečka, 1984, p. 141).

Compromising majority, thus behaving as if the emperor had clothes helped to perpetuate the *status quo*. The regime accepted the *as if* behaviour of the silent majority and the silent majority continued its double life and became even oblivious to that fact. Here apparently the minority accepted the role of a stable and a passive object, at least superficially. It was because the silent majority behaved as if they agreed and were compliant the regime could continue its totalitarian activities. In this case, no external dialogue took place, or if it did, it was only a faked dialogue (Chapter 4) in which authors did not take responsibility for their words. These were 'dialogues' without dialogicality, in which the three-component processes were only faked.

NOTES

1. Peirce's semiotic theory of the growth of knowledge is triadic. Knowledge cannot be instantaneous and intuitive. All intuitions are determined by previous cognitions and there is no exception to this claim. He uses the concept of sign in two senses. First, in a broad sense, a sign is a triadic relation between the object, the interpretant and a sign proper (representation). The second sense of sign is therefore the sign proper (representation). It refers to the representative function only and 'representation' means both the mind and thought.

2. As in George Herbert Mead's theory of conversation of gestures, speech actions are co-produced rather than created by single individuals. Bühler echoed Humboldt's conception of language as *ergon* and *energeia*, the product and the process of language. Language as a relatively stable social phenomenon (ergon) and language as the speech of individuals (energeia) are two interdependent aspects of language, rather than two parallel phenomena, existing in isolation one from another. For this reason Bühler was critical of the treatment of language in terms of independent elements. He argued that 'separation into aspects can never be accomplished in the concrete with a dismembering instrument such as the butcher's knife' (Bühler, 1982, p. 103). This quote reminds Humboldt's (1836/1971) insistence that language cannot be studied like a dead body by an anatomist. In addition, it was Bühler's conviction that language should never be regarded as a self-contained system but as a system, which inter-relates with, and represents an extra-linguistic reality. He argued that although language communities have their 'inner language forms' (Bühler, 1982, p. 152), it is also essential to recognise that language is not a Kantian thing-in-itself, but that the language of each community represents the world in its own manner.

3. These films were discovered by Fritz Heider a long time after Kurt Lewin's death. Their scientific and educational value cannot be emphasised enough.

4. I am grateful to Sarah Collins for her insightful analysis of the case. She also did the transcription of the extract below as part of our ESRC research project.

5. Valsiner (1998) has drawn attention to this important point. There are different ways in which we can consider the relation of unity between two entities, for instance person-environment or person-person. Valsiner (1998, p. 14f.)

points out that sometimes, notions like 'socially situated activities', 'direct perception' or 'socially aided learning' suggest 'an immersion of the person in the undifferentiated environment'.

6. Following on this point, Valsiner explains the difference between exclusive and inclusive separation between non-dialectic and dialectic oppositions.

7. Relativistic epistemologies are different from pluralistic epistemologies. Pluralism in epistemology refers to different kinds of knowing in different social realities. Relativism, in contrast, denies possibility of knowing.

8. This contrasts with philosophical and linguistic analyses, which are often concerned with beliefs as mental states of a fleeting nature and their expression in language. Such analyses often focus on contents of propositions that are straightforward like 'it is raining'. For example, Bernard Williams (1973), in his influential paper on *Deciding to believe* explains:

> I am not going to take religious and moral beliefs, but cases of more straightforward factual belief; the sort of belief one has when one just believes that it is raining, or believes that somebody over there is one's father, or believes that the substance in front of one is salt (Williams, 1973, p. 136).

Others, however, like Wittgenstein, would not treat such language expressions as beliefs (e.g. Wittgenstein, 1953, pp. 191–2). It seems reasonable to assume that durable mental states are of different kinds than are mental states of a fleeting nature like believing or supposing that it rains.

9. There have been different ways in philosophy and the social sciences to distinguish between knowledge and beliefs. For example, Ryle (1949, p. 134) points out, even if the content is the same in the case of knowledge and belief, it is the 'because' in each of the two cases that is different. A person who believes that ice is thin and the person who knows that the ice is thin will use a different kind of explanation to that effect: Beliefs are like habits and inclinations, while knowledge is a skill. We may ask what may make people believe something but not what makes them know that something is or is not the case.

10. Some years ago I have suggested (Marková, 1987b, 1990) a three-step process as a unit of analysis in dialogue. This suggestion was inspired by the idea of George Herbert Mead (1934) of 'conversation of gestures'. I have characterised the three-step process as an epistemological unit that could not be subdivided physically into three parts but could be understood only as a whole. The three steps are internally related and take place both simultaneously and sequentially. The main idea of the three-step process is that dialogue is not a shifting of positions between the participants, or 'an exchange' of gestures but that it is a co-authorship. Co-authorship leads to co-development of dialogical perspectives of both participants. The third step in this process accounts for changes in the participants' awareness. The third step is, at the same time, speaking conceptually, the first step of the next three-step process.

The third step, representing changed perspectives in the mind of both participants, involves a special kind of knowing. It is the knowledge about the participants themselves. We can say that through the third step the participant becomes the object to himself as he reflects both on his own perspective and on the perspective others have of himself. In other words, while the three-step process was about self as an object of knowledge, the three-component process is about any *Object* of knowledge.

11. This essay is published in the French version of *Psychologie des Minorités Actives* (1979) but not, unfortunately, in the English version of the book published under the title *Social Influence and Social Change* (1976).

7 Understanding themata and generating social representations

In this chapter I shall turn attention to what should be considered, to-day, the main concepts of Moscovici's theory of social representations: *themata* and *thematisation*. The concept of themata (or thema in singular) brings into focus the question of dialogical antinomies in new perspectives. This concept explicitly shows commitment of the theory of social representations to language and communication as well as the historical and cultural specificities of the *Ego-Alter-Object* and its dynamics.

1 The structure of social representations: core and periphery

The theory of social representations presupposes that contents and meanings of social representations are structured and the aim of the theory is to identify, describe and analyse these structured contents and meanings. The study of *contents or materials that are structured* and communicated in real life situations[1] of ordinary people differs from the study of structures as abstract and general concepts as it is the case in various forms of structuralism. Neither does the theory of social representations examine processes or rules of behaviour in general terms as do, for example, functionalism, behavioural approaches or social cognition.

In studying concrete social phenomena, for example, social representations of AIDS, madness or personal identity as structured, the researcher attempts to discover the manner in which history, culture and contemporary circumstances all contribute to the stability and dynamics of this or that social phenomenon. She examines why the social representation, e.g. of AIDS, is structured and thematised in a particular way in a specific epoch, or which aspects of content and meaning are foregrounded and why some components of the structured content change faster or slower than others. In other words, the theory of social representations conceives of the phenomenon in question as a whole. It studies it in a holistic manner and in relation to the contents and meanings of other social phenomena.

When specific groups share a social representation, it does not mean that they share *contents* and *meanings* of that representation in their entirety and that they conceive them in identical manners. Wilhelm von Humboldt (1971/1836) had already discussed such an obvious matter in the eighteenth century when he argued that nobody conceives a word and its meaning in exactly the same way as does his neighbour. In this context Humboldt compared language to concentric ripples over water. The centre of the ripple is well marked but as we move further away from the centre, the ripples are less and less clear. When we move far enough, they are no longer recognisable. In a similar manner we can conceive of the meaning of a word. For example, Humboldt maintained that in naming an animal 'a horse' everyone means the same kind of an animal but at the same time, everyone has his own idiosyncratic content attached to the core meaning that is associated with the name. The image of 'concentric ripples over water' indicates that humans are likely to share the centre of the ripple but that more peripheral aspects of the meaning are more idiosyncratic and less commonly shared. In other words, 'sharing' mental phenomena involves both sharing and non-sharing and therefore, 'sharing' must imply not only comprehension but also mis- and non-comprehension of such meanings.

The image of concentric ripples suggests that the overlaps between individuals' contents of concepts and meanings of words are not arbitrary. In fact, one could say that this Humboldtian image pre-dates, at least to some extent, the structural approaches in the study of social and cultural phenomena in the 1960s and 1970s. At that time, several different approaches, among them Lotman's theory of culture and the School of Social Representations in Aix-en-Provence both worked with concepts of the central core and periphery in their respective approaches. These concepts, which came from the theory of information and cybernetics, inspired the imagination of social and human scientists at the time.

The Estonian semiotician Yuri Lotman applied the idea of the core and periphery in his semiotic theory of culture (Lotman, 1976, 1992). Lotman viewed the core of the cultural space as being tightly knit and relatively inflexible and monovalent. If a researcher takes a synchronic approach in the study of culture, Lotman argued, he studies above all its core, i.e. the space of semiotic norms. Periphery, in contrast, is the space of semiotic practices. It is vaguely organised and ambivalent. The focus on periphery, Lotman insisted, is more valued in diachronic approaches, which are concerned with cultural changes. The more we move from centre to periphery, the more the cultural system, e.g. communication, becomes strained by tension between sometimes artificially sustained norms and peripheral genres that oppose those norms. Through these tensions, for example, marginal forms of art can be drawn into conflict with mainstream art. Thus Lotman showed that the avant-garde in arts starts as a rebellious fringe and through negotiating conflict it moves to the centre and changes the semiotic sphere of culture (see also Chapter 6 on this point). Lotman called his approach a *cultural dynamism*.

Historians of art like Mukařovský (1936/1970) and Gombrich (1968) also referred to such shifts (cf. Chapter 6) but they used different theoretical frameworks than did Lotman. Mukařovský and Gombrich both argued that the individual's vision in art is largely determined by shared social representations and by collective vision of cultural phenomena. They both discussed conditions under which shifts between the fringe and centre could take place. Mukařovský discussed these issues in the context of norms and avant-gard theatre, using in an eclectic way the ideas from Durkheim and from the Marxist dialectic.

The School of Social Representations in Aix-en-Provence has developed, over the last few decades, an original structural approach to the study of social representations. According to that approach, social representations are organised into a structured body of information, beliefs, attitudes and opinions, which consist of the central core and peripheral elements (Abric, 1994, 2001, 2002; Flament, 1994a, 1994b, 2002; Guimelli, 1994, 1998). The central core, Abric argues, gives social representation its meaning. It is a unifying and stabilising organisation of a representation, most resistant to change. According to this point of view, two social representations differ from one another if the contents in their cores are structured differently. For example, we can imagine the core of a social representation of AIDS to be organised around antinomies like dirt/cleanliness, morality/immorality, life/death, or even around several antinomies at the same time.

Peripheral elements are organised around the central core and they constitute an interface between the core and a concrete situation, in which the representation manifests itself, e.g. in the discourse. Peripheral elements serve a concretising function of the representation. By being more flexible than the central core and by being relevant to concrete situations, e.g. to fear of HIV infection, peripheral elements render the representation comprehensible and transmissible to other concrete situations. Peripheral phenomena, relevant to concrete situations, might include, e.g. the fear of touching a person with the HIV infection or avoidance of any social association with him. Moreover, peripheral elements play an essential role in the manner in which the representation adapts itself, not only to the actual environmental context, but also to its historical evolution (Abric, 2001, p. 44). Indeed, any new information and any transformation of information in the environment could be integrated into the periphery elements. Periphery elements keep the representation dynamic and at the same time they serve as a defence or as a regulating system resisting a total overhaul of a representation. Because it functions as a defence of a representation, Flament (1994b) compared the peripheral system to a 'shock absorber'. Imagine, for example, that the core elements of a hypothetical social representation of democracy are freedom, justice and human rights. Peripheral elements could be, for example, the education towards citizenship, the social responsibility of citizens and incorruptibility of the local government. If, for the sake of argument, the local government becomes corrupt, citizens may search for reasons of corruptibility in human nature or in bad policies, rather than in democracy as such. In this manner peripheral elements absorb the shock by reference to other phenomena, thus defending their existing social representations of democracy.

Abric (2001, p. 42) declares that the structural approach to the theory of social representations, which he and his colleagues have developed, is a direct extension of Moscovici's theory developed in the early 1960s. In the late 1950s and the early 1960s, cybernetics and theory of information inspired many of Moscovici's ideas. Like other social scientists at the time, e.g. Piaget, so Moscovici viewed cybernetics as a new type of science with tremendous possibilities for natural, social and human sciences. Moreover, cybernetics also made suggestions of how to combine the mathematical theory of information with the 'socio-physical' theory of communication. Moscovici commented that at the time, both information theory and communication theory brought him closer to the idea of representation (Moscovici and Marková, 2000, p. 232).

However, the promise of the 1960s did not materialise and both cybernetics and communication theory based on information processing later developed along formalistic lines that could not be easily transformed into the theory of social representations. Communication is a broadly based concept that refers to highly heterogeneous phenomena. Communication systems in cybernetics include both humans and machines. Information theory involves interaction between humans and machines or imitates machine communication in humans. In contrast, communication in the theory of social representations requires a very specific theoretical basis: dialogicality. Therefore, what originally appeared to be a convergence between cybernetics and the theory of social representations became a matter of divergence in subsequent development.

The structural approach based on the concepts of core and periphery continues to develop (Abric, 2002; Flament, 2002). Nowadays it is concerned with different functions of the core and periphery and it examines relations, from the point of view of core and periphery, between different social representations.

Questions that the core and periphery approach pose are different from those based on the dialogical approach in the theory of social representations. Just like Newton's and Einstein's approaches co-exist in contemporary physics, each of them being suitable for solving different kinds of problem, so the core and periphery and the dialogical approaches are fit for posing and solving different kinds of problem of social representations.

After the 1990s Moscovici has re-conceptualised the theory of social representations and communication in terms of themata and thematisation. Themata are dialogical concepts that significantly contribute to the theoretical development of the theory of social representations as a theory of social knowledge.

2 Themata as the bases of structured contents in social representations

Oppositional antinomies, e.g. freedom/oppression or justice/injustice, we have seen, appear to be essential to human thinking, language and communication and can be found throughout aeons of human history. Yet so far, we have not posed the question as to whether some of these oppositional antinomies might play a more decisive role in thinking and communication generally, and in social representations specifically. This is the question to which we shall now turn.

2.1   Themata in scientific thinking

The idea that certain oppositional antinomies might determine the development of scientific theories is central to *thematic analysis* of Gerald Holton (1975, 1978). In order to understand the content of scientific products, e.g. of laboratory records, the published papers or transcripts of interviews, Holton argues, we need to explore them from a variety of angles. For example, we must evaluate whether there are valid reasons, at that time, for certain scientific claims, in view of the state of shared scientific knowledge. We also need to consider the personal circumstances of the scientist in question, as well as the historical, sociological, cultural and logical conditions in which that scientific event took place. Nevertheless, while recognising the value of all these facets, Holton claims, the direction of scientific thought is determined above all, by a small number of antinomies of thought, which he calls *themata*.

Terms like 'theme' (singular) and 'themes' (plural), and 'thema' (singular) and 'themata' (plural), have been used in a variety of disciplines ranging from literature to music, linguistics and anthropology. However, Holton gives the notions of 'thema' and 'themata' specific meanings. By a thema Holton (1975, 1978) means preconceptions in science which usually involve dyads or triplets such as atomicity/continuum, simplicity/complexity, analysis/synthesis, or constancy/ evolution/catastrophic change. Such oppositional antinomies help to explain the formation of traditions of schools of thought, and the course of controversies (Holton, 1978, p. ix).

He points out that his findings of thematic analysis seem to be related to the dialectic of science, which seeks consensus between 'two themata in antithetical modes'. He explains that antithetical couples, such as evolution and devolution, stability and change or complexity and simplicity, guide the direction of scientific thinking. Scientific imagination, according to this view, seems to be prompted by implicit fidelity to one or more such themata (Holton, 1975), e.g. atoms versus continuum. Holton is a specialist in the history and philosophy of physical sciences and he has developed his theory of themata through case studies, in exploring lives and scientific development of scientists in physics throughout European history.

Merton (1975) commented that Holton developed his thematic analysis in scientific theories inductively rather than from an already established preconception. Holton studied, case by case, the scientists' ways of thinking throughout their theories and in each case he arrived at some kinds of themata. For example, Holton identified the main themata, simplicity and complexity in the work of Mikulas Copernicus. These themata facilitated the mutual accommodation of theory and data in Copernicus' work. In contrast to Copernicus, another famous physicist, Millikan, was committed to the thema of atomism. However, this prevented him from seeing the opposite thema, that of the quantum of light. Adherence to a preconceived thema can both facilitate and impede the scientist's work.

Holton insists on a difference between Kuhn's (1962/1970) concept of scientific revolutions and his concepts of themata. Thematic analysis, Holton argues, reveals certain kinds of constancy and continuities in the history and progression of science. These constancies extend themselves throughout and over Kuhnian scientific revolutions. In other words, a thema, e.g. stability/change could operate both in the Newtonian and in the Einsteinian scientific paradigm. However, it is the actual *content* of this thema in different scientific paradigms that will differ from one paradigm to the next. For example, the thema stability/change in the Newtonian paradigm would derive its content from mechanistic principles, whilst in the Einsteinian paradigm stability/change would be based on the principles of the theory of relativity.

Themata affect scientific thinking implicitly. They are usually theoretical presuppositions, which guide and constrain scientific thinking from inside. They are not usually explicit in scientific terminologies and can be revealed largely through meta-analysis. This is why, as Holton (1978) comments, thematic concepts can rarely be found in the indexes of text-books.

Themata are sometimes of a very long duration. Some of them, like atomism/continuity, have affected scientific thinking for centuries, or even for thousands of years. Holton argues though, that in the history of physical sciences one can identify only very few crucial themata, perhaps no more than a hundred or so. He also points out that it is relatively rare for a totally new thema to emerge in scientific thought. To give a rare example of a recently discovered thema, he points to Bohr's principle of complementarity in the early part of the last century. However, one would wish to question the veracity of this particular example because, as we have seen in Chapter 1, Bohr maintained that it was the ancient Chinese antinomy of yin and yang that brought the concept of complementarity to his attention. It seems, therefore, that in this particular case, Bohr was dealing with a thema of a very long duration.

Holton observed that the scientist's commitment to a particular thema could be long lived throughout the scientist's own life. In fact, a scientist may adopt a thema in childhood. Although there is not enough evidence for the generality of such a claim, we can illustrate it by an observation made by the linguist Roman Jakobson. Analysing Einstein's ideas about mathematics and linguistics, Jakobson (1972/85, pp. 81ff) refers to Einstein's adolescent years when he became acquainted with the work of the linguist Jost Winteler. Having failed the entrance examination to the Federal Institute of Technology in Zurich, young Einstein studied for a year in Aarau. There he became a boarder in the home of the linguist Jost Winteler, who at the time, wrote, a dissertation in which he made a distinction between 'accidental features' in language (variability) and 'essential properties' (invariance). Einstein was apparently influenced by this idea to the extent that he acknowledged later on, on various occasions, that 'the germ of relativity theory' was already contained in the paradoxical reflections which first inspired him during the Aarau year (Jakobson, 1979/85, p. 259).

Holton (1978) also refers to Einstein's devotion to another thema, that of continuity and atomic discreteness. He points out that Einstein's interest in the continuum was not exceeded by any other thema, 'except possibly of symmetry and invariance (that is, of 'relativity' itself)', which goes back to the influence of the Aarau linguist. Holton suggested that themata can be found in other sciences.

With respect to psychology, Holton draws attention specifically to Piaget and to his concepts of accommodation and assimilation as examples of themata. Jahoda's (1999) penetrating anthropological analysis of images of savages suggests that modern prejudice in Western culture reflects the existence of antinomies in human thought like human/animal or human/child. Although Jahoda does not refer specifically to these antinomies as themata, they express a very similar idea.

2.2   Themata in common sense

Scientific themata, we can suppose, originate from common sense. Moscovici made this supposition when he proposed that themata, by which he means taxonomies of oppositional nature, constitute the basis of common sense thinking and by implication, also of social representations (Moscovici, 1992; Moscovici and Vignaux, 1994/2000).

The idea of themata takes us back to antinomies of thinking that we discussed in Chapter 2. Thinking is by nature antinomic. Antinomies of thinking that shape the mental activities of humans, for example, the formation of concepts, meanings in language and images, can be present in human thought for a very long time. Examples of such antinomies in common sense thinking would be those like we/them, freedom/oppression, human/non-human and fear/hope.

However, if thinking is by nature antinomic and if themata are antinomies of common sense thinking, is it not the case that all antinomies of thinking are themata? We shall propose that not all antinomies of thinking become themata.

Although thinking is by nature antinomic, antinomies in thinking are not always explicitly foregrounded. Antinomies in common sense thinking can be dormant. Being embedded in common sense thinking, they are transmitted from generation to generation as part of cultural communication, but without reflection. We adopt thinking in oppositions or antinomies implicitly. For example, being born into a particular culture, the child learns quite naturally to make discriminations and to distinguish, e.g. between things she can eat and those, which should not be consumed.

Antinomies in common sense thinking become themata if, in the course of certain social and historical events, e.g. political, economic, religious and so on, they turn into problems and become the focus of social attention and a source of tension and conflict. It is during such events that antinomies in thinking are transformed into themata: they enter into public discourse, become problematised and further thematised. Then they start generating social representations with respect to the phenomenon in question.

We need to examine why, and under what circumstances, an oppositional taxonomy or an antinomy in common thinking, can become a thema. When is it that it starts generating social representations?

2.3   All antinomies can become themata

Animals, like humans, have a capacity to make distinctions. For example, animals, like humans, have a good sense of what, for their species, is edible and what is poisonous. Nevertheless, making biologically based distinctions is different from creating dialogical antinomies. What makes an antinomy dialogical, is its symbolic nature in communication. If we continue with our previous example of the antinomy edible/inedible, we find in human cultures, that only 'clean' but not 'dirty' food could be consumed. However, although probably all cultures have an antinomy clean/dirty, the content of what is and what is not considered 'dirty', differs from one culture to another. For example, if food is dropped on the ground, it is no longer edible in some cultures but is still edible in others. This might depend not only on the economic conditions of this or that country, but also on religious beliefs, e.g. 'food should not be thrown away' (cf. Josephs and Valsiner, 1998) or on cultural habits. Thus it appears that the antinomy edible/inedible is related to the antinomy clean/dirty.

Continuing with the same theme, people in some cultures do not eat living creatures, like oysters, while for others this is not only acceptable but it is a delicacy. Avoidance of eating meat, or certain kinds of animal, certain parts of animal and so on, all testify to the existence of an antinomy edible/inedible as something basic in daily living, something that is culturally and historically determined.

When a crisis occurs, the antinomy edible/inedible will change its boundaries and will be dialogically transformed. The Chernobyl disaster, the mad cow disease, the pollution of animal feed – all such events rapidly change the content of what becomes categorised as 'edible' and 'inedible'. At the other end of the spectrum, urine and excrements may become 'edible' if there is nothing else to eat, and if the only alternative to consuming such 'normally inedible' things is death. Clearly, the antinomy itself may give rise to public discussions, disputes and arguments. It may, subsequently, become a thema from which social representations of phenomena like food, the animal, health, dirt, life and death, are generated.

Many antinomies exist implicitly in our common sense thinking for centuries and they may never be brought to explicit awareness. This is so, because there may never be any reason, or at least there may not be any reason for generations, for their problematisation and thematisation. Although in principle all antinomies can become themata, that is, the issues for public debate and dispute, many of them do not reach that level.

Despite the fact that some antinomies may not get thematised during our life-time and even during generations, it would be difficult to think about an antinomy, which could never be thematised. We can imagine that social antinomies, like justice/injustice or equality/inequality, will easily become topics of public discourse because we cannot discuss the *Ego-Alter* relations for long without arriving at questions of a direct social concern like social recognition, morals and so on. However, even antinomies that might be considered relatively 'neutral', like sensory and perceptual antinomies, give rise to themata. Throughout history we can find that some of those more 'neutral' antinomies have given rise to rich thematisation in the past. For example, the history of colour tells us fascinating stories about the symbolic meanings of perceptual antinomies and their thematisation.

2.4   Colour as a thema

Colours can be viewed in terms of different perspectives. For example, antinomies like blue/not blue, red/not red or black/not-black may be considered as no more than perceptual distinctions of biological or neuro-visual significance. Alternatively, colour can have an aesthetic significance. Preferences for certain colours during the history of mankind have been related to technological advances enabling colours to be extracted from plants, animals or rocks. On the other hand, technological progress does not explain the social meanings of colours, their symbolic values, representations of ideas, beliefs and activities.

Let us consider thematisation of the colour blue. As early as in the second millennium before Christ, the blue colour had a social and mystical significance in Egypt and the Near East. It was a thema: blue was a preferred colour, because it was believed to keep away evil forces. It was also the colour of funeral ceremonies, because it was believed to protect the dead in the next world. In contrast, for ancient Greeks and Romans, blue/not blue was hardly an antinomy. Historians tell us that Greek and Latin vocabularies had very few words for the colour blue, that these words were ambiguous and did not separate blue from other colours like green, violet or grey. We can even find suggestions in the literature that ancient Greeks may not have had the category 'blue'. To be clothed in blue in ancient Rome was considered to be inferior or eccentric; or at least it was a sign of mourning. Having blue eyes was a physical disgrace. Until the mediaeval times, religious colours in Europe were white, red and black. In religious paintings even the sky was coloured white, red, gold or even black. A blue sky was to be avoided.

Since the eleventh century the situation has dramatically changed and blue became re-thematised. It was now the colour *à la mode*. It became the preferred colour of the Virgin Mary's clothes. The development of the cult of the Virgin Mary in the late mediaeval times and in the early Renaissance had a great impact on the preference for blue. Paintings of the early Renaissance are characteristic of this prevalence for blue. However, it was not only religious symbolism, but changed aesthetic feelings and art also contributed to this radical change in representations of blue. Blue became the colour of fashion and this influenced many important spheres of social life. Moreover, different shades of blue were associated with different social events. Azure became incarnated in armoires, heraldry and in coats of arms. Later on, the royal blue of the King of France introduced a different and a highly significant shade to azure. Royal blue became part of the ceremonies of European aristocracies. Its thematisation has penetrated literature, arts and ordinary life. In general, blue remains a favourite today (Pastoureau, 2000).

A different story applies to the Scottish national flag, the St Andrew's white cross on a blue background. Interestingly, the shade of blue has not been prescribed over centuries for the Scotland's national flag and, today, the new Scottish parliament refuses to lay down a recommended colour. 'Blue is blue' and according to the minister Wallace the regulations on this matter are seen as unnecessary because they 'would create more difficulty than they might solve' announced the Scottish daily newspaper, *The Herald*, on 9 October 2002. The opponent of this view, who lodged the petition with the Scottish parliament, argues, however, that 'no other country's flag is made with varying backgrounds' and that you can see on television Scotland's flag in 'every shade of blue, from duck egg to navy blue' (*The Herald*, 2002). No doubt, the dormant antinomy is becoming a thema!

Equally interesting, but very different, is the history of the colour red. In contrast to blue, red seems to have always been thematised in European cultures; it has been a triumphant colour in the history of art, religion and it has always been seen as a social symbol of one kind or other. Since ancient Greece and Rome, red has been one of the three religious colours apart from white and black. However, it seems that it is in Slav history where the colour red has been more significant than in many other cultures. Red, which has always been a colour of blood and of fire, became the colour of the Soviet Revolution. In November 1917 Lenin chose it as the colour of the Soviet State. Since then it has been identified with communism and Red Square in Moscow became the symbol of the Soviet regime and Soviet life.

In 1998 a very special exhibition of Russian art took place in St Petersburg. This exhibition, launched in the post-Soviet era, was based on the thema of the colour red. Some of the exhibits were abstract paintings that were condemned during the Stalinist era. The exhibition drew attention to the fact that red has been a favourite colour of Russians for centuries. It has been considered a beautiful colour and it has always dominated the colours of cultural products, decorative art and clothes. One can trace it to the art of the monks of Novgorod in the fifteenth century and to icons of the Russian Orthodox religion. Red also dominated naturalistic paintings in the eighteenth and nineteenth centuries, whether clothes of aristocracy or the background of war scenes. It was also a favourite colour in the early twentieth century. One of the most significant paintings was the phantasy of the red horse by Petrow-Wodkin. Red also prevails in abstract paintings by Gontcharova, Malevitch and Chagall (Brugger *et al.*, 1998).

Lexically, there is an association in Slav languages between the words 'red' and 'beautiful'. 'Krasnyj' in the old Russian language meant not only 'red' but also 'beautiful'. In today's Russian, there is still a similarity between the two words, with 'krasivyj' meaning 'beautiful' and 'krasnyj' referring to 'red'.

In another Slav language, in Czech, 'krásný' means 'beautiful'. The linguistic confusion between the Czech and Russian 'red' and 'beautiful' shows in the Czech film *Kolja*. The film is based on a story of a little Russian boy Kolja, who was left in Czechoslovakia by his mother. She emigrated from Czechoslovakia to West Germany during the occupation of Czechoslovakia in 1968 by the Russian and East European troupes. Kolja lived in Prague with a Czech musician. The musician did not speak Russian and Kolja did not speak Czech.

At one point in the film the musician felt obliged to pacify the communist regime. As was the habit at the time, he decorated his windows with the Soviet and the Czech flags in order to celebrate one of the political events. At one crucial moment in the story Kolja pointed his finger at the red Russian flag and said: 'naš krasnyj' (in Russian 'ours is red'). The musician responded: 'I beg your pardon? What is beautiful about it? It is red like training shorts! Ours is beautiful [in Czech 'Náš je krásný']. You understand nothing'.

3   Social recognition as a basic thema

Clearly, some themata play a more important role in social life than others. Some themata seem to be almost eternally foregrounded in public discourse while others emerge, live for a while and disappear.

Some themata arise directly from dialogicality of the *Ego-Alter* and these, we can propose, appear to be conceived in social thinking as essential for the survival and enhancement of humanity. We can refer to such themata as *the basic themata*. The example of such a basic thema is *social recognition and its denial.* I propose that social recognition is a basic thema because it involves realisation of two fundamental dialogical potentials. One potential refers to the *Ego*, who desires that the *Alter* treat him with dignity. The other potential refers to the *Alter*, who desires that the *Ego* treat him with dignity.[2] Social recognition, therefore, is a basic social drive – or desire – directed towards other human beings. Through social recognition, social and historical realities can be conceived as the human history of desired desires (Kojève, 1969, p. 9). As Kojève clarifies, there is an essential difference between animal 'desires' and human desires. For humans, an object, quite useless as a physical entity, e.g. a piece of paper or a cheap medal, can become a symbol of social recognition. It can become an object through which social recognition is transmitted – and therefore, an object of other people's desire. The thema of social recognition, whether the struggle for social recognition or an attempt to deny others' social recognition hides behind many social representations. This should not be surprising because dialogicality of the *Ego-Alter* involves judgements, evaluation and passions and these are concerned with the desire for and the denial of social recognition. For example, those social representations that are focused on the *Ego*, e.g. self-identity, personal responsibility, morality and rights, just like those that foreground the *Alter*, e.g. disabilities, AIDS, democracy and totalitarianism, are all judgemental and evaluative of the *Ego-Alter*. In fact, the *Object* of these representations *is* not an object 'in the world', the *Object* actually *is* the *Ego* and/or the *Alter*. Communication about the self and others can be nothing but judgemental.

Much of social psychology research, like that on social comparison, violence, the desire to be attractive and socially approved of, attribution and intergroup processes could all be re-conceptualised in terms of the struggle for or the denial of social recognition. Moscovici (1976b) explicitly analyses the interdependence between majorities and minorities as the struggle for social recognition by the 'invisible' and 'unattractive' minorities. Moscovici also gives credit to the philosophical and historical meaning of social recognition and he elaborates its social psychological significance. In order to become liked, be chosen as a source of comparison, become socially approved and become someone, who 'counts', active minorities manipulate a variety of forceful strategies to affect majorities' perceptions and their existing social representations.

The history of mankind, from ancient times until today, could be described and analysed in terms of the search and the struggle for social recognition. Social recognition has been continuously thematised in connection with other themata like we/them, freedom/oppression, justice/injustice and equality/inequality and so on, with their contents transforming from one period of time to another. Let us consider, as examples, some thematisations of social recognition in terms of interconnected themata.

3.1   Honour and social recognition

Among terms relating to social recognition, 'honour' has a particularly rich history. The subject of honour and its history displays itself in a multitude of scholarly studies in anthropology and sociology of different cultures as well as in literature. The concept of honour, or the code of honour, existed in pre-modern societies since ancient times all over the world. It has taken different forms through the course of history. In all its manifestations, it has formed a buffer against insult, damage to the self and the injury of one's self-esteem. It has been associated with different hierarchical orders in various societies. For example, it was mandatory in the medieval codes of chivalry and it was part of the social structures of feudalism. Different codes of honour were bound to different social groups, to men and to women. While honour of men in some societies was to express manliness, honour of women was to express shame. The function of honour was not only to maintain status among the socially equal but its role was also to maintain boundaries between different social strata. There were codes on how one should behave with respect to the socially inferior and with respect to those of the same rank according to the principles that 'to each his due' (Berger, 1973). While there were different codes of honour for different social groups, prescribing specific behaviour and etiquette in social contexts, it was the aristocratic concept of honour together with the pursuit of glory, which attracted great literature in mediaeval and Renaissance Europe. Honour became more important than life. Dramatists like Corneille, Shakespeare and Molière, among others, eternalised the concept of honour and showed that it was above the law and life itself. As Corneille says in *Le Cid*: 'Who dares to threaten my honour yet fears to threaten my life?' Even when duels and murders in response to insult became forbidden, in many European countries this custom continued illegally.

Whilst aristocratic honour was a favourite literary genre, anthropological studies have shown how honour manifests itself in poor communities. Campbell's (1964) study of the Greek shepherd community of Sarakatsani shows that even now the community continues to live by quite a severe code of honour. In this little community only members of the kin are honoured and trusted while strangers are treated as enemies. Honour is highly personalised and it is not applicable to anonymous strangers. Campbell points out that this code is very different from the prescriptions of Christian charity and fellowship. Hostility is expressed in aggressive denigration of the reputation of others, theft and physical violence. In conversations with strangers both parties look for hints of the other's intentions or activities that might transgress the code of honour.

3.2   From honour to dignity

Although one can find that social recognition is expressed throughout history in very different terms, in the course of modernity, it has been analysed throughout the transition of the concept of honour into dignity (Berger, 1973). With the transition to modernity, approximately from the sixteenth century onwards the hierarchical order of society and unequal rights among people became obsolete. Specifically, themata like equality/inequality, freedom/oppression and justice/injustice became problematised and thematised both in daily life and in philosophy and social sciences. A number of the eighteenth century philosophers like Rousseau and Montesquieu were preoccupied with the idea of changing society based on hierarchies into a society based on egalitarian principles, i.e. on the principles of dignity. As Berger (1973) argued, dignity meant that all people, regardless of race, beliefs, colour or gender shared the same humanity and that human identity was independent of institutional roles. Berger also observed that insult as an assault on honour and coping with it can hardly be understood in modern societies because motives for honour have no standing in the modern legal system, in which punishment is de-personalised and the subject of scrutiny and proof. Reasons for these changes must be seen in the rise of demands for human rights and dignity, which leads to introducing new morals. All these changes problematised the concept of honour, which as a result became an old-fashioned concept unable to cope with the new humanism, which involves the historically unprecedented concern with dignity, human rights and equality.

Berger explicitly related dignity to the modern concept of self-identity and to problems arising from the *Ego-Alter* relations. The breakdown of pre-modern society not only brought freedom, equality and human rights but it also shattered the pre-modern identity which was closely tight to institutions, kinship, family and in general, to social structures. Pre-modern identity was a stabilised identity in which the individual's identity merged with her social and family roles. It was passed from generation to generation and was not questioned. As identities were given to individuals and were not questioned, so, Taylor (1995e, p. 231) argued, the problem of social recognition did not arise. It could arise only when this stabilised identity disappeared.

For the solitary self that emerged in Europe towards the end of the eighteenth century, the struggle for dignity became associated with equality, freedom, justice and rights. Only when people started to create their individualised identities and when their expectations of recognition of these identities were not fulfilled, could the search for social recognition have become a thema. We can say that our identity is shaped not only by social recognition but, perhaps, and even more, by its opposite, i.e. by non-recognition or misrecognition by others. It can be felt as harm, oppression, and imprisonment in a reduced humanity (cf. Taylor, 1995e, p. 225).

Despite his concern with transition from honour to dignity as an aspect of modernity, Berger makes it clear that it would be a mistake to talk about dignity as something new and modern. He points out that the principles of dignity exist already in the Hebrew Bible, for example, in the confrontation between Nathan and David ('Thou art the man'). The same principles are also to be found in the confrontation between Antigone and Creon in the ancient drama of Sophocles. In both cases, although it is expressed in different ways, behind the roles and the norms imposed by society, there is an understanding that humans should be treated with dignity. As Berger (1973, pp. 82–3) states, 'this humanity as profound dignity, is not a modern prerogative. What is peculiarly modern is the manner in which reality of this intrinsic humanity is related to the realities of society'. What is new in the modern concept of dignity, is that humans have, or should have, their rights irrespective of their position in society, irrespective of race, colour or creed. We can translate Berger's analysis into the hypothesis of the dialogicality *Ego-Alter*. Social recognition expresses itself differently in specific historical conditions. Alternatively, we could say that while the thema of dignity, through which social recognition expresses itself, is as old as humanity, its content keeps changing as well as its boundaries.

3.3 Thematisation of morality/immorality in relation to social recognition

The search for and the denial of social recognition often takes place through thematisation of specific antinomies. One of them is morality/immorality. It is a thema that is judgemental and evaluative of the *Ego-Alter*. Evolutionary epistemology provides evidence for its biological origins in phylogenesis, and its transformation in socio-cultural history.

Throughout the history of humanity, disease and death have often been surrounded by myths related to morality/immorality. In ancient societies disease was collectively represented as an activity of supernatural forces. It was believed that violation of social taboos resulted in illness and illness was a social marker of the boundaries of acceptable behaviour (Dubos, 1968). The rise of Christianity in Europe reinforced links between sin and moral transgression, punishment and illness, and apocalypse and plague. While the thema of morality/immorality has existed throughout history and culture, the ways in which it has been problematised and thematised, have been unique to specific societies and cultures.

In the last two decades, morality/immorality has been amongst the most important themata that have generated social representations of AIDS. During the 1980s the epidemic of the 'new' killer disease AIDS, spread rapidly throughout the world. The disease, caused by the human immunity deficiency virus, is due to the breakdown of immunity. It leads to various kinds of illnesses like cancers, pulmonary problems and exhaustion, from which the patient is likely to die. In the first stage of the epidemic in the 1980s the disease primarily affected homosexuals and drug users and it became quickly associated, for the general public, with immorality, 'misbehaviour', sin and punishment.

Research findings concerning social representations of AIDS, analysis of the media and public discourses, have all led to the basic thema: morality/immorality. 'Morality back in fashion' announced the *Daily Express* on 2 January 1987. '*Churchmen attack war on AIDS as immoral*', wrote the *Daily Mail*, 17 June 1987. The governmental campaign in the UK, focusing on provision of education about sexual protection, 'Don't die of ignorance' was blamed for encouraging promiscuity and immorality. Other newspaper headlines emphasised that AIDS victims were outcasts who did not deserve to live: '*AIDS sufferer tried suicide after doctor said: Cut your wrists*' (*Daily Express*, 6 March 1987).

However, due to active and consistent behavioural styles of homosexual communities, the thema morality/immorality became challenged and problematised. As a result, morality/immorality has continued to be re-thematised. The terminology, originally GRID (Gay Related Immune Syndrome) was changed into AIDS (Acquired Immunity Deficiency Syndrome). Newspaper articles that related AIDS to morality/immorality and punishment gradually disappeared. Today, it would be unthinkable that newspaper headlines such as those above could appear in the press. Social representations of AIDS have kept changing accordingly; social representations are rarely generated from a single thema. In the case of AIDS, re-thematisation of morality/immorality was associated with re-thematisation of values related to sexuality, promiscuity in the general public, discrimination of minorities and with social recognition, among other issues (Marková *et al.* 1995). While the antinomy of morality/immorality itself was not questioned, it was its content, context and boundaries that were thematised and re-thematised in the context of changes of social representations.

3.4   Thematisation of freedom/oppression

Thematisation of freedom/oppression in post-communist Europe can serve as another example of generating social representations that are closely linked to social recognition. In 1989 the world experienced an un-expected event: the collapse of the Soviet bloc. After forty years of Soviet rule, the countries of Central and Eastern Europe overthrew their politi-cal, social and economic systems and chose their own ways of transform-ing 'people's democracies' to the democracies of Western style. Europe became a 'natural laboratory' in which social psychologists could explore social representations of phenomena related to this radical change, like the formation and transformation of social representations of democracy.

In political terminology, 'democracy' and 'return to Europe' became a frequent rhetoric of the time with reference to these dramatic changes. Market economy and privatisation replaced the socialist command econ-omy and state ownership. Political parties were mushrooming, appearing overnight in their dozens, contradicting the one-party system in the Com-munist regime. Streets and institutions were renamed and the names of the martyrs of the past regime replaced those of the communist heroes. Statues of Lenin and other creators of the past regime disappeared.

The main finding of social psychological research at the time was that in contrast to professional definitions of democracy, social repre-sentations of democracy were above all associated with social recog-nition. In a series of studies that was carried out over a decade from 1990, the same finding was repeatedly confirmed. While professional definitions of democracy usually referred to political representation, the rule of majorities and the government of people, the contents of social representations of democracy included above all the thematisation of freedom/oppression, justice/injustice and human rights (Marková et al., 1998b). Apart from equality/inequality which, after the collapse of com-munism had very low currency in post-communist countries, the the-mata dominating social representations of democracy, referred to similar issues that Berger (1973) found in his analysis of human dignity. Other research at the time corroborated these results. For example, the popular concept of democracy in Poland differed from the normative textbook meaning. In searching for the underlying dimensions of these socio-political perceptions, it was found that despite prolonged attempts to change the meanings of the 'traditional European notions of freedom and democracy', citizens described the new democracy primarily in terms of attained freedom (Buchowski *et al.*, 1994, p. 555; Reykowski, 1995). In Bulgaria, Patzeva (1994) found that in her research, the most frequent response to 'democracy' was 'freedom'. Simon (1997), in a multi-lingual twelve-nation survey of political culture in Central and Eastern Europe asked his participants what democracy meant to them. He found, once again, that freedom was the most common meaning of democracy (see also Miller *et al.*, 1997).

As in the case of morality/immorality, a brief historical reference with hindsight could help us to understand the relations between social recognition and social representations of democracy. When de Tocqueville wrote about *Democracy in America* (1835/1945) it did not look like 'democracy' was a word used in ordinary language (Naess *et al.*, 1956, pp. 119–20). Naess and his colleagues thought that de Tocqueville introduced the term because it had been used in France and he considered it suitable for a description of American society. As Naess observes, in the eighteenth century democracy was in nearly all civilised countries 'identical with a "rule of terror" in the style of the French Jacobins' (Naess *et al.* 1956, p. 107). However, after the French Revolution 'democracy' became anchored, in public thought, to 'liberty', 'fraternity', 'equality', 'human rights', 'justice' and all those ideals of humanity that were desired by the oppressed, i.e. by those who were not socially recognised. Therefore, democracy became associated with social recognition and with the dialogical antinomy of the *Ego-Alter*. Thus it was then that the word 'democracy' obtained currency in ordinary language.

Although antinomies like freedom/oppression, justice/injustice and equality/inequality appear to be shared by many cultures and societies, their problematisation and thematisation is determined by specific social conditions in each culture and society. In the first years after the political revolution, social representations of democracy in post-communist countries were contrasted with the oppression of the 'people's democracy' of the past. Democracy was a matter of passion, of hopes and optimism for the future.

However, as the reforms did not progress as fast as expected and as economic problems of the transition to the market economy mounted, the positive feelings changed into negative ones, and into the expression of disillusion and disappointment. The meaning of new democracy became associated, again, with being treated without dignity, i.e. without social recognition. These feelings had several sources. On the one hand, our respondents expressed fear of the Mafia, deception and corruption, they commented on the sharp increase in criminality. On the other hand, they felt a general insecurity and a fear of expressing their opinion. The situation as they experienced it reminded them of the totalitarian system of the past. However, whether emotions were positive or negative, democracy was in the public discourse. It was the issue of relevance to citizens' life and its quality (Marková *et al.* 2001).

While our respondents in the UK and France expressed social representations of democracy primarily in terms of freedom, justice, equality and human rights, our respondents from post-communist countries included, in addition, free market, privatisation and all new economic and financial institutions. The latter were introduced in post-communist countries at the same time as their new democratic systems after the fall of the Berlin Wall. Not surprisingly, they were viewed as features of new democracies. None of these issues formed the contents of social representations in the UK and France. Moreover, participants' responses in post-communist countries implied that anything that was disliked about society and anything that did not fit their expectations of the new political system was a lack of democracy.

Although respondents both from traditional and new democracies shared antinomies like freedom/oppression, justice/injustice and equality/inequality, problematisation and thematisation of their contents were determined by specific social and political conditions. For example, what may be considered as freedom in one country, could be considered as oppression in another country. However, even in the same country, after some passage of time, what is considered as freedom at a certain period of time, could be felt as oppression in another time.

Participants' thematisation of freedom/oppression, justice/injustice and equality/inequality presents a rich panorama of expectations, beliefs and common sense knowledge about democracy. We can conclude that re-conceptualisation of the structured contents of social representations in terms of themata will enable us to see their potential for further development of ideas relating to the theory and, more generally, to social psychology. Through thematisation we can learn about processes of the self, identity, influence and group dynamics as well as about many other social psychological issues. These phenomena, moreover, will require examination of communication and speech genres through which they are thematised.

4   Thematisation through communication genres

Social representations involve a multitude of ways in which humans think, imagine and communicate about their social realities. In other words, thematisation and re-thematisation of social representations take place through different styles of thinking and communicating. These styles differ according to specific local situations, institutional rules, group norms and cultural traditions. Some activities are more or less culturally or institutionally fixed, e.g. legal procedures, education or doctor–patient consultations, others are more informal, e.g. public gatherings, conversations in cafés or family talks. These styles of thinking and communication also differ with respect to what purposes they serve. They are framed by social positions of interlocutors, by their personal interrelations, by norms and rules of politeness and tradition (Linell, 1998).

4.1   Communication genres

Researchers characterise such styles of thinking and communicating in different ways and using different terms, e.g. 'contextualisation conventions', 'activity types', 'communicative projects' and 'speech or communication genres'. Some researchers focus on pragmatic, others on linguistic (semantic, syntactic, phonological) or content based characteristics of communication (for a scholarly review see Linell, 1998). We shall call these styles communication genres.

Although they are expressed through the mouth of the individual, genres are social conventions (Luckmann, 1992). There is no genre that belongs to a sole individual but through genres the individual conveys her belonging to a certain culture, a group or her commitment to a certain social practice. For a communicative activity to be called a genre, it must be recognised as such, even if only implicitly, by members of the community of which it is a part. Genres correspond 'to typical situations of speech communication, typical themes, and consequently, also to particular contacts between the meanings of words and actual concrete reality under certain typical circumstances' (Bakhtin, 1979/1986, p. 87). Children adopt speech or communication genres naturally in their social environment as they acquire language. They learn to speak in different genres without even realising that they do so. Through genres they learn to view social realities from particular perspectives. For Medvedev, 'seeing and representation merge' and 'new means of representation force us to see new aspects of visible reality' (Medvedev, 1934/1985). In order to be creative, the artist must see realities with the eyes of the genre. In this perspective, the notion of genre repudiates 'neutrality' in language and thought and refocuses attention on heteroglossia in language and polyphasia in thought.

The diversity of genres stems from their embeddedness in specific local situations (e.g. the family, therapy, social and political groups etc.) which are framed by social positions of interlocutors and their personal interrelations. Voloshinov (1929/1973) noted the proliferation of different communication genres in all life situations. Therefore, he spoke about behavioural genres, thus interconnecting communication with action. Behavioural genres just like communication genres are facts of the social milieu, they are conventional and institutional.

Despite being conventionalised and institutionalised, speech and communication genres have a double orientation: they are relatively stable and dynamic organisations of thought and language. While genre is a relatively stable social convention that is embedded in its socio-historical background, it changes through communicative practices. Referring to Dostoyevsky's work, Bakhtin characterises genre as living in the present yet remembering its past: genre is representative of creative memory in the process of literary evolution, which is precisely why genre is capable of guaranteeing some unity and the continuity of this evolution (Bakhtin, 1984a, p. 142). This means that like the linguistic means, vocabulary, grammar and morphology, communication genres are transmitted through history and reconstituted in local situations. To learn language, therefore, is not only to learn vocabulary and grammar but also genres. By adopting genres one also adopts the styles of thinking.

Genres are meaningful only in relation to another genres or to communication styles. This point already captured Jurij Tynjanov, one of the Russian formalists of the early part of the twentieth century. He argued that it is incorrect to conceive of genre as something static because a new genre forms itself out of conflict with a traditional genre. It emerges, has its time and disappears or changes into rudiments of other systems. A new phenomen takes the place of an old one. It is impossible to study isolated genres outside the system in which they are implicated (Tynjanov, 1929b/1971, p. 106). In other words, it is not enough simply to want to know what a genre is without relating it to its particular context, for example to a poem in the twentieth century.

Because communication genres are relational social phenomena, we do not acquire them through learning language in the language laboratory. A Czechoslovakian dissident Šimečka (1984) presented a communication genre that was part of the situation called 'normalisation' after 1968 in Czechoslovakia. 'Normalisation' was a term applied officially by the communist regime after the invasion of the country by the foreign troops of the Soviet bloc. It meant returning to a normal life by accepting the *status quo* and pretending that there was nothing wrong with the fact that the country was occupied. It was supposed to be seen not only as a normal situation but also as a 'thank you' to the Soviet regime for saving the country from the influence of Western ideology and Western practices. Šimečka pointed out that to a stranger coming to Czechoslovakia during that period, that situation was difficult to grasp. Strangers did not share the local genre. Foreign troops occupied the country and the post-totalitarian and dictatorial regime legitimised its authority from their presence. The regime exerted pressure on everybody who appeared to express any con-conformist ideas. Šimečka gives a social-psychological account of the situation, in which citizens did not protest, behaved as if everything was normal, as if they did not see the absurd and senseless system that dictated their behaviour in daily life and in which they were immersed. It appeared that no tension existed there and that everybody played the game. By ignoring the system and by not engaging in communication, citizens allowed the regime to continue its existence. They prolonged the regime's continuous monologue in which no change took place.

4.2   Relations between social representations and communication genres

How social representation is thematised through genre depends on the kind of *Ego-Alter* relations. Some communication genres are similar to monologues with a dominant voice, e.g. in ceremonies, whether religious, political, social or otherwise. Other genres are based on 'thematisation' that involves re-statements and recycling of what is already known. For example, propaganda uses strategies of repetition, re-statements and re-gurgitation of information. Such genres often have specific aims, like changing political or religious ideologies into social representations. Yet other genres thematise topics that speakers conceive as problematic. Thematisation can appear spontaneously in public discourse. Thematisation, in this case, expresses the effort a speaker makes to understand and appropriate the meaning which is at the heart of the matter.

In *La Psychanalyse: son image et son public*, Moscovici (1961, 1976a) identifies three systems of communication, namely, diffusion, propagation and propaganda[3] according to the source, the goal and the logic of messages. Moscovici shows that each system of communication has its rules of logic, lexical means, syntax, form of argument and means of influence. For example, diffusion of psychoanalysis in journals proceeded by using a style, which could be described as concrete, attractive and quick. It focused on the use of the vocabulary of the reader, and it showed that application of short sentences raised attention and was amusing. For example, titles like 'Divers into the unconsciousness' attempted to elicit new and unusual images. In contrast, propaganda used adjectives and specific phrases, like 'psychoanalysis as pseudo-science', 'bourgeois pseudo-science' or 'American pseudo-science'. Rather than focusing on images, it focused on producing an ideological, verbal or a conceptual effect. The intention of propaganda was to disqualify psychoanalysis as a science and the linguistic means were to serve this purpose. Once the connection between undesirable states of affairs and psychoanalysis was made through such means, e.g. 'pseudo-science' or 'bourgeois', the connection could then be generalised to psychoanalysis as such. Once the effect of generalisation was achieved, adjectives and other linguistic means could be removed. The word 'psychoanalysis' has obtained its negative meaning through propaganda and it no longer needs to make a connection between 'bourgeois pseudo-science' and 'American pseudo-science'.

Another example of propaganda is related to the notion of 'democracy' used during the Cold War in the 1950s. Since the First World War, all politicians, from Nazis to Communists, all defined democracy in positive terms. The politicians of the Soviet bloc, just like politicians in the West, declared that their political system was democratic. However, they clearly distinguished Soviet definitions of democracy from those by Western politicians. They practically never used 'democracy' in an unqualified manner but they usually combined it with an adjective, for example 'bourgeois democracy', 'proletarian democracy' with the 'Soviet democracy' representing the highest form of all democracies (Naess et al. 1956; Moodie, Marková and Plichtová, 1995). They felt it necessary to demonstrate that democracy in the Soviet bloc countries was a different kind of democracy than that in Western countries and linguistic means served such aims well.

An extreme case of thematisation or lack of thematisation may refer to situations in which the phrase or an utterance becomes inexpressible for fear of its effect. The semantic power of words can be omnipotent whether uttered or written down. Douglas (1966) maintains that certain kinds of images evoked by some words do not allow people to spell them out for fear that the very words might bring about calamity. In a similar vein Sontag (1979) refers to the names of diseases as having a magic power over people. Among her examples are Stendhal's *Armance*, in which the hero's mother refused to say 'tuberculosis'. By pronouncing the word she could bring about her son's death. Similarly, in Menninger's *The Vital Balance* the very word 'cancer' prematurely killed some patients.

Communication genres, just like in hidden polemic, may use a 'sideward glance' and may refer to seemingly unconnected phenomena or may even remain tacit and unverbalised. Yet, they *are* genres as long as their tacit meaning is collectively understood. Záviš Kalandra, a Czech intellectual murdered in 1951 in one of the monster-trials, knew the genre of political trials in 1937 in the USSR and during a Nazi process in 1939. He had previously analysed these events and their linguistic features in his publications (Kalandra, 1994). When he himself was put on trial by the communist regime in Czechoslovakia he recognised that communists used the same genre that was used in Nazi and Soviet political processes and which led to the execution of the accused. Therefore, despite the disbelief of his friends and colleagues, he knew, from the very beginning of the process, that he too would be executed.

In his paper on social representations and pragmatic communication Moscovici (1994) shows a very special communicative genre. He analyses the sentence 'The Bororo are arara' by which Lévy-Bruhl illustrates his vision of the mystical participation of Bororo individuals in various spheres of life:

[This sentence] utters the Bororo individual's creed: at one and the same time he is both himself, a man, and something different from himself, a bird (Moscovici, 1994, p. 163).

Moscovici points out that the communication power of this sentence, which, with a minimum of semantic material transmits a number of representations, emotions and poetry, goes far beyond semantic meaning. Its intense communicative power lies in its capacity to express rich images filled with mythical narratives which are shared by the Bororo and which represent their social reality. These images are framed within particular speech genres, which are likely to be transmitted from generation to generation and institutionalised as forms of communication filled with mythical narratives. The Bororo share these images and they represent their social realities. Language framed in these genres plays an integrative role in the context of mythic invention and in the formation and maintenance of people's representations of their social world.

Therefore, behind genres, there is our shared social past as well as open and unlimited potential for new enquiries.

NOTES

1. Social sciences often conceive the phenomena under study as *structures and processes*. For example, linguistics studies linguistic phenomena in terms of linguistic structures like syntactic, semantic, grammatical or pragmatic, the structures of conversations, their openings and closings, and so on. Anthropology defines the phenomena of its study with respect to the structures of kinship, family, tribe organisations and so on. Psychology, too, identifies structures, like structures of personalities or groups, cognition, etc. In general, structures and processes are conceived as hierarchies, levels and stages, which can be classified, categorised and sub-categorised. The study of structures and processes in social science has been largely motivated by the search for general principles and laws in social sciences, enabling the understanding and prediction of the phenomena in question. Structures in these cases are viewed as relatively stable conglomerations of elements and structuralists are usually quick to add that structures are more than the sums of their parts. Those with more

dialectic tendencies, like Anthony Giddens, attempt to view structures and processes as dynamic and interdependent entities, e.g. as structure/processes. They argue that structures and processes are not separate from one another but that structures are shaped by processes and that they, themselves, shape processes. Overall, the study of structures and processes in the social science foregrounds abstract, generalised or generalisable aspects of the phenomena in question.

2. In modernity it was Hegel who explicitly defined social recognition in dialogical terms. In his explicit formulation, the individual has the capacity to acknowledge the other as a human and he or she has the desire to be acknowledged in the same fashion. Hegel explains the meaning of these two dialogical aspects of social recognition in his allegory of the Master and Slave. This allegory shows that the need and desire for social recognition forms the very foundations of any human relationship in civilised, that is, non-totalitarian and non-terrorist societies. For the completeness of my argument, I shall reiterate briefly this well-known allegory. Hegel articulates the relation between *Ego-Alter* as follows: one of them, the master, has freedom and power; the other, the slave, lives oppression and is dependent on the former. The dependence of the slave on his master, the fear for his life and the desire to be valued by his master leads him to act, to learn skills and to create things. Through fear he learns not only to value the products of his own work and to discipline himself, but also to become conscious of himself as a free human being. As a result, he demands to be acknowledged by his master. It is through his dependence on the other who is more powerful, and through self-realisation of his own potential that, in the end, he gains. The master, in contrast, cannot look up to the slave because he considers him to be inferior. However, because he cannot recognise the slave as a human consciousness that is equal to his over, he does not satisfy his own basic need for social recognition. Only those who consider themselves as worthy of recognising one another, satisfy the condition for social recognition through mutual acknowledgement. The master loses because he does not acknowledge the slave as being worthy of acknowledgement. An important message of this allegory is that one cannot achieve self-recognition at the expense of the other. Recognition has to be mutual if it is to be a true and satisfactory recognition. And the struggle and conflict between conscious human beings are for Hegel a logical necessity for the development of self-consciousness (Marková, 1982).

3. Moscovici (2000, in Moscovici and Marková) remarked that what he called in *La Psychanalyse* 'systems of communication' he would now call 'communication genres'.

8   Conclusion: social representations and dialogicality

I have arrived at the end of the journey on which I set out by drawing attention to the basic capacity of living organisms to make distinctions. Many researchers before me started their enquiries in a similar way. However, focusing on organisms' ability to make distinctions opens up options for many different routes. For example, for Western philosophers, from Aristotle through to Kant and Russell, the capacity of making distinctions was the starting point for posing metaphysical questions about the nature of the world. Making distinctions opened for them the route for thinking in categories, which they conceived as independent principles of the presumably objective world consisting of, e.g. substances, quantities or relations. Making distinctions can also constitute the basis for the formulation of typologies, the development of different kinds of logic and the search for order and hierarchical structures.

In focusing on making distinctions, I have chosen yet another route. My starting point of enquiry was not ontology in a metaphysical sense, like the ontology of being in the natural world. Instead, the capacity of making distinctions has led me to making a hypothesis about the *Ego-Alter* as the ontology of the human world based on communication. I have first conceived of antinomies in human thinking, language and dialogue. But then I have turned the question round. Why do we think and speak in antinomies? Because, I hypothesise, thinking and speaking in antinomies is an expression of dialogicality of the human mind. Dialogicality is the capacity of the *Ego* to conceive and comprehend the world in terms of the *Alter* and to create social realities in terms of the *Alter*.

Scientific theories are human theories however 'scientific' they may be. They live and transform themselves as long as there are researchers who are attracted by the ideas that they propose. The theory of social representations originated in the study of a specific social phenomenon, psychoanalysis in France in the 1950s. However, it was the emphasis of this theory on communication and on common thinking that has provided the

203

basis for the transformation of the specific theory of social representations of psychoanalysis into the theory of social knowledge.

In this book I have implied but not explicitly discussed that the notion of the theory of social representations as used today, has two distinct, yet interconnected meanings. In the first instance, I have referred to the theory of social representations as the theory of social knowledge. The second meaning of the theory of social representations is more specific. It is the theory concerned with the study and explanations of specific social phenomena that appear in public discourse. This point may not be easily understood because the two meanings of the theory of social representations have been developing over the years together and have cross-fertilised one another. Nevertheless, it is important to distinguish between these two meanings for the following reasons.

The theory of social representations as the theory of social knowledge defines the field of social psychology. It is a unifying epistemological force binding the discipline together. This theory of social knowledge is based on dialogicality. Dialogical knowledge is generated from the three-component processes of the *Ego-Alter-Object* (social representation) in their many manifestations and dynamics rather than from a monological *Ego-Object*. The *Ego-Alter* is a communicative and a symbolic relation. In this sense the theory provides our discipline with an epistemological coherence. This does not mean that it aims at a theoretical homogeneity of our field. On the contrary, the theoretical diversity of social psychology is essential for studying the multiple social realities in which we live. By insisting on different styles of thinking and communicating and by emphasising the multifaceted natures of social realities, the theory of social representations as a theory of social knowledge provides the grounds for the theoretical diversity in social psychology. For example, theories of influence based on this theory of social knowledge would involve three-component processes consisting of the *Ego* (for example, a minority) – the *Alter* (for example, a majority) – the *Object* (for example, the shade of blue of the Scottish national flag). This would exclude the possibility of focusing only on the majority influence while neglecting the minority influence; it would exclude the possibility of discourse being considered only at the level of external dialogue rather than as an internal dialogue. Theories of the self and identity, using the dialogical theory of social knowledge would focus on oppositions of identity, on the mutuality of social recognition, on multiple kinds of *Ego-Alter* and on the culturally embedded themata pertaining to personal identities and personal change. Being underpinned by the dialogical theory of social knowledge, social psychological theories will develop their specific theoretical concepts, pertinent to their particular approaches. For example, theories of influence develop their own specific concepts, e.g. of the behavioural style, power, conflict, speech and communication genres, subjectivity and so on.

The second meaning of *the theory of social representations refers to the study of the phenomena that are thematised in public discourse.* In this sense, the theory of social representations is one among other social psychological theories that are based on the theory of social representations as the theory of social knowledge. The theory in its specific sense examines phenomena in the centre of social life and daily realities, whether they are political, ecological, health related and so on. Indeed, its force manifests itself through the study of phenomena, which touch in some fundamental ways upon daily life, of phenomena, which disrupt routines or even, turn them upside down. For example, how do people socially represent, exchange and create ideas about health (e.g. Jovchelovitch and Gervais, 1999)? About madness (e.g. Jodelet, 1989; de Rosa, 1987)? About human rights (Doise *et al.*)? About adolescence (e.g. Palmonari, 1993)? About democracy (e.g. Galli, 2001; Uribe and Acosta, 1992)? About citizenship (Lozada, 2000; Acosta and Uribe, 2000)? About the quality of life (Liu, 2002)?

Like other theories in social psychology, the theory of social representations in its specific sense develops its own concepts, e.g. anchoring, objectification and normative or hegemonic representations. The theory is also concerned with social action. For example, in his study of the social representations of psychoanalysis, Moscovici (1961) studied communicative actions like propaganda and propagation. Jodelet (1989), in her study of social representations of madness studied not only representations as thoughts but as social practices resulting from representations. By studying people in action, the researcher makes the theory.

The theory of social representations in this specific sense reconceptualises the traditional differentiation between 'pure' and 'applied' social psychology. 'Pure' social psychology often studies 'processes' and 'structures' in the laboratory setting without paying attention to real people, their problems, passions and interests. A researcher doing 'pure' research can carry out laboratory experiments throughout his life. He can study 'subjects' and their 'processes', e.g. judgements in imaginary situations, information processing and linguistic biases without seeing 'people' in their social realities. Berkowitz (1999, p. 163) guesses that the overwhelming majority of studies that were published in the last decade in the main journals of social psychology 'were stimulated by other laboratory experiments rather than by naturalistic observation'.

Social representations in society are perhaps best explored in public discourse; phenomena that are problematic raise tension and become, therefore, subjects of debates. If the researcher intends to study phenomena that are not relevant to the concerns of society here-and-now, however hard he tries, he does not find social representations! Since the theory concerns social realities in which people live, it has become of major interest in the developing countries and in countries where democratisation has a major value and where health and values aiming to extend and improve human life are primary goals. For example, the theory of social representations is much advanced in Latin America; it is also of interest in post-Communist European countries and in Asia.

The two meanings of social representations, i.e. the theory of social representations as the theory of social knowledge and the specific theory of social representations cross-fertilise one another. There are many possibilities for their theoretical development and for creating new social practices. The study of linguistic aspects of thematisation, polyphasia in thinking and knowledge, explorations of speech and communicative genres is only beginning. Equally, interdependencies between modern technology, dialogicality and the relevant macrosocial phenomena will present new challenges for the theory of social representations as a theory of social knowledge, as well as in its specific sense.

In addition to the possibility of eliminating fragmentation of social psychology, the theory of social representations makes a very specific and fundamental contribution. It places language and communication at the centre of social psychology.

References

Abelson, R.P., Aronson, E., McGuire, W.J., Newcomb, T.M., Rosenberg, M.J. and Tannenbaum, P.H. (1968). *Theories of Cognitive Consistency: A Sourcebook.* Chicago: Rand McNally.

Abric, J-C. (1994). L'organisation interne des représentations sociales: système central et système péripherique. In C. Guimelli (ed.) *Structures et Transformations des Représentations Sociales*, pp. 73–84. Neuchâtel: Delachaux et Niestlé.

Abric, J-C. (2001). A structural approach to social representations. In K. Deaux and G. Philogène. *Representations of the Social.* Oxford: Blackwell.

Abric, J-C. (2002). L'approche structurale des représentations sociales: développements récents. *Psychologie & Societé*, 4, 81–103.

Acosta, T. and Uribe, J. (2000). El pandemónium en la ciudad de México. In J. Juárez and S. Arciga (eds.) *La Ciudadanía: Estudios de Psicología Política y Representación Social*, 111–41. México: Unidad Iztapalapa.

Arbib, M.A. and Hesse, M.B. (1986). *The Construction of Reality.* New York: Cambridge University Press.

Arendt, H. (1955/1973). Introduction. Walter Benjamin: 1892–1940. In W. Benjamin: *Illuminations*, pp. 7–55. London: Fontana Press. Trans. from *Schriften* (1955): Frankfurt-am-Main: Suhrkamp Verlag.

Aristotle, *Metaphysica. The Works of Aristotle*, Vol. VIII. Trans. and ed. W.D. Ross (1908). Oxford: Clarendon Press.

Aristotle, *Analytica Posteriora.* Trans. J. Barnes (1975). Oxford: Clarendon Press.

Aronsson, K. (1991). Facework and control in multi-party talk: a pediatric case study. In I. Marková and K. Foppa (eds.) *Asymmetries in Dialogue*, pp. 49–74. New York & London: Harvester Wheatsheaf.

Atkinson, J.M. and Heritage, J. (eds.) (1984). *Structures of Social Action.* Cambridge University Press.

Bain, A. (1868). *Mental and Moral Science: A Compendium of Psychology and Ethics.* London: Longmans Green.

Bakhtin, M.M. (1981). *The Dialogic Imagination.* Four essays by M.M. Bakhtin. Ed. M. Holquist. Trans. by C. Emerson and M. Holquist. Austin: University of Texas Press.

Bakhtin, M.M. (1979/1986). *Estetika SlovesnovoTvorchestva.* Moskva: Bocharov. Trans. by V.W. McGee as *Speech Genres and Other Late Essays* (eds. C. Emerson and M. Holquist). Austin: University of Texas Press.

Bakhtin, M.M. (1984a). *Problems of Dostoyevsky's Poetics.* Ed. and trans. by C. Emerson. Manchester University Press.

Bakhtin, M.M. (1984b). *Rabelais and His World*. Trans. by H. Iswolsky. Bloomington: Indiana University Press.

Bakhtin, M.M. (1986/1993). *Towards a Philosophy of the Act*. Trans. and notes by Vadim Liapunov. Austin: University of Texas Press.

Baldwin, J.M. (1895). *Mental Development in the Child and the Race: Methods and Processes*. New York and London: Macmillan.

Baldwin, J.M. (1897). *Social and Ethical Interpretations in Mental Development*. London: Macmillan.

Baldwin, J.M. (1910). *Darwin and the Humanities*. London: Swan Sonnenschein.

Baldwin, J.M. (1911). *The Individual and Society*. London: Rebman.

Batnitzky, L. (2000). *Idolatry and Representation: The Philosophy of Franz Rosenzweig Reconsidered*. Princeton University Press.

Beer, G. (1993). Wave theory and the rise of literary modernism. In G. Levine (ed.) *Realism and Representation*, pp. 193–213. Madison: University of Wisconsin Press.

Beilin, H. (1992). Piaget's new theory. In H. Beilin and P. Pufall (eds.). (1992) *Piaget's Theory: Prospects and Possibilities*, pp. 1–17. Hillsdale, J.J.: Lawrence Erlbaum.

Benjamin, W. (1955/1973). Theses on the philosophy of history. In *Illuminations*, pp. 245–55. London: Fontana Press. Trans. from *Schriften* (1955): Frankfurt-am-Main: Suhrkamp Verlag.

Benveniste, E. (1966). *Problèmes de Linguistique Générale*. Paris: Gallimard.

Berger, P. (1973). On the obsolescence of the concept of honour. In P. Berger, B. Merger, and H. Kellner (eds.). *The Homeless Mind*, pp. 78–89. Harmondsworth: Penguin Books.

Berger, P. and Luckman, T. (1966). *The Social Construction of Reality*. New York: Doubleday Anchor Books.

Bergson, H. (1932/1935). *Two Sources of Morality and Religion*. Trans. R. Ashley Audra and Cloudesley Brereton. London: Macmillan.

Berkowitz, L. (1999). On the changes in US social psychology: some speculations. In A. Rodrigues and R.V. Levine (eds.). *Reflections on 100 Years of Experimental Social Psychology*, pp. 158–69. New York: Basic Books.

Berlin, I. (1976). *Vico and Herder. Two Studies in the History of Ideas*. London: The Hogarth Press.

Bernstein, N.A. (1967). *The Co-ordination and Regulation of Movements*. Oxford and London: Pergamon Press.

Billig, M. (1996). *Arguing and Thinking: A Rhetorical Approach to Social Psychology*. Cambridge New York: Cambridge University Press. Paris: Editions de la Maison des Sciences de l'Homme.

Billington, J. (1966). *The Icon and the Axe. The Interpretative History of Russian Culture*. London: Weidenfeld and Nicolson.

Böhme, J. (1623/1958). *Mysterium Magnum oder Erklärung über das erste Buch Mosis*. Sämtliche Schriften, 7–8. Stuttgart: Frommanns Verlag.

Brugger, I., Kiblitsky, J., Petrova, J. and Schröder, K. (eds.) (1998). *Rot in der Russischen Kunst*. Milano: Skira Editore. Wien: Kunstforum.

Buber, M. (1923/1962). *I and Thou*. Edinburgh: T&T Clark.

Buchowski, M., Kronenfeld, D., Peterman, W. and Thomas, L. (1994). Language, *Nineteen eighty-four* and 1989. *Language in Society*, 23, 555–78.

Budgen, F.S.C. (1972). *James Joyce and the Making of 'Ulysses', and Other Writings*. London: Oxford University Press.

Bühler, K. (1934). *Sprachtheorie*. Jena/Stuttgart: Gustav Fischer Verlag. *Theory of Language: The Representational Function of Language*. Trans. D.F. Goodwin. Amsterdam: John Benjamins, 1990.

Bühler, K. (1982). The axiomatization of the language sciences. In R.E. Innis (ed.), *Karl Bühler, Semiotic Foundations of Language Theory*, pp. 75–164. New York: Plenum Press.

Butera, F., Legrenzi, P., Mugny, G. and Pérez, J.A. (1991–92). Influence sociale et raisonnement, *Bulletin de Psychologie*, 45, 144–54.

Campbell, J.K. (1964). *Honour, Family and Patronage: A Study of Institutions and Moral Values in a Greek Mountain Community*. Oxford: Clarendon Press.

Campbell, L. and Garnett, W. (1882). *The Life of James Clerk Maxwell with a Selection from His Correspondence and Occasional Writings and a Sketch of His Contributions to Science*. London: Macmillan.

Chapman, M. (1992). Equilibration and the dialectics of organization. In H. Beilin and P. Pufall (eds.). (1992) *Piaget's Theory. Prospects and Possibilities*, pp. 39–59. Hillsdale: Lawrence Erlbaum.

Chomsky, N. (1980). *Rules and Representations*. Oxford: Blackwell.

Chomsky, N. (2000). *New Horizons in the Study of Language and Mind*. Cambridge University Press.

Cohen, H. (1919). *Religion of Reason: Out of the Sources of Judaism*. Trans. with an introd. by Simon Kaplan. Introductory essay by Leo Strauss. New York: F. Ungar Publishing Company (1972).

Collins, S. and Marková, I. (1995). Complementarity in the construction of a problematic utterance in conversation. In I. Marková, C. Graumann and K. Foppa (eds.) *Mutualities in Dialogue*, pp. 238–63. Cambridge University Press.

Collins, S. and Marková, I. (1999). Interaction between impaired and unimpaired speakers: intersubjectivity and the interplay of culturally shared and situation specific knowledge. *British Journal of Social Psychology*, 38, 339–68.

Cummins, R. (1996). *Representations, Targets and Attitudes*. Cambridge, MA and London: The MIT Press.

de Cusa, N. (1954). *Of Learned Ignorance*. London: Routledge & Kegan Paul.

Danziger, K. (1997). The varieties of social construction (Essay review). *Theory & Psychology*, 7, 399–416.

Darwin, C.R. (1859). *On the Origin of Species*. London: John Murray.

Descartes, R. (1628). *Rules for the Direction of the Mind*. In E.S. Haldane and G.R.T. Ross (trans. and eds.), *The Philosophical Works of Descartes*, Vol. 1, London and New York: Cambridge University Press (1911).

Descartes, R. (1641a/1970). Letter to Mersenne, 16th June 1641. In A. Kenny (trans. and ed.). *Descartes Philosophical Letters*, pp. 22–3. Oxford: Clarendon Press.

Descartes, R. (1644). *The Principles of Philosophy*. In E.S. Haldane and G.R.T. Ross (trans. and eds.), (1911). *The Philosophical Works of Descartes*, Vol. I. London and New York: Cambridge University Press.

Dodds, A.E., Lawrence, J.A. and Valsiner, J. (1997). The personal and the social: Mead's theory of the 'Generalized Other'. *Theory & Psychology*, 7, 483–503.

Doise, W., Spini, D. and Clémence, A. (1999). Human rights studies as social representations in a cross-national context. *European Journal of Social Psychology*, 29, 1–29.

Douglas, M. (1966). *Purity and Danger: An Analysis of Concepts of Pollution and Taboo*, Routledge and Kegan Paul, London.

Dubos, R. (1968). *Man, Medicine and Environment*. London: Pall Mall.

Durkheim, E. (1898). Représentations individuelles et représentations collectives. *Revue de la métaphysique et de morale*, 6, 273–302.

Durkheim, E. (1901). *The Rules of the Sociological Method*. W.D. Hall (trans.). Basingstoke: Macmillan, 1982.

Durkheim, E. (1914). Le dualisme de la nature humaine et ses conditions sociales. *Scientia*, XV, pp. 206–21. Reprinted in E. Durkheim (1970). *La science sociale et l'action*, pp. 314–32. Introduction et presentation de Jean-Claude Filloux, Paris: Presses Universitaires de France.

Durkheim, E. (1915). *The Elementary Forms of Religious Life*. New York: Free Press.

Durkheim, E. (1955). *Pragmatisme et sociologie: Cours inédit prononcé la Sorbonne en 1913–14 par Armand Cuvillier d'après des notes d'étudiants*. Paris: Vrin.

Durkheim, E. (1957). *Professional Ethics and Civic Morals*. London: Routledge and Kegan Paul.

Eccles, J.C. (1989). *Evolution of the Brain: Creation of the Self*. London and New York: Routledge.

Einstein, A. (1949). *Albert Einstein: Philosopher-Scientist*. Vol. I. P.A. Schilpp (ed.). London: Cambridge University Press.

Estes, W.K., Koch, S., MacCorquodale, K., Meehl, P.E., Mueller, C.G., Schoenfeld, W.N. and Verplanck, W.DS. (1954). *Modern Learning Theory*. New York: Appleton-Century-Crofts.

Evans-Pritchard, E. (1981). *A History of Anthropological Thought*. London and Boston: Faber and Faber.

Faron, L.C. (1962). Symbolic values and the integration of society among the Mapuche of Chile. *American Anthropologist*, 64, 1151–64.

Farr, R.M. (1995). Representation of health, illness and handicap in the mass media of communication: a theoretical overview. In I. Marková and R.M. Farr (eds.). *Representations of Health, Illness and Handicap*, pp. 3–30. New York: Harwood.

Farr, R.M. (1996). *The Roots of Modern Social Psychology*. Oxford: Blackwell.

Flament, C. (1994a). Aspects péripheriques des représentations sociales. In C. Guimelli (ed.). *Structures et Transformations des Représentations Sociales*, pp. 85–118. Neuchâtel: Delachaux et Nestlé.

Flament, C. (1994b). Structure, dynamique et transformation des représentations sociales. In J-A. Abric (ed.). *Pratiques Sociales et Représentations*, pp. 37–57. Paris: Presses Universitaires de France.

Flament, C. (2002). L'approche structurale et aspects normatifs des représentations sociales. *Psychologie & Societé*, 4, 51–80.

Fodor, J. (1980). Methodological solipsism considered as a research strategy in cognitive science. *Behavioral and Brain Sciences*, 3, 63–73.

Fodor, J. (1981). *Representations: Philosophical Essays on the Foundations of Cognitive Science*. Brighton: Harvester.

Fodor, J. (2000). *The Mind Doesn't Work That Way*. Cambridge, MA/London: The MIT Press.

Fontaine, P.F.M. (1986). *The Light and the Dark, A Cultural History of Dualism*, Vol. I. Amsterdam: Gieben.

Fontaine, P.F.M. (1987). *The Light and the Dark, A Cultural History of Dualism*, Vol. II. Amsterdam: Gieben.

Fontaine, P.F.M. (1988). *The Light and the Dark, A Cultural History of Dualism*, Vol. III. Amsterdam: Gieben.

Formigary, L. (1988). *Language and Experience in the 17th Century British Philosophy*. Amsterdam: Benjamin.

Freud, S. (1900). The interpretation of dreams. In J. Strachey (ed.). *The Complete Works of Sigmund Freud*, Vol. IV, V. London: The Hogarth Press, 1953.

Freud, S. (1905). Jokes and their relation to the unconscious. In J. Strachey (ed.). *The Complete Works of Sigmund Freud*, Vol. VIII. London: The Hogarth Press, 1960.

Freud, S. (1910). The antithetical meaning of primal words. In J. Strachey (ed.). *The Complete Works of Sigmund Freud*, Vol. XI. London: The Hogarth Press, 1957.

From, F. (1971). *Perception of Other People*. New York and London: Columbia University Press.

Galli, I. (2001). *Dalla I Alla II Repubblica*. Napoli: Redizioni Scientifiche Italiane.

Gellner, E. (1992). *Reason and Culture*. Oxford: Blackwell.

Gellner, E. (1998). *Language and Solitude*. Cambridge University Press.

Gergen, K.J. (1973). Social psychology as history. *Journal of Personality and Social Psychology*, 26, 309–20.

Gergen, K.J. (1994). *Realities and Relationships: Soundings in Social Construction*. Cambridge, MA & London: Harvard University Press.

Gombrich, E. (1968). *Art and Illusion*. London: Phaidon.

Gopnik, A. and Meltzoff, A.N. (1997). *Words, Thoughts, and Theories*. Cambridge and London: The MIT Press.

Gould, S. J. (1996). *Full House*. New York: Three Rivers Press.

Gruber, H.E. (1973). Courage and cognitive growth in children and scientists. In M. Schwebel and J. Raph (eds.). *Piaget in the Classroom*, pp. 73–105. London: Routledge and Kegan Paul.

Gruber, H.E. (1974). *Darwin on Man, together with Darwin's early and unpublished notebooks*. Transcribed and annotated by P.H. Barret, London: Wildwood.

Guimelli, C. (1994). Transformation des représentations sociales, pratiques et schèmes cognitifs de base. In C. Guimelli (ed.). *Structures et Transformations des Représentations Sociales*, pp. 171–98. Neuchâtel: Delachaux et Niestlé.

Guimelli, C. (1998). Differentiation between the central core elements of social representations. *Swiss Journal of Psychology*, 57, 209–24.

Hacker, P.M.S. (1990). Chomsky's problems. *Language and Communication*, 10, 127–48.

Haldane, K. (1897). Jacob Böhme and his relation to Hegel. *The Philosophical Review*, 6, 146–61.

Harris, J. (1751/1968). *Hermes: or, a Philosophical Inquiry Concerning Language and Universal Grammar*. London: H. Woodfall. Reprinted in the series *English*

Linguistics, no. 55, 1500–1800. Selected and edited by R.C. Alston. Menston, England: The Scholar Press.

Havel, V. (1979). O počátcích Charty 77. In V. Havel, *O Lidskou Identitu*, pp. 50–4. Praha: Rozmluvy.

Havel, V. (1985). *Dopisy Olze*. Toronto: Sixty-eight Publishers.

Havel, V. (1992). *The Power of the Powerless*. New York: Vintage Books.

Hegel, G.W.F. (1830). *The Encyclopedia of the Philosophical Sciences* (Part 1). *The Science of Logic*. In W. Wallace (trans.) *The Logic of Hegel*. London: Oxford University Press (1873).

Hegel, G.W.F. (1807). *The Phenomenology of the Spirit*. Trans. by A.V. Miller. Oxford University Press (1977).

Hegel, G.W.F. (1837). *The Philosophy of History*. Trans. by J. Sibree, New York: Dover (1956).

Heidegger, M. (1954). *Was Heisst Denken?* Tuebingen: Max Niemeyer Verlag. *What is Called Thinking?* Trans. by G. Gray and F. Wieck. Harper Colophon (1968).

Heider, F. (1958). *The Psychology of Interpersonal Relations*. New York and London: Wiley.

Heider, F. and Simmel, M. (1944). An experimental study of apparent behavior. *American Journal of Psychology*, 57, 243–59.

Henderson, L.D. (1998). *Duchamp in Context*. Princeton University Press.

Herder, J.G. (1771/1967). *Abhandlung über den Ursprung der Sprache*. In J.G. Herder, *Sämtliche Werke* V, (B. Suphon, ed.). George Olms.

Hermans, H.J.M. and Kempen, H.J.G. (1993). *The Dialogical Self*. London and New York: Academic Press.

Holton, G. (1975). On the role of themata in scientific thought. *Science*, 188, 328–34.

Holton, G. (1978). *The Scientific Imagination: Case Studies*. Cambridge New York: Cambridge University Press.

von Humboldt, W. (1836). *Linguistic Variability and Intellectual Development*. Trans. by E.C. Buck and F.A. Raven. Coral Gables: University of Miami Press (1971).

Hunt, M. (1993). *The Story of Psychology*. New York and London: Doubleday.

Inwood, M. (1992). *A Hegel Dictionary*. Oxford: Blackwell.

Jackendoff, R. (1992). *Languages of the Mind. Essays on Mental Representation*. Cambridge MA and London: The MIT Press.

Jahoda, A. (1995). Quality of life: hope for the future or an echo from the distant past? In I. Marková and R.M. Farr (eds.) *Representations of Health, Illness and Handicap*, pp. 205–14, New York: Harwood.

Jahoda, G. (1992). *Crossroads Between Culture and Mind. Continuities and Change in Theories of Human Nature*. New York and London: Harvester Wheatsheaf.

Jahoda, G. (1999). *Images of Savages*. London and New York: Routledge.

Jakobson, R. (1932). Phoneme and phonology. In S. Rudy (ed.) *Roman Jakobson Selected Writing*, Vol. I, pp. 231–3. The Hague and Paris: Mouton (1971).

Jakobson, R. (1960). Linguistics and poetics. In S. Rudy (ed.) *Roman Jakobson Selected Writing*, Vol. III, pp. 18–51. The Hague and Paris: Mouton (1981).

Jakobson, R. (1971). Linguistics in relation to other sciences. In S. Rudy (ed.) *Roman Jakobson Selected Writing*, Vol. II, pp. 655–96. The Hague and Paris: Mouton (1985).

Jakobson, R. (1958). The Kazan School of Polish linguistics and its place in the international development of phonology. In S. Rudy (ed.) *Roman Jakobson Selected Writing*, Vol. VII, pp. 394–428. The Hague and Paris: Mouton (1985).

Jakobson, R. (1972). Verbal Communication. In S. Rudy (ed.) *Roman Jakobson Selected Writing*, Vol. VII, pp. 81–92. Berlin, New York & Amsterdam: Mouton (1985).

Jakobson, R. (1979). Einstein and the Science of Language. In S. Rudy (ed.) *Roman Jakobson Selected Writing*, Vol. VII, pp. 254–64. Berlin, New York & Amsterdam: Monton (1985).

Jakobson, R. (1982). La Théorie Saussurienne en Retrospection. In S. Rudy (ed.) *Roman Jakobson Selected Writing*, Vol. VIII, pp. 391–435. Berlin, New York & Amsterdam: Mouton (1988).

Jakobson, R. and Waugh, L.R. The sound shape of language. In S. Rudy (ed.) *Roman Jakobson Selected Writing*, Vol. VIII (1), pp. 1–315. Berlin, New York & Mouton (1988).

Janet, P. (1926). *De l'angoisse a l'extase. Etudes sur les croyances et les sentiments.* Paris: Librarie Felix Alcan.

Jodelet, D. (1989). *Folies et représentations sociales.* Paris: Presses Universitaires de France.

Jones, F. (1952). *The Life and Work of Sigmund Freud.* Vol. II (1955) *Years of Maturity.* New York: Basic books.

Josephs, I.E. and Valsiner, J. (1998). How does autodialogue work? Miracles of meaning maintenance and circumvention strategies. *Social Psychology Quarterly*, 61, 68–83.

Jovchelovitch, S. and Gervais, M.C. (1999). Social representations of health and illness: The case of the Chinese community in England. *Journal of Community & Applied Social Psychology*, 9, 247–60.

Jung, C.G. (1961). Freud and psychoanalysis. *Collected Works.* Vol. IV. Trans. by R.F.C. Hull. London: Routledge and Kegan Paul.

Jung, C.G. (1966). The practice of psychotherapy. *Collected Works.* Vol. XVI. Trans. by R.F.C. Hull. London: Routledge and Kegan Paul.

Jung, C.G. (1979). General Index. *Collected Works.* Vol. XX. trans. by R.F.C. Hull. London: Routledge and Kegan Paul.

Kalandra, Z. (1994). *Intelektuál a Revoluce.* J. Brabec (ed.) Praha: Český Spisovatel.

Kant, I. (1763). Versuch den Begriff der Negativen Grössen in die Weltweisheit einzuführen. *Kant's Werke, Band II*, pp. 165–204. Berlin: Georg Reimer.

Kant, I. (1781 and 1787). *Critique of Pure Reason*, trans. N.K. Smith. London: Macmillan; New York: St Martin's Press (1929).

Karcevskij, S. (1927). *Système de verbe russe.* Prague: Plamja.

Karcevskij, S. (1929). Du dualisme asymétrique du sign linguistique, *Travaux du Cercle Linguistique de Prague*, 1, 33–8. Reprinted as The asymmetric dualism of the linguistic sign, in F. Steiner (ed.), *The Prague School: Selected writings, 1919–1946*, pp. 47–54. Austin: University of Texas Press, 1982.

Kelley, H.H. (1999). Fifty years in social psychology: some reflections on the individual-group problem. In A. Rodrigues and R.V. Levine (eds.). *Reflections on 100 Years on Experimental Social Psychology*, pp. 35–46. New York: Basic Books.

Kessler, S. (1980). The psychological paradigm shift in genetic counselling. *Social Biology*, 27, 167–85.

Kirk, G.S. and Raven, J.E. (1957). *The Presocratic Philosophers*. Cambridge University Press.

Klicperová, M., Feierbend, I.K. and Hofstetter, C.R. (1997). In the search for a post-communist syndrome: a theoretical framework and empirical assessment. *Journal of Community and applied Social Psychology*, 7, 39–52.

Kojève, A. (1969). *Introduction to the Reading of Hegel*. New York and London: Basic Books.

Kosík, K. (1963). *Dialektika konkrétního*. Praha: Nakladatelství Československé Akademie Věd.

Kratochvíl, Z. (1997). Roots of alchemy, hermetic doctrines and gnosis. In V. Zadrobílek, *Opus Magnum*, pp. 41–3 and 274–5. Prague: Trigon.

Kuhn, T.S. (1962). *The Structure of Scientific Revolutions*, 2nd edn. 1970. University of Chicago Press.

de Lasenic, P. (1997). Alchemická filosofie. In V. Zadrobílek, *Opus Magnum*, pp. 88–91. Prague: Trigon.

Lele, J. and Singh, R. (1987). Panini, language theories and the dialects of grammar. In H. Aarsleff, L.G. Kelly and H-J. Niederehe (eds.) *Papers in the History of Linguistics: Proceedings of the Third International Conference on the History of the Language Sciences*, pp. 43–51. Amsterdam: John Benjamins.

Lévi-Strauss, C. (1962). *La Pensée Sauvage*. Paris: Plon.

Lewontin, R.C. (1990). How much did the brain have to change for speech? Commentary on Pinker and Bloom. *Behavioural and Brain Sciences*, 13, 740–1.

Linell, P. (1998). *Approaching Dialogue*. Amsterdam: John Benjamins.

Linell, P. and Marková, I. (1993). Acts in discourse: from monological speech acts to dialogical inter-acts. *Journal for the Theory of Social Behaviour*, 23, 21–43.

Liu, L. (2002). *Quality of life in China: a social representational approach*. Thesis submitted in partial fulfilment of the degree of Doctor of Philosophy. Department of Social Psychology: London School of Economic and Political Science.

Lloyd, G.E.R. (1966). *Polarity and Analogy*. Cambridge University Press.

Lloyd, G.E.R. (1990). *Demystifying Mentalities*. Cambridge University Press.

Lloyd, G.E.R. (1994). New perspectives on ancient science. *European Review*, Vol. 21/(2): 91–8.

Lloyd, G.E.R. (2000). On the 'origins' of science. In *Proceedings of the British Academy, 105. 1999 Lectures and memoirs*. Oxford University Press, pp. 1–16.

Locke, J. (1690). *An Essay Concerning Human Understanding*. Ed. and introduction by Peter H. Nidditch. Oxford: Clarendon Press (1975).

Lotman, Y.M. (1976). Un modèle dynamique du système sémiotique. In Y.M. Lotman and B.A. Ouspenski (1976) *Travaux sur les systèmes de signes*, pp. 77–93. Traduits du russe par A. Zouboff. Bruxelles: Editions Complexe.

Lotman, Yu. (1990). *Universe of the Mind. A Semiotic Theory of Culture.* Trans. by A. Shukman. London and New York: Tausis.

Lotman, Yu. M. (1992). Vmesto zaklucenija o roli slucajnuych faktorov v istorii kultury. In: Yu. M. Lotman. Izbrannyje stati v trech tomax. Vol. I. pp. 472–9. Tallinn: Alexandra.

Lozada, M. (2000). Discurso político e ideología *light. ¿*Fin del compromiso? J. Juárez and S. Arciga (eds.). *La Ciudadania: Estudios de Psicología Política y Representación Social,* 43–62. México: Unidad Iztapalapa.

Luckman, T. (1990). Social communication, dialogue and conversation. In I. Marková and K Foppa (eds.) *The Dynamics of Dialogue,* pp. 45–61. New York & London: Harvester Wheatsheaf.

Luckmann, T. (1992). On the communicative adjustment of perspectives, dialogue and communicative genres. In A. Heen Wold (ed.). *The Dialogical Alternative. Towards a Theory of Language and Mind,* pp. 219–34. Oslo: Scandinavian University Press.

Luria, A.R. (1976). *Cognitive Development: Its Cultural and Social Foundations.* Trans. by M. Lopez-Morillas and L. Solotaroff. Cambridge MA and London: Harvard University Press.

Marková, I. (1982). *Paradigms, Thought and Language.* Chichester & New York: Wiley.

Marková, I. (1987a). *Human Awareness.* London and Melbourne: Hutchinson.

Marková, I. (1987b). On the interaction of opposites in psychological processes. *Journal for the Theory of Social Behaviour,* 17, 279–99.

Marková, I. (1990). A three-step process as a unit of analysis in dialogue. In I. Marková and K. Foppa (eds.) *The Dynamics of Dialogue,* pp. 129–46. New York & London: Harvester Wheatsheaf.

Marková, I. (1991). The concepts of the universal in the Cartesian and Hegelian frameworks. In A. Costall and A. Still (eds.) *Against Cognitivism,* pp. 81–101. Hemel Hempstead: Harvester Wheatsheaf.

Marková, I. (1995). Quality of life and human agency: A theoretical overview. In I. Marková and R.M. Farr (eds.), *Representations of Health, Illness and Handicap,* pp. 191–204. New York: Harwood.

Marková, I., Forbes, C. and Inwood, M. (1984). Consumers' views of genetic counselling in haemophilia. *The American Journal of Medical Genetics,* 17, 741–52.

Marková, I., McKee, K., Power, K. and Moodie, E. (1995). The self, the other and perceived risk: Lay representations of HIV/AIDS in Scottish prisons. In I. Marková and R.M. Farr (eds.) *Representations of Health, Illness and Handicap,* pp. 111–29. New York: Harwood.

Marková, I., Moodie, E., Farr, R., Drozda-Senkowska, E., Erös, F., Plichtová, J., Gervais, M-C., Hoffmannová, J. and Mullerová, O. (1998). Social representations of the individual: a post-communist perspective. *European Journal of Social Psychology,* 28, pp. 797–829.

Marková, I., Moodie, E., Plichtová, J., Mullerová, O. and Hoffmannová, J. (2001). La démocratie dans ses relations entre langage et pensée. *Bulletin de Psychologie,* 54, 611–21.

Marr, N. J. (1977). *Jazyk i myslenie.* Letchworth Herts.

Mathesius, V. (1911/1964). "O potenciálnosti jevů jazykových". *Věstník královské české společnosti nauk, třída filosoficko-historická*. Reprinted in J. Vachek (ed.), *A Prague School Reader in Linguistics*, pp. 1–32. Bloomington: Indiana University Press.

Mead, G. H. (1927). The objective reality of perspectives. *Proceedings of the Sixth International Congress of Philosophy*, pp. 75–85. (ed. E.S. Brightmann). New York: Longmans.

Mead, G.H. (1934). *Mind, Self and Society*. Chicago and London: University of Chicago Press.

Medvedev, P.N. (1934/1985). *The Formal Method in Literary Scholarship. A Critical Introduction to Sociological Poetics*. Cambridge, MA: Harvard University Press.

Merton, R.K. (1975). Thematic analysis in science: notes on Holton's concept. *Science*, 188, 335–8.

Meyerson, (1934). De l'analyse des products de la pensée. *Revue Philosophique*, CXVIII, pp. 135–70.

Middleton, D. and Brown, S. (2001). The baby as virtual object: Agency and stability in a neonatal care unit. Presented at the symposium on the 'Social Psychology of the Virtual' at the British Psychological Society Social Psychology Section Annual Conference, University of Surrey, 18–20 July 2001.

Middleton, J. (1968). Some categories of dual classification among the Lugbara of Uganda. *History of Religions*, 29, 187–208.

Mihailovic, A. (1997). *Corporeal Words: Mikhail Bakhtin's Theology of Discourse*. Evanston, IL: Northwestern University Press.

Moodie, E., Marková, I. and Plichtová, J. (1995). Lay representations of democracy: A study in two cultures. *Culture and Psychology*, 1, 423–53.

Morson, G.S. and Emerson, C. (1989). *Rethinking Bakhtin*. Evanston: Northwestern University Press.

Moscovici, S. (1961). *La Psychanalyse: son image et son public*. Paris: Presses Universitaires de France.

Moscovici, S. (1976a). *La Psychanalyse: Son image et son public*. Paris: Presses Universitaires de France.

Moscovici, S. (1976b). *Social Influence and Social Change*. Trans. by C. Sherrard and G. Heinz. Cambridge University Press.

Moscovici, S. (1979). Psychologie des minorités actives. Paris: Presses Universitaires de France.

Moscovici, S. (1980). Towards a theory of conversion behavior. In L. Berkowitz (ed.). *Advances in Experimental Social Psychology*, Vol. XIII, pp. 209–39. New York and London: Academic Press.

Moscovici, S. (1984a). Introduction: le domaine de la psychologie sociale. In S. Moscovici (ed.) *Psychologie Sociale*, pp. 5–22. Paris: Presses Universitaires de France.

Moscovici, S. (1984b). The phenomenon of social representations. In R.M. Farr and S. Moscovici (eds.) *Social Representations*, pp. 3–69. Cambridge University Press.

Moscovici, S. (1988). La machine à faire des dieux: sociologie et psychologie. Paris: Fayard. Trans. by W.D. Hall as *The Invention of Society*. Cambridge: Polity Press, 1993.

Moscovici, S. (1992). Communication introductive à la première conférence internationale sur les représentations sociales. Ravello: Italy.

Moscovici, S. (1994). Social representations and pragmatic communication. *Social Science Information*, 33, 163–77.

Moscovici, S. (1998a). Social consciousness and its history. *Culture & Psychology*, 4, 411–29.

Moscovici, S. (1998b). The history and actuality of social representations. In U. Flick (ed.) *The Psychology of the Social*, pp. 209–47. Cambridge University Press.

Moscovici, S. (2002a). Pourquoi l'étude des représentations sociales en psychologie? *Psychologie & Societé*, 4, 7–24.

Moscovici, S. (2002b). *De la nature*. Paris: Métailié.

Moscovici, S., Lage, E. and Naffrechoux, M. (1969). Influence of a consistent minority on the responses of a majority in a color perception task. *Sociometry*, 32, 365–79.

Moscovici, S. and Marková, I. (2000). Ideas and their development: a dialogue between Serge Moscovici and Ivana Marková. In S. Moscovici, *Social Representations*, pp. 224–86. Ed. G. Duveen. London: Polity Press.

Moscovici, S. and Personaz, B. (1980). Studies in social influence V: minority influence and conversion behavior in a perceptual task. *Journal of Experimental Social Psychology*, 16, 270–82.

Moscovici, S. and Personaz, B. (1991). Studies in social influence VI: is Lenin orange or red? *European Journal of Social Psychology*, 21, 101–18.

Moscovici, S. and Vignaux, G. (1994). Le Concept de Thêmata. In Ch. Guimelli, *Structures et transformations des représentations sociales*, pp. 25–72. Neuchatel: Delachaux et Niestlé. Reprinted in S. Moscovici, *Social Representations*, pp. 156–83. Ed. G. Duveen. London: Polity Press.

Mukařovský, J. (1936). *Estetická funkce, Norma a Hodnota jako Socialni Fakty*. Trans. by M.E. Suino as *Aesthetic Function, Norm and Value as Social Facts*. Ann Arbor: Michigan Slavic Contributions, 3, 1970.

Mukařovský, J. (1940). Two Studies of Dialogue. In J. Burbank and P. Steiner (eds.). *The Word and Verbal Art, Selected Essays by Jan Mukařovský*, pp. 81–133. New Haven and London: Yale University Press, 1977.

Naess, A., Christophersen, J.A. and Kvalø, K. (1956). *Democracy, Ideology and Objectivity*. Oslo University Press; Oxford: Blackwell.

Needham, J. (1962). *Science and Civilisation in China*. Volume 4, part I: Physics. V. Cambridge University Press.

Needham, J. (1970). *Clerks and Craftsmen in China and the West*. Cambridge University Press.

Needham, R. (1973) (ed.). *Right & Left. Essays on Dual Symbolic Classification*. Chicago and London: University of Chicago Press.

Nerlich, B. and Clarke, D.D. (1996). *Language, Action and Context*. Amsterdam and Philadelphia: John Benjamins.

Newell, A. (1990). *Unified Theories of Cognition*. Cambridge MA and London: Harvard University Press.

Newson, J. (1979). The growth of shared understandings between infant and caregiver. In M. Bullowa (ed.). *Before Speech: The Beginning of Interpersonal*

Communication. pp. 207–22. Cambridge and New York: Cambridge University Press.

Nicolson, M. (1950). *The Breaking of the Circle: Studies in the Effect of the "New Science" Upon Seventeenth Century Poetry.* Evanston: North Western University Press.

Ogden, C.K. (1932/1967). *Opposition: A Linguistic and Psychological Analysis.* Bloomington: Indiana University Press.

Orwell, G. (1949). *Nineteen Eighty-Four.* Oxford: Clarendon Press.

Paoletti, G. (2000). Representation and belief: Durkheim's rationalism and the Kantian tradition. In Pickering, W.S.F. (ed.) (2000). *Durkheim and Representations,* pp. 118–35. Routledge: London.

Parsons, T. (1974). Durkheim's life and work. In E. Durkheim, *Sociology and Philosophy,* pp. xliii–lxx. New York: The Free Press.

Pastoureau, M. (2000). *Bleu. L'histoire d'une couleur.* Paris: Editions du Seuil.

Patzeva, M. (1994). The creation of new meaning in the process of democratisation of Eastern Europe. *Journal of Russian and East European Psychology,* 32, 5–12.

Peirce, C.S. (1931). *Collected Papers of Charles Sanders Peirce.* Vol. I. Eds. C. Hartshorne and P. Weiss. Cambridge MA: The Belknap Press of Harvard University Press.

Pérez, J.A. and Mugny, G. (1986). Induction expérimentale d'une influence minoritaire indirecte. *Cahiers de psychologie sociale,* 32, 15–24.

Piaget, J. (1965). *Etudes Sociologiques.* Genève: Droz.

Piaget, J. (1970). *The Principles of Genetic Epistemology.* Paris: Presses Universitaires de France. Trans. by W. Mays, London: Routledge and Kegan Paul, 1972.

Piaget, J. (1985). *The Equilibration of Cognitive Structures.* University of Chicago Press.

Palmonari, A. (1993). *Psicologia dell'adolescenza.* Bologna: Il Mulino.

Pickering, W.S.F. (2000a). Introduction. In W.S.F. Pickering (ed.) (2000). *Durkheim and Representations,* pp. 1–8. Routledge: London.

Pickering, W.S.F. (2000b). Representations as understood by Durkheim. In W.S.F. Pickering (ed.) (2000d). *Durkheim and Representations,* pp. 11–23. Routledge: London.

Pickering, W.S.F. (2000c). What do representations represent? The issue of reality. In W.S.F. Pickering (ed.) (2000d). *Durkheim and Representations,* pp. 98–117. Routledge: London.

Pickering, W.S.F. (ed.) (2000d). *Durkheim and Representations.* Routledge: London.

Pinker, S. and Bloom, P. (1990). Natural language and natural selection. *Behavioral and Brain Sciences,* 13, 707–84.

Plato (1975). *Philebus.* Translated with notes and commentary by J.C.B. Gosling. Oxford: Clarendon Press.

Plato. *Gorgias.* Translated, with an intro., by W.C. Helmbold. New York: Library Arts Press, 1952.

Plato. *The Republic.* Trans. by A.D. Lindsay. London: Dent (1976).

Prendergast, C. (2000). *The Triangle of Representation.* New York: Columbia University Press.

Putnam, H. (1988). *Representation and Reality*. Cambridge MA and London: The MIT Press.

Pynsent, R. (1994). *Questions of Identity. Czech and Slovak Ideas of Nationality and Personality*. London: Central European University Press.

Reykowski, J. (1995). Popular concept of democracy and perception of the socio-political situation. Paper presented at the 'East-West conference of the European Association of Experimental Psychology'. Prague 19 April, 1995.

Richards, I.A. (1967). Introduction. In C.K. Ogden (1932/1967). *Opposition: A Linguistic and Psychological Analysis*. Bloomington: Indiana University Press.

Rieff, P. (1979). *Freud, the Mind of the Moralist*. University of Chicago Press.

de Rosa, A.S. (1987). The social representations of mental illness in children and adults. In S. Moscovici and W. Doise (eds.). *Current Issues in Social Psychology*, Vol. II, 47–138. Cambridge University Press.

Rommetveit, R. (1974). *On Message Structure. A Framework for the Study of Language and Communication*. London: Wiley.

Rommetveit, R. (1990). On axiomatic features of a dialogical approach to language and mind. In I. Marková and K. Foppa (eds.) *The Dynamics of Dialogue*, pp. 83–104. New York and London: Harvester Wheatsheaf.

Rommetveit, R. (1991). Dominance and asymmetries in *A Doll's House*. In I. Marková and K. Foppa (eds.). *Asymmetries in Dialogue*, pp. 195–220. Chichester: Harvester Wheatsheaf.

Rommetveit, R. (1992). Outlines of a dialogically based social-cognitive approach to human cognition and communication. In A.H. Wold (ed.) *The Dialogical Alternative: Towards a Theory of Language and Mind*, pp. 19–44. Oslo: Scandinavian University Press.

Rommetveit, R. (1998). On divergent perspectives and controversial issues in studies of language and mind. In M. Janse (ed.) *Productivity and Creativity. Studies in General and Descriptive Linguistics in Honor of E.M. Uhlenbeck*, pp. 179–89. Berlin and New York: Mouton de Gruyter.

Rorty, R. (1980). *Philosophy & the Mirror of Nature*. Oxford: Basil Blackwell.

Rosenblueth, A., Wiener, N. and Bigelow, J. (1943). Behavior, purpose and teleology. *Philosophy of Science*, 10, 18–24.

Rosenstock, E. (1924). *Angewandte Seelenkunde, eine pragmatische Übersetzung*. Darmstadt: Roetherverlag.

Rosenstock, E. (1963–64). *Die Sprache des Menschengeschlechts: eine leibhaftige Grammatik*. I, II. Heidelberg: Schneider.

Rosenzweig, F. (1921). *Stern der Erlösung*. Frankfurt: Kauffmann.

Rosenzweig, F. (2001). *Foi et Savoir*. Introduit, traduit et annoté par G. Bensussan, M. Crépon et M. de Launay. Paris: Librairie philosophique J. Vrin.

Ryle, G. (1949). *The Concept of Mind*. London: Hutchinson.

Rychlak, J.F. (1968). *A Philosophy of Science for Personality Theory*. Malabar, Florida: R.E. Krieger.

Rychlak, J.F. (1994). *Logical Learning Theory*. Lincoln and London: University of Nebraska Press.

Saint Augustine. *Confessions*. Trans., introduction and notes by H. Chadwick. Oxford University Press (1991).

Saint Augustine. *The Trinity*. Trans. by S. McKenna. Washington: Catholic University of America Press (1963).

Salazar-Orvig, A. (1999). *Les mouvements du discours*. Paris: L'Harmattan.

Salazar-Orvig, A. (2000). La reprise aux sources de la construction discursive. *Langages*, 140, 68–91.

de Saussure, F. (1915/1959). *Course in General Linguistics*. Glasgow: William Collins.

de Saussure, F. (1910–1911/1993). *Troisième Cours de Linguistique Générale* (1910–1911). Saussure's *Third Course of Lectures on General Linguistics* (1910–1911). (From the notebooks of Emile Constantin). French text ed. by E. Komatsu; English Trans. by R. Harris. Oxford and New York: Pergamon.

Schutz, A. (1970). *Reflections on the Problem of Relevance*. New Haven and London: Yale University Press.

Schutz, A. (1972). *The Phenomenology of the Social World*. Trans. by G. Walsh and F. Lehnert. London: Heineman Educational Books.

Shpet, G. (1927). *Vnutrennjaja Forma Slova. Etjudyi Variacii na Temy Gumboldta*. Moskva: Gosudarstvennaja Akademija Chudožestvennych Nauk.

Šimečka, M. (1984). *The Restoration of Order: The Normalisation of Czechoslovakia, 1969–1976*. London: Verso.

Sontag, S. (1979). *Illness as Metaphor*. Allen Lane (page references to Penguin edition, 1983), London.

Stalin, J.V. (1972). *Marxism and Problems of Linguistics*. Peking: Foreign Languages Press.

Stedman Jones, S. (2000). Representation in Durkheim's masters: Kant and Renouvier. I. Representation, reality and the question of science. In Pickering, W.S.F. (ed.) (2000). *Durkheim and Representations*. Routledge: London, pp. 37–58.

Tarde, G. (1897). *L'opposition universelle*. Paris: Alcan.

Tarde, G. (1922). *L'opinion et la foule*. Paris: Alcan.

Taylor, C. (1989). *Sources of the Self*. Cambridge University Press.

Taylor, C. (1995a). Preface. In C. Taylor (ed.), *Philosophical Arguments*, pp. vii–xii. London & Massachusetts: Harvard University Press.

Taylor, C. (1995b). Overcoming Epistemology. In C. Taylor (ed.), *Philosophical Arguments*, pp. 1–19. London & Massachusetts: Harvard University Press.

Taylor, C. (1995c). The importance of Herder. In C. Taylor (ed.). *Philosophical Arguments*, pp. 79–99. London & Massachusetts: Harvard University Press.

Taylor, C. (1995d). To follow a rule. In C. Taylor (ed.), *Philosophical Arguments*, pp. 165–80. London & Massachusetts: Harvard University Press.

Taylor, C. (1995e). Politics of Recognition. In C. Taylor (ed.), *Philosophical Arguments*, pp. 225–56. London & Massachusetts: Harvard University Press.

The Oxford Modern English Dictionary (1992). Oxford: Clarendon Press.

Théses présentées au Premier Congrés des philologues slaves (1929). In *Travaux Linguistiques de Prague*, 1, 5–29.

Thom, F. (1987). *La langue de bois*, Paris: Julliard.

de Tocqueville, A. (1835/1945). *Democracy in America*. New York: Random House.

Trevarthen, C. (1979). Communication and cooperation in early infancy: a description of primary intersubjectivity. In M. Bullowa (ed.). *Before Speech: The*

Beginning of Interpersonal Communication, pp. 321–47. Cambridge University Press.

Trevarthen, C. (1992). An infant's motives for speaking and thinking in the culture. In A. Heen Wold (ed.). *The Dialogical Alternative*, pp. 99–137. Oslo: Scandinavian University Press.

Trilling, L. (1972). *Sincerity and Authenticity*. London: Oxford University Press.

Turner, M.B. (1967). *Philosophy and the Science of Behavior.* New York: Appleton-Century-Crofts.

Tynjanov, J. (1929b/1971). O literaturnoj evoljucii. In L. Matejka (ed.). *Readings in Russian Poetics*, pp. 99–113. Michigan Slavic Materials. Ann Arbor: Department of Slavic Languages and Literature.

Tynjanov, J. and Jakobson, R. (1928). Problems in the Study of Literature and Language. In *Roman Jakobson, Selected Writings. Vol. III*, pp. 3–6. The Hague: Mouton, 1981.

Uribe, P.F.J and Acosta, A.M.A.T. (1992). Los referentes ocultos de la democracia, *Fundamentos y Cronicas de la Psicologia Social Mexicana*, 5, 8–9, 43–50.

Vachek, J. (1964). *The Linguistic School of Prague*. Bloomington and London: Indiana University Press.

Valsiner, J. (1989). *Human Development and Culture*. Lexington: D.C. Heath.

Valsiner, J. (1998). *The Guided Mind: A Sociogenetic Approach to Personality.* Cambridge, MA & London: Harvard University Press.

Valsiner, J. and Lawrence, J.A. (1996). Human development across the life-span. In J.W. Berry, P.R. Dasen and T.S. Saraswathi (eds.). *Handbook of Cross-cultural Psychology: Vol. 2 Basic Processes and Developmental Psychology*, pp. 69–106. Boston: Allyn and Bacon.

Vico, G. (1744/1968). *The New Science of Giambattista Vico*. Trans. by T.G. Bergin and M.H. Fisch. Ithaca, NY: Cornell University Press.

Vodička, F. (1976). Response to verbal art. In L. Matejka and I.R. Titunik (eds.) *Semiotics of Art. Prague School contributions*. Cambridge, MA: MIT Press, pp. 197–208.

Voloshinov, V.N. (1929/1973). *Marxism and the Philosophy of Language*. Trans. L. Matejka and I.R.Titunik. New York and London: Seminar Press.

Wallon, II. (1945). *Les origines de la pensée chez l'enfant*. Paris: Presses Universitaires de France.

Walsh, W.H. (1975). *Kant's Criticism of Metaphysics*. Edinburgh University Press.

Wellek, R. (1976). Vilém Mathesius (1882–1945). Founder of the Prague Linguistic Circle. In L. Matejka (ed.), *Sound, Sign and Meaning*, pp. 6–14. (Michigan Slavic Contributions, 6). Ann Arbor: Department of Slavic Language and Literature, The University of Michigan.

Wertsch, J.V. (1991). *Voices of the Mind: A Sociocultural Approach to Mediated Action*. Cambridge, MA: Harvard University Press.

Williams, B. (1973). Deciding to believe. In B. Williams, *Problems of the Self Philosophical Papers 1956–1972*, pp. 136–51. Cambridge University Press.

Wittgenstein, L. (1953). *Philosophical Investigations*. Trans. G.E.M. Anscombe. New York: The Macmillan Company.

Index

Printed in the United Kingdom
by Lightning Source UK Ltd.
114640UKS00001B/243